Meet Me at the Oasis

Kim Halberg

Written by: Kim Halberg (copyright 2006)
ISBN # 0-9772913-0-8

PO Box 48340
Minneapolis MN 55448-0340

All Scripture quotations not specified by (NIV) are taken from the King James Version.

The author wishes to thank John and Patti Worre for permission to use material from the JESUS PEOPLE MUSIC collection including *Psalms Hymns & Spiritual Songs* Copyright © 1980 (#116 *Great is the Lord* by Robert Ewing) and *The Gospel According to Scrooge* and *The Jesus People Singers Present...Memories* album covers. Photo credits for *Scrooge*: Phil Osterhus, Mark Lundeen, and Collins Photography; and *Memories*: Phil Osterhus.

Top cover photo of hands under water by Casey Schutrop taken in India at a well done through partners of Oasis World Ministries.

All other photos were supplied by Tom and Vicki Elie, their family, friends, and Oasis World Ministries. Any omission of credit where credit is due was not intentional and forgiveness is requested.

Meet Me at the Oasis

Leaving a Legacy to Echo in Eternity

Kim Halberg

A Letter from Tom and Vicki Elie

First of all, we give any and all glory to our Lord and Savior Jesus Christ. We also give heartfelt thanks to our wonderful parents, our families and our partners. We give a special thank you to our four sons, Troy, Ryan, Jon and Darren, who have been in ministry right along with us. We could not have accomplished what we did without them. We are grateful for the times they willingly shared their father while he ministered to others, even though it meant he was often away from home.

Recently while in India, we asked a 23-year-old college student if he was a Hindu. He said, "Yes, I was, until last night at your Festival. I saw a man on your stage that everyone knows as the town 'blind man.' Jesus opened his eyes and he saw his wife for the first time in 15 years. That's the kind of God I want to serve."

As we interact with the faith-filled people of India, it seems that our eyes continue to open to behold the glory of the Lord in greater ways. Why do we lack faith or boldness? He is ready to do so much more than we ever imagined possible! We must not let fear or finances hinder us from moving out of our comfort zone. God has a legacy waiting to be built in each of us.

By God's grace, we have now built more churches and drilled more wells than we ever thought possible. We have given training to thousands of pastors, and seen over 300,000 people confess Jesus as their Lord. An average of 1,000 new believers are attending the local churches after each of our open-air Festivals. If our partners will continue to send us and pray for us, we will continue to go. We are on our way to our goal of seeing one million people coming to know Christ as their Savior. By God's grace, it will happen! Thank you.

Intentional for souls,

Tom and Vicki Elie

P.S. If you would like to join us on a short-term missions outreach contact us at:

Oasis World Ministries
P.O. Box 27893
Minneapolis, MN 55427 USA
763-425-9355
Email: oasisworldministries@juno.com

FORWARD

I first met Tom and Vicki Elie in the mid 1980's. I was so impressed with this young couple who were planting an urban church during an era when most of the church world seemed to be abandoning the inner cities for the suburbs. This church plant [in Northeast Minneapolis] was not only successful, but served to challenge other young pastors to take steps of faith in church planting.

People like Tom and Vicki challenge me. I want to know what "makes them tick." What fuels their passion? What is it that makes them stand apart from the crowd and go on to do great things for God? Tom is not only an extremely gifted individual, but he is a man with a mission and vision to touch people with the gospel. He has had a dynamic and effective ministry here at home and overseas. His burden for India is literally changing the nation one life and city at a time.

This book, Meet Me at the Oasis, gives the reader a glimpse not only into the major events that have served to shape Tom's life and ministry, but into some private moments as well. The reader is put on the inside track of circumstances involved in bringing Tom and Vicki to the place of influence that they enjoy today.

Those who already know and love Tom and Vicki will enjoy reading about their varied ministry experiences. Those who are meeting them for the first time will soon feel like they have met new friends that they can trust.

Clarence St. John
District Superintendent
Minnesota District Council of the Assemblies of God

PREFACE

In 1905 a circuit-preaching evangelist rode his horse into Lake Bronson, Minnesota. The evangelist gave the message of a new life in Christ and left the rest for God to finish. Perhaps he knew, or perhaps he didn't know, that a man gave his life to Jesus Christ. All the stubbornness, rebellion, and resistance to following God melted. The real thing, the Light, had come into his soul and dispelled the darkness. He was known for being the town drunk and wife beater, but now he would be known for something different: a trumpet for God. He was now a child of God and he meant to pass that legacy onto his daughter and her children and he would pray for his great-grandchildren too. He could not see into the future far enough to know that one day his great-grandson would become an evangelist who would use modern means of transportation to reach the destinations where the Light was needed. All he knew was that he needed to teach his daughter the great stories of the Bible and pray that each generation would in turn teach their children.

That is how Meet Me At the Oasis really began: with Tom Elie's great-grandfather. Or did it begin with the horseback riding evangelist and his mother and father? In any case, we are all leaving a legacy that will echo. What will our echo sound like in the ears of those who follow in our footsteps?

The following story was told to me through many different people's account. They did not always match, but an effort has been made to be accurate and fair in portraying all events and characters as much as possible.

With thanksgiving to my Heavenly Father,
Kimberly Ann Halberg

DEDICATION PAGE

For my parents, Gene and Arlene Simons, who taught me to love books and learning. And for opening my eyes to the rest of the world through many yellow trimmed issues of The National Geographic.

There is an acknowledgment page in the back of book, but just incase my husband, Sheldon, forgets to look, I want him (and the world) to know how much I appreciate his support. Thank you dearest for believing in me, even when it's not your dream.

CONTENTS

Part One

Tom and Vicki
The Foundation Years

Chapter One

A Call From the East

Lakshamakka pulled her brightly colored saree around her and ate a breakfast of rice before starting her morning chores. The hot Indian sun baked the ground during her long and tedious walk to the low-caste well two kilometers away. The high cast well in her village was forbidden to those of lower social standing. All morning Lakshamakka would help her mother carry water, placing the clay pots on their heads. And then the cooking and gardening would begin. The Hindu gods were demanding and they also needed attending to. She enjoyed being with her mother as they talked, sang, and laughed. Back at home she watched her mother go through the rituals.

"Why don't we know what we will be in our next life, Mother?" she asked softly in Telegu.

"Because no one knows how much good karma they have, my daughter. If you have lived a good life then you will come back as something good. If you have lived a bad life then you will come back as something bad."

"But, Mother, how can we know if we are good enough?"

"No one knows. That is the way the gods want it," she answered.

As Lakshamakka followed her mother, she began to get tired and fell behind a few steps. She watched her mother so strong and tall carry the water with the clay pot securely positioned on her head like a crown. Six yards of the silky material of her saree floated now and then in the light breeze with the pallav gracefully falling over the left shoulder, as she swished in rhythm with her mother's stride. A thought came into her mind. No, maybe it was a question. Did she dare ask her mother? She was taught to respect their Hindu faith. To be truly Indian one must worship as their ancestors did, appeasing millions of gods. But she secretly wondered something. Would the gods hear her thoughts and think she is doing something bad? Like a criminal, she thought about it again. Why were there millions of gods and not one who was loving? Why did they feel so far away? She shook the thought from her mind as best she could. It was supposed to be that way. The gods were powerful and important, and she was only a girl.

Chapter Two

A Victorious Second Chance

This is the story of Vicki.

In 1950 the winds swept through Aberdeen, South Dakota, with a change of season for Mrs. Wolden and her two daughters. With Linda, at twelve, and Gretchen, nine years old, Mrs. Wolden knew the years would pass by quickly and they would be graduating from high school. She had enjoyed their companionship in the absence of her traveling husband. Although the changing of districts often made it necessary to move, it had been a decent enough life for them with his salary from Shell Oil Company. She and the girls seemed to adapt to change readily. Maybe all the moving made them closer as a family. Recently, though, her husband had settled down as the owner and president of Aberdeen Nash Auto and it seemed his traveling days were over.

She thought about how to fill her time when the girls left, perhaps a part-time job would help. Many were married at eighteen these days. It wouldn't be long. Her thoughts turned back to moving. Why couldn't they live near a big city like Minneapolis or St. Paul? Her husband had talked favorably about the Twin Cities when he had traveled or visited relatives living in Minnesota. Then there was her other idea. He had raised his eyebrows when she first suggested another little addition to the family, but lately he seemed amused by the whole thing. It almost seemed to make him look younger when they discussed it.

"Are you sure you want to have another child, honey?" he had smiled at her, picking up his leather briefcase. "You better think it over while I'm at work today. Maybe we can talk about it after I get a home-cooked meal tonight?"

Ruth Marie let out a laugh. "And which kind of meal would make you the most agreeable, Mr. Ralph Fred Wolden?"

"Sirloin steak, if the budget will allow for it, Mrs. Ruth Marie Wolden."

Later that evening, after the girls had gone to bed, Ruth Marie glanced at her wedding picture she kept on the nightstand. Had they really looked that young back in 1935? No, she thought, I can't have another child; I'm thirty-eight.

The summer came and went. Autumn faded into winter and Ruth Marie began taking out the Christmas decorations for their home. They had not made it to the big city yet, but when they did a new little one would be going with them. A soft glow on her face appeared as she thought about the future. On Christmas Eve she worked on a family favorite: pork chops, sauerkraut, and a German dish of drop dumplings called nefffels. Suddenly she felt a sharp pain. A few minutes later she felt another. Soon they were fifteen minutes apart. "Ralph—something's wrong—this is too much like real labor."

"I'll let the girls know we need to go to the hospital, Ruth," he replied with a concerned look.

"Honey," Ruth Marie called to her husband, "don't let the girls see you so worried."

Linda and Gretchen ran up to their mother with a small package in their hands. "Please, Mother, before you go to the doctor, could you open our Christmas present to you?"

Ruth Marie calmly opened the package, her eyes glistening as she looked at the beautiful bracelet they had bought for her. Despite the labor pains she embraced her girls and relished the moment. "Thank you, you're both my sweethearts. I'll try to be home as soon as I can." She kissed them both in a bittersweet way one does when things are uncertain.

At the Catholic hospital Ruth Marie's face was white, but she was surprisingly calm as the Catholic Sisters packed ice around her lightly-clothed body. She thought of Mary in the stable in Bethlehem and how all she had was Joseph and a few animals around her. She could hear the nuns praying softly, always praying. Her mother had come from a Pentecostal background, but she had prayed with the same determination. Somehow it felt as though her mother and even her grandmother were there in that hospital with her. By morning the labor pains finally subsided. It was truly a Christmas miracle.

"She must be on bed rest for the duration of her pregnancy," the oldest nun had said, looking deep into Ralph's bloodshot eyes. "You have two daughters to help you until a relative can come to help. She must not do anything." Then with warm hands she grasped his hands. "You have been given a second chance with this little one. It will be interesting to see what God will do through this life."

Three months later on March 30, 1951, their second chance was born—Victoria Lynn Wolden. "She has been a victory for me in a battle I almost lost," Ruth Marie said to her husband, who was watching her rock the baby in the hospital room.

"Let me know when Victoria is ready to travel," Ralph replied to Ruth Marie, "and we will take a trip to Minneapolis and St. Paul. I think there could be a house she might like in one of those cities."

When the happy couple arrived home with their third girl, Linda and Gretchen met them at the kitchen door. Slowly Ruth Marie unwrapped the blanket so both the girls could see their new sister. Linda was very pleased and seemed proud to be the big sister, but nine-year-old Gretchen scrunched up her face in a knot. After one look at the bald-headed bundle, she declared, "What do we need her for?"

Soon, though, Gretchen was enjoying the role of being big sister. Now instead of playing dolls, she had Victoria to dress up like a little princess. Gretchen was happy to have little Vicki with them wherever they went and would fuss over her making sure her clothes were just right. At the family gathering, Gretchen was so proud and protective of her new little sister that it brought a few smiles to the adults. Ruth Marie was talking to her siblings about plans to move to the Twin Cities. Talk turned to the Korean War and then the newly crowned Queen Elizabeth at age twenty-five. The afternoon passed and it was time to bundle everybody up and go home. As they drove along the country road, Ruth Marie thought about moving again. "What about your brother and sister?" Ruth Marie asked her husband. "Do you think they are really serious about moving to the Twin Cities nearer to relatives? It would be so nice to have them move there when we do, wouldn't it?"

Ralph agreed. Both of them felt family was one of God's gifts not to be forgotten or seldom seen. Not only was it good to share holidays and special events together, the family was like a safety net when the world fell apart.

A short time later, two and one-half-year-old Vicki scampered around the room "helping" her mother pack. "Thank you for bringing Mommy some newspaper, sweetheart! You're such a big helper." Ruth

Marie glanced through the newspapers as she rolled glasses, plates, and cups into old issues of the Minneapolis Tribune. Ralph had been picking up the five-cent copies for her to read when he would pass through in search of possible real estate. One headline from June 2, 1953, told of the two mountain climbers who were the first to reach Mount Everest.

"Oh, look at this, Vicki," her mother said.

Vicki's large soft hazel eyes moved from her toy dishes she was pretending to pack to her mother's gentle face.

"Remember when Daddy brought this newspaper home for me? July 27, 1953. Truce Signed in Korea. Fighting Stops."

Vicki nodded in agreement and began babbling back a response, her flaxen curls bobbing with every enigmatic word.

"Just think," Ruth Marie continued, "the war lasted three whole years, yet it took only eleven minutes to sign the truce. Well, I'm glad that's over. It's happier times for all of us."

Ruth Marie was tired of moving, but after so many times of relocating she was good at it. Besides, her husband had promised her they would be putting roots down in the Twin Cities. Even he was getting tired of wanderlust. Finally, Ruth Marie's dream of living close to her relatives and the big city opportunities for Linda and Gretchen would be within reach. And family picnics with cousins to play with would be in store for little Victoria.

Chapter Three

Thomas Gregory Elie

This is the story of Tom.

On June 6, 1952, Al and Ruth Elie gazed at their little boy, Thomas Gregory Elie, and thought he was the most perfect baby they had ever seen. After two weeks the happy couple proudly attended church Sunday night, while Tom rested peacefully through the service and the socializing afterwards. Later that night Ruth checked on him before going to bed and prepared herself for several night feedings. To her amazement, she awoke in the morning and realized she hadn't gotten up once all night. When Al got home from work that evening Ruth gave him the report, "That baby of ours is so easy. Why, he slept all through the night until this morning!"

Al and Ruth Elie had been married almost five years when they decided it was time for Ruth to quit her job at the Sears and Roebuck Company in Minneapolis, Minnesota, and start a family. Now they would be totally dependent on Al's job of selling office supplies to provide for their needs. However, they knew that their real dependence was on their Heavenly Father. Both of them had been raised in families where faith was lived out vibrantly rather than just a dull duty of going to church once a week to avoid feeling guilty. It was a fun time for Al and Ruth and they looked forward to adding another little one to their nest.

Months passed and Al and Ruth were becoming experienced parents, learning all the tricks of the trade, or so they thought. One day while driving along one of the busier streets in Bloomington, Al noticed a Kiddies' Carnival on the right side of the road. Not wanting two-year-old Tom to notice and then fuss about going to it, Al pointed to the driver's side of the road. "Tom, look at the swamp on the left."

Tom replied, "Daddy, look at the swamp on this side." His parents burst out in laughter at his creative reply.

Hospitality was a regular occurrence in their home and Tom would get excited to the point of not knowing what to do with himself when they were having company. Once when the doorbell rang, Tom ran to the door to help his mother greet the company.

"Come see my room!" he exclaimed to the children as soon as they had passed the threshold. Not getting a response fast enough for this energetic two-year-old, Tom repeated, "Come see my room!" With legs built of springs, he bounded toward his bedroom, proud to have his own room with a small chest of drawers, rocking chair, crib, and an assortment of toys. But instead of getting out his toys he jerked open the lower drawers of his chest tossing out all the carefully washed and folded clothes. Soon the floor was a kaleidoscope of scattered little boy's clothes.

Betty and Pete Peterson were familiar visitors at the Elie home, knowing Al and Ruth before they were married. After Ruth graduated from high school she left Alexandria and moved to the cities to work. Al had come down to the cities from a small northern township. Pete had met Betty after finishing his term in the Air Force flying on missions during WWII. All four young adults attended Minneapolis Gospel Tabernacle on 13th and Lake Street and had become life-long friends, even going on vacations together through the years. Even as a young child, Betty saw something in Tom that caught her interest. "You know, Pete, there's something special about Tom. His love for the Lord is so earnest. I bet God's going to have some kind of calling on that young man."

Tom began having adventures early in life. The first one was when Al decided to do some repair work while almost three-year-old Tom was in his crib sleeping. He propped the metal ladder against the two stories of siding to the roof of their home. It was their first house and Al wanted to keep it in good shape. Ruth was away on an errand and he was in charge of Tom until she got back. All of a sudden there was a rattle on the ladder. Before Al could look down the ladder, a small brown-haired head appeared, "I'm here too, Daddy."

Al's heart skipped a beat. He considered how to get his young son up the last two steps, but realized he couldn't reach him. Silently praying he watched Tom take those last two steps toward the roof and then scooped him up into his arms and onto the roof. As Al sat in stunned silence Tom looked around and said, "Daddy, you sure can see a lot up here!"

Next Al had to figure out how to get his son down. The ladder had a steep angle with a metal web-like cyclone fence directly below it. Slowly he crawled past Tom and got onto the first rung of the ladder and then worked with Tom to get him to step down. Once Tom's little frame was tucked in close to Al's chest, they gingerly made their way down the ladder. Al was never so relieved as when they set foot on solid ground. He quickly put the ladder away and kept a steady eye on Tom until Ruth returned home. Alas, Tom's adventures with his Dad would continue to the dismay of Ruth!

It was nearing Christmas and Ruth was expecting their second child. One morning when Ruth was picking up Tom from Sunday School, the teacher approached her.

"Hello, Mrs. Elie. I wanted to let you know that Tom will be singing a solo in the Christmas program."

Ruth let out a laugh. She knew Tom loved to sing, he was always singing around the house. He knew every chorus sung at church as if he had purposely memorized the book, but sing in front of a large audience? Her doubt of Tom getting shy and backing out grew. "I don't think he'll do that in front of a crowd," she said.

Undeterred, the Sunday School teacher replied, "You leave that up to me."

The night of the program Ruth nervously dressed Tom in a gray wool Ethan suit. Her fingers almost trembled as she fastened the shorts and placed little shiny black shoes over the knee-high white socks.

"You look cute as a button!" she said, her eyes gleaming. Well, at least he would look nice if nothing else, she thought to herself.

Ruth had been told by Tom's Sunday School teacher that he would proceed up to the platform before his class and sing his part of the song first and then wait for the rest of the class to come to the front. After taking their places they would all sing the song together. Al and Ruth sat down in one of the crowded church pews. Ruth looked over the audience of grandparents and church members and tried to rest her hands peacefully on her growing abdomen with the hope of their second child.

Al looked at her, "All we can do is wait and see what will happen."

Soon the music started and a cute and confident toddler came striding down the center aisle like he owned the place. He was handed the microphone and began to sing his little heart out. Tom sang the solo without a hitch, but then something unexpected happened. As his classmates began marching up to the front Tom began to sing the solo again. It took a little while for all the children to make their way to the front, so Tom sang the solo a third time, and then again while the children found their places. By now the audience was snickering and enjoying the extra encores by the little gentleman in the gray wool suit. Finally, the class joined Tom and sang their part of the song and Tom had to relinquish the microphone back to the emcee of the program.

The Elie nest grew by another son and it was time to show Tedd off to the relatives. Ruth and Al were finishing up another visit with Ruth's parents in Alexandria and saying their good-byes before driving home in their 1954 Oldsmobile. They had purchased it used, but the green sedan with the cream-colored top had a smooth ride, and was still in good shape. By this time Tom was a mature four-year-old and already fascinated with cars. He followed his father outside to warm up the Olds. Tom watched his father start the car and reach down to release the emergency brake. Al had recently heard the WCCO radio announcer, Cedric Adams, give advice that a person should let the engine run in cold weather before driving it and make sure not to set the emergency brake. Just leave it in park. Al looked directly into Tom's innocent large hazel eyes. "I'm going to help your mother with your new little brother. I'll be right back. Don't touch anything."

When Al and Ruth came out the door with baby Tedd, Ruth let out a scream. The car was missing! It had rolled down a gentle hill into a ditch and the front tire was lodged in between a tree and fence post. Al ran to the car and flung open the door. Tom was crying and shaking.

"He's safe!" Al yelled as he pulled Tom out of the Olds. Ruth's brother-in-law came over with his tractor to pull the slightly scratched car back onto solid ground.

"So much for free advice," Al quipped to no one in particular.

Chapter Four

That's My Girl!

After moving to the suburb of Hopkins, Ruth Marie registered Linda and Gretchen at the local high school, while Vicki would go to grade school the following year. Linda came in the door one day wearing a cheerleading uniform, "Hi, Vicki! Ready for more cheerleading practice?"

Vicki got so excited she nearly tripped as she ran to hug her big sister, Linda, who had been teaching Vicki a few small cheers. Vicki's chubby little hands would push out, as she yelled out in her best little five-year-old voice, "Push 'em back! Push 'em back! Way back!"

Linda's voice was enthusiastic that day as she called out, "Mom, where are you?"

"Right here, dear. How was school today?" Ruth Marie came around the corner just as Linda started eating the after-school snack her mom had set out and gave Vicki a bite. "Mom, do you think it would be all right if Vicki helped cheerlead at some of the football games?"

Ruth Marie's puzzled expression matched her tone, "What ever are you talking about?"

"Some of the girls were over last week practicing and Vicki kept following us around and imitating everything we were doing. She looked so adorable that we all thought it would be fun to have her help; kind of like a mascot. I asked Mrs. Brown and she thought it would add interest. We could sew a little outfit to match ours. What do you think?"

Ruth Marie went to work cutting and sewing all week. For the finishing touch she sewed a large letter H for Hopkins on the front of the top.

The next week after Ralph had gotten back from another business trip, he was greeted by a cheerleading trio. He couldn't believe how cute Vicki's little outfit looked on her. After giving Linda and Gretchen a warm embrace he scooped up Vicki and carried her into the house laughing and tickling her.

"Ruth, I'm home…and look what I found in the front yard. My little cheerleader princess!" he beamed.

Ruth Marie's eyes lit up with joy. "Hi, honey! Isn't she just adorable? You wouldn't believe all the routines she can do and she's memorized every word."

As if on cue, Vicki cheered for her dad, "Go Warriors! Hopkins High!"

Sunday came and after the Wolden family settled into the church pew at Mt. Olivet Lutheran Church, Vicki asked to hold the hymnal. Although she couldn't read, she wanted to sing like everyone else. So at age five, Vicki began her life-long career of singing in church choirs and other special productions. Faith was an important ingredient in the Wolden household and both parents were active in serving in the church. Ralph would attend church even if he was out of town.

Ruth Marie began volunteering as a cook at the summer church camp. "Vicki," she asked, "how would you like to help me in the kitchen this summer at camp?"

Vicki was full of questions. "What else do you do at camp? Where is it? Is Daddy coming?"

"One question at a time, dear!" Ruth Marie laughed at her daughter's inquisitive mood. "When we are not cooking we can hike down to Lake Superior. It's so large that it sounds like the ocean when the waves come in. The camp is located in Lutsen, a few hours northeast of Duluth."

"Lutsen." Vicki tried out the name of the town.

"You'll like driving through Duluth, Vicki. It's a harbor town with huge ships coming and going filled with iron ore."

After they were all packed up, Vicki's dad gave her a squeeze and kiss. "Throw in a few rocks for me when you get to the lake."

"Okay, Daddy. I'll find the biggest rock I can and throw it in for you."

"That's my girl! I want you to be a big help to your mother, too."

"I will." Vicki didn't know what camp was all about, but it seemed like fun already. After that first year it became the summer ritual to go to church camp on the North Shore, as many people called it.

After camp was over the Wolden household became alive with romance. Linda was always doting on Vicki, so it was no surprise when she asked Vicki to be her junior bridesmaid at her wedding. Vicki confidently walked down the aisle almost stealing the show from the bride and groom. Her dress matched the other attendants dressed in white with pink-scalloped hems. The small bouquet of red roses she carried blended perfectly with her satin sash. Vicki quickly grew to love her new brother-in-law, Don, and thought he was the best husband a girl could want. Maybe someday she would find somebody like Don. The three sisters stood for a photo with matching winter wheat hair and creamy alabaster faces lit up with joy. The only sad part was Linda would be moving to California with her new husband. Soon 1961 came around the corner and Vicki's other sister Gretchen was married. Vicki was so happy to have Dick for another older brother, who along with Don, gave her just as much attention as her sisters.

The changes in the family kept coming. Gretchen and Dick announced they were moving to California, too. "Why is all my family leaving? I feel like an only child," Vicki's eyes teared up.

"I know, honey, it's hard for me too." Ruth Marie comforted her daughter as best she could and prayed a prayer of thanks that she still had one in the nest.

Now that Linda and Gretchen had married and begun carving out their own lives, Vicki was left to herself with Mom and Dad. She needed more action. Kneeling with her elbows on the back of the couch, her chin in her hands, she waited for the station wagon to pull in across the street. Because the car could only accommodate half the family, the Framptons would attend Catholic Mass in two shifts. Her hazel eyes were impatiently fixed on her target across the street. As soon as the car pulled in the driveway she zipped across the street. Knock, knock, knock! Vicki's ten-year old frame bounced up and down, her golden hair bobbing in rhythm as she waited for her neighbors to answer the front door and come out to play.

With twelve kids, the Framptons were an instant baseball team, a group for Kick the Can, or companions for climbing trees. No matter what they did Vicki joined in and she always wanted to be with them. She had been raised Lutheran, but her parents had taught her to respect Catholics and had reminded her many times about the Catholic nuns in South Dakota helping them in their time of need. Following the nuns' example, Vicki's mom was always helping someone else. Experiencing hard times for herself, Ruth Marie could be moved to tears just listening to someone else's troubles.

It had been a good life for Vicki living in Hopkins until the news of the move came to her ears. "Why?" Her confusion spilled out in tears, "I like living here! Why do we have to move?"

"Now, honey, try to understand. With Linda and Gretchen married this house is too much for just the three of us. Your father and I found this wonderful apartment close to my sister and our church. It's right in the heart of the big city where there are all kinds of opportunities waiting for you!" Vicki could tell by the look in her mother's face that the matter was settled. Vicki didn't realize it, but her destiny was right around the corner. Living in south Minneapolis would be both wonderful and tragic.

Chapter Five

Seeds for the Future

Once again the school Christmas program rolled around with Al and Ruth waiting to see what their second grader Tom would end up doing this year. The year before, Tom had kept it a secret when his first grade teacher had asked him to do a solo. This year the curtains opened up and there in the center of the stage was their son with the microphone in his hand ready to emcee the program. Again Tom had never said a word to his parents and neither had the teacher. The entire program went smoothly with Tom confidently emceeing the entire production. Would the surprises ever end with this boy?

It was Saturday and that meant one thing. It was chore day at the Elie home. Tom huffed and puffed as his eight-year-old arms lifted the large bag of garbage up each step from the basement. Al came up the steps and asked Tom to bring up some other items from the basement they were clearing out. Tom's shoulders dropped, "I can't do that!"

Al placed his hand on Tom's sagging shoulder. "Look at me, Tom." Tom looked into his father's eyes. There wasn't anger, just firmness and patience.

"I would never give you something to do you can't do."

The words burned into Tom's mind and spirit. He would go back to this moment often when challenges seemed too overwhelming. Already at this tender age Tom was learning more than perseverance by being asked to obey the assignment given. He had to learn to trust his earthly father. Next, he would learn to trust his Heavenly Father. Obedience through trust and faith would lead to a life hallmarked in one word often used by others to describe Tom: integrity. But there would be many lessons along the way.

Tom was excited. Grandpa was coming down for a visit from Alexandria, the small Minnesota farming town in which his mother had grown up. That meant there would be music. After one of Mom's great home-cooked meals, Grandpa would gather the family around and play his six-string guitar and sing Gospel melodies. Tom would join along singing his nine-year-old heart out unashamed. His younger brother Tedd and his baby sister, Barbara, clapped their hands as best they could in time with the music. Ruth's side of the family was musical; his cousins were all taking instrument lessons. Naturally, it stirred a bit of curiosity in Tom about learning to play an instrument; soon Tom began taking piano lessons from the pastor's wife where they attended church. At first the songs seemed fairly easy to Tom, but the difficulty increased when he began to play the bass and treble notes together and his half-hour practice each day seemed a little longer. Soon, however, he noticed that even those pieces were beginning to be played with ease and he enjoyed playing the piano even more. There was only one exception—when the weather was nice and his friends would want to play ball outside.

Tom grabbed his football and was about to run out the door when he heard the familiar voice of his mother.

"Tom, you haven't practiced the piano yet today."

"Oh, Mom, can't I do it after I play ball?"

"Now, Tom, if you don't practice you are going to have to pay for your own lessons."

Tom thought about it. Two dollars and fifty cents was a lot to part with. "Oh, all right. I'll practice."

His friend stood outside the door shuffling from one foot to the other. "Tom, can we use your football until you're done with your piano practice?"

"Okay..." Tom said reluctantly and handed him his football. Usually Tom derived quite a bit of satisfaction from conquering a new song. But today it was pure torture! It pained Tom to think that every minute of his thirty-minute practice his friends were outside in the glorious sunshine with his football having the time of their lives.

Tom's ten-year-old eyes opened with excitement. Today was Saturday morning. He was free from school for two whole days to play ball with his friends! Two days to ride his bike—his thoughts were interrupted by his mother's cheery voice.

"Tom, time for breakfast and chores, so please come to the kitchen." A determined and organized woman, Ruth never seemed to run out of energy or ideas as to what her three children needed to do in order to become responsible and productive citizens one day. Tom made his way to the warm breakfast waiting for him. Slipping into his spot next to his brother, Tedd, he waited for the prayer of blessing over the food.

He watched his father bow his head. "Heavenly Father, thank you for Calvary, for sending Jesus to die for our sins. Thank you for this food we are about to eat. Amen."

His father's faith was perhaps a little quieter than his mother's, but it was just as intense. After the blessing, Tom's mother, with her brunette hair neatly in place, passed around the food as she went over the chore list for Saturday morning.

"Tedd, take out the garbage and then sweep the basement. Barbara, you can help me wash the breakfast dishes and then you need to check under your bed." Barbara couldn't look her mother in the eye, knowing she had been found out after having stuffed items under her bed rather than putting them in their proper places. Tom thought he noticed a brief smile in his father's pale blue eyes. A little bit of syrup dripped off Tom's pancakes and landed on his pants. Grabbing his napkin he managed to rub it off, but got some stuck on his hand. Bothered by anything dirty or sticky on his hands, Tom worked with his napkin until the gooey substance was completely gone.

"And, Tom, your room needs a thorough cleaning also." Ruth settled into eating her breakfast with confidence that once again the Elie ship would be in great shape by noon.

After washing his hands Tom slowly walked around his room moving things here and there. Why did they have to do chores every single Saturday? Couldn't there be a Sabbath on Saturdays for boys who needed to play ball with their friends after being in school all week? And what about his favorite TV shows? Didn't his parents know that Lassie and the Lone Ranger were on TV Saturday mornings? Everyone was busy; household family sounds of work and voices drifted through the house. Suddenly Tom had an idea. Why couldn't he just live somewhere else where there weren't any chores to do on Saturday morning? A plan was forming in his mind. First, he would need to pack a few things. A person needed clothes, a ball, and a sandwich. The breakfast dishes were done and the kitchen was empty. He made a peanut butter and jelly sandwich, and after washing his hands, he packed the sandwich in his bag, grabbed his jacket, and slipped out the door without anyone noticing. Excitement filled his small ten-year-old frame as he walked down the street ready for adventure. He would show them!

Still early, not one of his friends was outside playing, so he kept walking toward the direction of the construction site with the newly-delivered sewer pipes. After tossing a few rocks, he found a large cement sewer pipe and ventured in. He called out, "Hello, in there," and listened to the echo of his voice. He found a spot to sit and pulled out his sandwich. The strawberry jelly tasted good with the brand of peanut butter that happened to be on sale when his mother had done her shopping.

"Hm-m-m..." he said to himself. Nothing like a peanut butter and jelly sandwich to make a boy feel good about the world. Things got a little boring after that and Tom didn't know what to do next. "Hmpf," he thought out loud, "I bet they are all worried about me. I guess they learned their lesson by now. I might as well go home."

To his surprise no one was in the front yard looking for him; in fact, there was no one at the windows or door looking for him. He imagined they must be at the table crying and calling the police. Expectantly he walked in. His shoulders drooped as he realized everyone was busy. He could hear his father downstairs patiently instructing his brother Tedd on how to change a fuse when the washing machine would blow it out occasionally. His mother was in the room where the ironing board was kept starching and pressing clean laundry. Tom could hear Barbara pulling stuff out from under her bed as he walked past her room. No one even noticed Tom hang up his coat and unpack his traveling bag. Here he was back in his room moving things around again. Some idea that had been. "What a lousy world!" he muttered to himself.

But Tom had other ideas that worked out better. Like the carnival he organized to raise funds for the fight against muscular dystrophy. A local television station was promoting carnival kits for kids packed with posters and ideas for neighborhoods in the Twin cities area. Homemade games could be set up with small prizes and the profits would be sent into the station. Many kids in the Minneapolis and

St. Paul communities were getting involved helping other kids with muscular dystrophy. Casey Jones, a Minnesota television icon of the 60's and 70's was so popular homemakers would continue to watch *Lunch With Casey* even after their children went off to school in the fall. After watching Casey Jones in his railroad overalls talk about where to get the Muscular Dystrophy Carnival kit, Tom waited for Casey to finish the TV program with the daily melody, "Happy, happy birthday to every girl and boy..."

During dinner that night Tom talked to his parents about the carnival idea and sent for his packet. After reading over all the illustrated pamphlets, he enthusiastically recruited his family and friends to help. The day of the carnival came and Tom was pleased with the turnout and felt thrilled at the end of the day when they counted up their earnings. Not only had he raised money for other kids in need, he had also derived satisfaction during the planning and execution of the carnival. All his lists in the packet were checked off and it made him feel good. His parents complimented him on a job well done. After the big clean up Tom asked himself, *What else could I do*?

"Mom, where's the telephone book?" Tom asked.

"It's in the drawer closest to the phone."

Tom sat down at the table with the telephone book and prayed silently to himself asking the Lord to direct his attention to the people who most needed to read a Gospel tract explaining God's plan of salvation for them. His ten-year-old fingers paged through the book. As he found an address he carefully copied the address from the phone book onto the white envelope. Looking through the assortment of little hand-sized Gospel booklets he had ordered, he selected one, inserting it into the envelope. Tom licked the unpleasant-tasting glue and sealed the envelope. Looking over the envelope he checked to be sure his own return address was in the left upper corner. His mom and dad had agreed to pay for the postage.

One day a letter arrived in the mail. "Tom, this came for you today. I don't recognize the name on the return address," his mother said, handing him the white envelope.

Tom glanced at the writing, "It's an address from one of the telephone book people."

Ruth was curious as to what the letter said, but Tom never shared the contents of the letter with her, and she felt she shouldn't press him about it. From the time he was a boy he was always looking to find people that didn't know Jesus. Ruth decided to continue praying for Tom and the desire he had to share the Gospel story with others.

Holidays were special times in the Elie home. Relatives would come and wonderful food would be served for the occasion. The adults would visit upstairs while the cousins played downstairs. Then the adults would come downstairs for the after dinner entertainment. Once again, Tom would be busy organizing and leading; this time it was a play. As director, he would oversee the whole production from blocking out the action, feeding lines, to organizing the chairs, with only one exception: the acting. For all his natural leadership tendencies, Tom was actually rather shy.

During one such holiday season, Tom wrote a poem about the Christmas Story in school and won first place in the class. "Tom, would you be willing to read your poem at the Christmas program this year?" his teacher asked. The poem was a simple story of how Christ Jesus was born the Son of God.

Tom came home from school excited, "Mom, guess what? I wrote a poem."

After Ruth read the poem, Tom said, "My teacher really liked my poem and I guess I won first place and I will read it at the Christmas program…but she changed one little thing."

"What did she change?" Ruth replied.

Tom pointed to the line. "Right here. I wrote Jesus, Son of God.

She erased 'God' and put in 'Mary' so it would read 'Son of Mary.'"

Ruth had to wait a while before she could make the telephone call. Once she felt she had had her emotions under control, she called the school and asked for the principal. In a determined, yet calm tone she explained to the principal what had happened and concluded with, "She cannot do that, because what she is doing is changing my son's viewpoint of who Jesus is. Sure, Mary is the mother of Jesus, but this was God's Son who was given to us."

The principal was quick to respond, "Oh, well, I'll let you talk to her. I'll leave a message and she'll call you right back."

Ruth received several phone calls of apologies. The teacher, Mrs. Tell, had no intention of doing anything wrong. "Mrs. Elie, I am so sorry. Please let me explain. I was raised Catholic and attended a private Catholic school. Because we were trained to call Jesus, the son of Mary, I just automatically wrote in the correction. I in no way intended to suggest to your son that Jesus is not the Son of God. I am really sorry about this."

Ruth considered the sincerity of the teacher and realized that is was a natural instinctive reaction of the teacher and was not meant to interfere with the way Tom was being raised. Yet, Ruth felt she needed to clarify one more thought, "I accept your apology, but I hope you understand that that's a very serious thing to do. It can confuse a child. If Tom sees Jesus as only the son of Mary and not the Son of God, then all we have taught him from the Bible doesn't mean much. It's sort of like watering down the truth. It's like only telling one part of the real story and leaving out the most important part."

The teacher was listening more than Ruth realized. Years later they would meet again. Mrs. Tell, who was now teaching fourth grade at the same grade school Barbara was attending, came up to Ruth, "Mrs. Elie, I've got to talk to you. Do you have a few minutes?"

"Of course I do," said Ruth, not knowing what to expect.

The teacher broke into a smile, "What you said to me that day made me stop and think. I didn't have a Bible, but I found one and read it, and I learned a lot that I hadn't known before. Not only about Jesus the son of Mary, but also about Jesus the Son of God. Reading the Bible gave me a greater understanding of who Jesus is and what God did in sending his Son to die for my sins. Thank you, Mrs. Elie, for bringing this to my attention."

Neither Ruth nor Mrs. Tell realized back then that this was the beginning of many Catholics and Protestants studying the scriptures. Years later it would become a common occurrence in many Catholic and Protestant churches to have Bible studies where the scriptures were read, studied, and even taught by lay people. But for now the Jesus People movement was just beginning to form its first wave that would soon crest and become a spiritual phenomenon of the 1970's and 80's. God's Holy Spirit was up to something that would surprise priests and church leaders all across the United States. The pioneering days of contemporary worship and the implementation of the arts, particularly in drama, would soon be coming in like a mighty rushing wind of the Spirit. And Tom Elie would be right in the middle of it, along with a certain special someone that destiny would bring together by the hand of God.

Chapter Six

Growing Pains

One day when Tom was twelve years old, his mother noticed an envelope that Tom had addressed to Billy Graham waiting to be mailed. Curious, she picked it up and discovered it was filled with change. Not wanting to send loose change in the mail, Ruth decided to open the letter and exchange the coins for dollar bills. To her surprise, inside was a serious letter Tom had written to Billy Graham. The Elie family had recently seen the Rev. Graham at the Minnesota State Fairgrounds in St. Paul. It had been an impacting event for all of them. She was delighted to read Tom's brief letter:

Dear Rev. Graham:

I'm only 12 years old, but I feel God is calling me into a life of ministry. I want to know how I can be certain that that's what God wants me to do. I want to win souls like you do.

Sincerely,

Tom Elie

Later as Ruth told Al about the letter, they both agreed to pray for Tom and God's direction for his life. Eventually Tom received a letter back from the Billy Graham organization with a reply that included:

You watch for open doors. When you feel compassion and an urging in your spirit to want to do something, watch for open doors to minister.

Tom began watching other evangelists and how they would minister to the lost. The coals of fire that would create a burning passion in his heart for souls to hear the saving message of eternal salvation through the death of Jesus Christ were getting more intense. One such evangelist was Lowell Lundstrom. A young man newly converted to following Jesus with all his heart, Lowell had a passion to see the lost come to Christ. Tom had prayed and felt his best friend could be ready to accept Christ. When they got to the church they noticed a well-used station wagon pull into the parking lot. Out jumped Lowell, his wife Connie, and his brother.

"Let's sit in the front row," Tom said to his friend.

"Okay." His friend had no choice but to follow Tom up to the front where all the action was. Tom's eyes locked onto Lowell. As the trio sang and Lowell preached from the Bible, Tom thought to himself: *This is what I want to do.*

When the time came to invite people to respond to the Gospel message, Tom's best friend made a decision to follow Christ. Tom was elated. The joy and satisfaction of seeing his friend and others turn from darkness to light, made Tom thirst and desire to see even more people receive this free gift of salvation. He began to dream of hundreds, no…thousands of people wanting to accept the Lord. Tom thought about the scriptures that described hundreds of thousands of people joining with the crowd of witnesses already gone before them. In the book of Romans Paul wrote about this crowd of witnesses cheering them on anxiously waiting to receive them at heaven's gates. Yes, Tom thought to himself, that's what this Christian life is all about: helping and leading thirsty souls to the well of salvation. It was mature thinking for a twelve-year-old, but Tom had a destiny to follow. Similarly, another twelve-year-old boy had astonished those at the Temple in Jerusalem, discussing theology with the Jewish scholars during the Passover celebration. Many marveled at Jesus that day wondering how such a young lad could know so much about Yahweh.

Although Tom had a calling to be an evangelist at a young age, he still struggled with his own spiritual life. He had prayed to make Jesus Christ his Lord and Savior, so why did he feel he kept needing to give his life to Christ? He had gotten "saved" many times over at church. Every time he would listen to a sermon about repenting and surrendering to God, he would feel a stir inside. Sometimes he would stay in the pew and other times he would walk to the front altar for prayer. He knew all the right words to say and what he believed in was true, so why was he doing this again? Was it for assurance of salvation? Was he sensing the Holy Spirit at work bringing in a harvest of souls? He couldn't figure it out. Then one day he chose to publicly demonstrate that he was a Christian by practicing the first-century Christian church model of baptism by immersion. After the pastor spoke the words, "I baptize you in the name of the Father and of the Son and of the Holy Spirit," Tom came up out of the baptismal waters changed. It seemed to drive a stake into the ground that meant *I have made Jesus Christ my own. I am His and He is mine. Forever. Wherever the road leads we're going together.*

Tom peered at his newest sister snuggled into her pink blanket. At age thirteen Tom was used to being a big brother. After Tedd came Barbara and now it was Beth Kathryn. The only one in the family feeling dethroned was seven-year-old Barbara until she learned that she was now her mother's assistant in caring for the new baby.

Tom didn't know quite what to do with Beth until she got older. Then he did what came natural for an older brother.

"Don't! Stop! No more! Leave me alone!" Beth protested, while

Tom dragged her five-year-old body across the carpet until she had rug burns.

"Stop teasing me!" Beth's eyes would fill with tears when Tom would go too far with his sarcastic jesting.

Snap went the towel again. This time, though, the end had been dipped in water and it stung like a scorpion. "Stop it! I'm telling on you, Tom!"

Beth ran out of the room crying for mom. But, all in all, Tom was a good older brother, helpful and loving. Although Tom was thirteen years older than Beth, moving out of the house when she was only six, Beth would become an ardent advocate for her older brother as the years unfolded.

Beautiful sounds of music filled the Elie home as Tom continued practicing on the Koehler Campbell console piano. The family's musical talent was apparent in Tom's ability to read the notes ahead as he played the music. After one of Tom's many piano lessons, his teacher took Ruth aside, "Tom is by far the best sight-reader I have ever had. It's amazing."

He had been taking lessons with Mrs. Kingsriter, the pastor's wife, since he was eight years old. For a while, Tom became a piano teacher and gave lessons. But like Mrs. Kingsriter, he had no patience for students who would not show dedication by practicing, so he soon retired from the piano instructor profession. Tom continued with his lessons from other teachers acquiring the versatility of sight-reading using piano sheet music or reading the chords on guitar sheets. After playing through the chords, Tom could then fill in the song with the melody line. By the time Tom was a junior in high school he began playing piano for Sunday morning church services at Bloomington Assemblies of God. He had also taken trumpet lessons and would often play that, as well as sing in school and church choirs.

A significant event impacting Tom's spiritual life happened at youth group when Tom was fourteen. Because his church was part of the Assemblies of God denomination, the youth groups were known as Christ's Ambassadors, or simply CA's. One Wednesday night at CA's, thirty teens gathered to hear a special speaker—an evangelist by the name of Reverend A. G. Dornfeld. He was a gentle man who would later remind Tom of Ichabod Crane in appearance. Rev. Dornfeld talked to the teens about the benefits of asking Jesus for the same infilling of the Spirit as the disciples had in the beginning of the early Christian church. He referred to scriptures such as in the second chapter of Acts, "The disciples were filled with power from on high to be bold in their witness of all Jesus had done." This caught Tom's attention.

Then Rev Dornfeld went on to say, "Before he returned to heaven, Jesus had told the disciples to wait in Jerusalem for the promised Holy Spirit."

Tom saw the connection between being a witness for Christ and what the Assemblies of God referred to as the Baptism of the Holy Spirit. At the conclusion of his talk, the evangelist asked, "How many want it?"

Tom and a girl raised their hands. They were then asked by Tom's pastor and the visiting evangelist to come into the pastor's office for prayer. In the office Pastor Kingsriter and Rev. Dornfeld laid hands on their heads and began to pray, asking Jesus to baptize these two youth not with water this time, but with the fire John the Baptist had spoken about, and that which Jesus had promised.

"Close your eyes, Tom," suggested his pastor.

When Tom did, he began to see a blue sky with clouds and three empty crosses. Then something else happened right out of the pages of the New Testament—Tom began to speak in another language he had never heard before! For Tom, it was a beautiful experience with the Lord. He felt infused with a new source of power to pray and to believe with greater faith for the lost souls who needed God's plan of salvation through Jesus Christ. When they were done praying, Tom saw his parents waiting in the hallway for him.

The pastor explained to Al and Ruth what happened, "Tom received the Baptism of the Holy Spirit!"

"Oh, really?" they asked in unison.

They were intrigued because both of them had been raised in the Pentecostal tradition of believing that the Holy Spirit and the gifts given by the Spirit were necessary for a productive Christian life. During times of family devotions they had talked to their children about the Holy Spirit, but had never prayed with Tom for this additional filling of God's Spirit.

However, Tom was not ready for what Pastor Kingsriter said next. "Go ahead, Tom, show them."

Tom looked at his parents and they waited happily as he mustered up the courage to speak in tongues. His parents' excitement helped to ease Tom's embarrassment and he prayed a little bit. As they left the church, he thought to himself that if he ever got into the ministry he would never do that to anybody.

Over the years the memory became more humorous to Tom and he always had a soft spot in his heart for the two men who were willing to pray with two teens to receive more of God. In the days to come, Tom would lean heavily on the supernatural power of God for what he called "winning souls." There would also be times of personal prayer in a heavenly language that would help Tom weather spiritual storms in the future.

Tom was surfing on the edge of excitement and things were going well for him at his youth group. Still, there was a longing to be where the ultimate action was—winning souls. There were souls out there who needed an opportunity to hear the Gospel and make a decision about Jesus Christ. The eternal destiny of these souls was hanging in the balance. Tom could feel it. Were there other young people like himself who had a passion to win souls? Tom had read in the New Testament how Jesus, walking with his disciples one day, had asked them to look at the wheat fields. Then Jesus had told them to pray to the Lord of the Harvest that he would send out laborers because the fields were ripe, waiting for harvest. Tom felt an urging to go to fields that were white, ready for the harvest of souls, and work with other fieldhands. But where were those fieldhands?

Ruth whispered a "thank you, Jesus" as she left the school building. It was hard work raising four children in the 1960's with the culture wars going on and the Viet Nam situation. Although Tom got raving reviews at conferences at the local high school in Burnsville for good grades and a positive attitude, he still was a basic teenager. At age sixteen Tom's dream to own a car came true the day he laid eyes on the light pea-green 1962 Chevrolet II Nova. He paid the owner $500 of his own hard-earned money. It was a whiner of a car, but it was his first car, and he drove it home proud as all get out. Tom painted a black racing stripe on the bottom to look cool with the Baby Moon hubcaps. Then he installed an orange shag fur all across the dash and rear window area. He souped it up, or tried to soup it up, by buying a new part for his distributor to make it go faster. But that idea ended up ruining his distributor.

Tom's friend taught him how to squeal rubber with the Nova. "This technique is known as the 'neutral drop.'" His friend tried to sound professional as he trained in the newcomer to the world of cars. "First, put the car in neutral and rev the engine. Then when it's revved up real good, drop it in drive. You'll burn a line of rubber from your tires a mile long!"

Tom learned how to squeal rubber and became quite efficient at it, but later found out that it was a good way to ruin the transmission or "tranny," as most of his friends called it. Instead of a neutral drop it could have been a tranny drop: leaving his transmission on the road.

One night while driving home after church youth group in his Chevy Nova, one of the four or five teens riding in the car had an idea.

"Hey, the light is turning red. Let's do the Fire Drill!"

Everyone started laughing, "Yeah, let's do it!"

Tom's sense of adventure got the best of him, and he said, "Sure, let's do it!" They came to a full stop at the red light and the car doors flew open. Everyone was laughing and yelling as they ran around the car once and then jumped back in before the light turned green. No one noticed the police car parked across the street. When the red flashing lights of the squad car came up behind Tom, he got so nervous he didn't know what to do. His first reaction was to turn off the car lights even though it was pitch black outside.

"Oh no! It's the cops!"

"We're busted, man!" said someone in the car.

Tom began to panic and decided to turn left onto a side street. Perhaps the police car was after someone else and he was merely in the way. After all, the squad car had seemed to come out of nowhere. Tom pulled over to the side of the curb. His heart sank as he saw the squad car pull in behind him and the police officer step out of his car. Tom's fingers shook as he retrieved his driver's license out of his leather wallet. The officer scolded him after looking the license over, "Thomas Elie, you are only sixteen and a new driver. I don't want you being a future menace on the streets."

Tom's face was a bit ashen when he came into the house that night. He dreaded telling his parents, he knew should. But, instead, he decided to watch the mailbox and try to intercept the ticket, only he missed one day of the mail because of the youth church convention. The next morning his mother ripped open the shades of his room to let the early morning light come in and to help with her interrogation. "It's time to get up, Thomas Gregory Elie!"

Tom could see the steam coming out of her ears.

Both his parents were stunned. They were not accustomed to their son having a brush with the law. "Where did you learn the Fire Drill?" Ruth asked, wanting to get to the bottom of this.

"From the youth pastor. He used to do it all the time."

Al gave the verdict, "Well, Tom, this is a serious thing. You will have to forgo your driving privileges for awhile."

"Yes, sir, I'm really sorry." Tom's repentant heart was written all over his face. Not only did Tom lose his wheels, but he also had to attend what some referred to as Ding Dong School. For two weeks one of Tom's parents had to drive Tom to a special driving class three times a week.

Ruth was so upset she didn't know what to do, so she called the pastor's wife. "Hello, Mrs. Kingsriter? This is Ruth Elie and I…I need to talk to you about something."

The voice on the other line was full of compassion. "Go ahead, Ruth, I'm listening."

Before Ruth could finish the whole story, the pastor's wife burst out laughing. Ruth struggled for words, "Well, I guess it's funny if it's not your son. I thought you would understand because you've raised boys and are more experienced than I am."

The pastor's wife heard the disappointment in Ruth, however, she knew this was nothing compared to what some parents had to go through. "Well, Ruth, I want to tell you something. Tom's a good kid. He's a teenager; nothing more, nothing less. You have to roll with it at this stage of the game. Another thing, remember, when you punish him you are punishing yourself. Having an extra driver in the family with three other children is a big help. He needs to be corrected, but don't make it so long and severe that it creates bitterness in his heart."

After Ruth hung up the phone she let out a sigh. Her burden had been lifted and Mrs. Kingsriter had given her a new perspective on raising boys. God was faithful to help Ruth through the growing pains of Tom becoming a young adult, and he would continue to help as the next big changes in their family came along.

Chapter Seven

The Ethnocentric Onion

For years Tom had felt God's strong call to be involved in evangelism. All the touch points of his young life were combining to shape his future destiny: the Billy Graham Crusade, water baptism, praying for the Baptism of the Holy Spirit, and seeing the young evangelist Lowell Lundstrom's passion for bringing souls into God's kingdom. Now at sixteen, Tom was looking for open doors to share his faith when he heard about mission trips that young people around the United States could take. The Assemblies of God denomination had a youth organization called Ambassador in Missions, or simply, AIM. Tom was so charged up with youthful zeal and energy he had to do something.

So when he heard about a team of students going on what was called a short-term outreach mission trip to Jamaica, he was ready to make a difference in the world for God's kingdom. Organized by AIM, their main focus would be evangelism or "house-to-house witnessing" as described in the brochure. No one else in the youth group was going, but other students from across America would be on the team. Tom liked the idea of meeting other people his own age who were hungry for God and eager to share their faith with the world. He began raising support by letting his friends and family know he was going and started saving his own money. He also spent time praying in preparation for the trip. Meanwhile, overseas immunizations were completed and the passport was on its way.

A few weeks before Tom left, he gathered around the family table to share the Sunday meal of pot roast and potatoes with gravy. Al prayed, "Lord Jesus, thank you for Calvary. We ask that you bless this meal and Tom's upcoming trip to Jamaica." Sunday meals were great times for conversation and often centered on what the Lord was doing in their lives. Beth might share about a friend in the neighborhood she helped and then was able to tell the mother about Jesus. Barbara and Tedd would share stories also.

Finally, the day came for Tom to go to Jamaica. He checked his passport picture. In his opinion, it wasn't a good one; still, he thought he looked older. His chin line was changing with the hint of a mustache over his upper lip. His sandy brown hair, cut short above his ears, was parted on the left side, and his hazel eyes were like his mother's. Tom's generous smile with good straight teeth didn't show much on the picture. In fact, it looked more like a mug shot, but one couldn't expect too much from a passport picture. He shrugged his shoulders, ran down the stairs, tossed his suitcase into the trunk of the car, and took off for the airport, his mom and dad riding along.

After the plane lifted off the Minnesota soil, Tom let out a sigh of contentment as he watched the houses and roads grow smaller. He could hardly believe he was on his first flight over an ocean!

After the excitement wore off, Tom dozed for a while until the captain announced the upcoming descent to Jamaica. Tom could feel the grinding of the landing gear go into action. Eagerly, he looked out the window and saw palm trees and buildings coming into view.

"Oh, my word!" His curiosity turned to shock when he noticed there were no normal houses like he was used to seeing, but only little huts fashioned together using local materials, such as palm fronds. Admittedly, some were artfully done, but they still looked as if the big bad wolf from *The Three Little Pigs* story could come by and blow down the entire block in two good puffs. When the brochure had described it as house-to-house witnessing, Tom had pictured something quite different! What had he gotten himself into?

As Tom stepped off the air-conditioned plane, he was hit with a wall of heat and humidity. Students his age were milling around in the airport. Tom met the leader of the team who took him and several other young guys to the pastor's study at a church. Tom tried not to let his mouth drop during the drive to the church. People with dark skin were everywhere wearing brightly-colored clothes of every Caribbean description. He saw men with long twisted hair known as dreadlocks. He wondered how his mother would feel about their hairstyles. Their driver commented, "Those men with the dreadlocks are called Rastafarians. It takes three years to get their hair like this. They use only natural products for washing their hair, and according to local rumors, this natural product is cow dung. Then they squeeze out the water like wringing out a sponge. They are very spiritual and don't like people taking their picture."

At the church Tom was relieved to learn that an air conditioner had been set up in the pastor's office that was temporarily converted into the boys' dorm room. Tom couldn't see the floor because it was covered with wall-to-wall mattresses. When he spread out the bed sheets he had brought from home, Tom tried not to think about how old the mattress was. While eating a meal and attending an orientation meeting, Tom met some of the other kids on the trip. Girls and guys from all over the United States were there; some looking excited, and some looking tired and a little unsure about the whole situation. Eventually, Tom and the guys headed back to their lodging feeling pumped up for the next day. After getting cleaned up in the simple bathroom accommodation, Tom laid down on what would be his new bed for the next month. The air conditioner droned on with a hint of mildew smell mixing with his thoughts of his first day in another culture. It was so different! But with God's help he could do this. He whispered to himself *I can live with this.* And by God's grace he did.

Every day groups of teens went hut-to-hut with a guide, sharing their faith and inviting people to evening meetings at the church. By the end of the month the entire group of teams saw 500 people come to the Lord. Tom was ecstatic! He still struggled with what his leader termed "culture shock;" nonetheless, it truly was an adventure similar to the Apostle Paul's missionary travels described in the Book of Acts and the Epistles of the New Testament. Yet Tom was torn by his growing love for the people and the camping-like conditions of his environment. As a child, Tom had insisted on bringing a washcloth with him when he played in the backyard sandbox. He didn't like the way the sand made his hands feel: gritty and dirty; so he would routinely clean the sand off his little hands with the washcloth and then go back to his sand project. It wasn't an obsession as much as liking the feeling of being clean.

Before leaving the exotic island, Tom was meandering through one of the many open-air markets where the Jamaicans were selling fresh vegetables, fruit, fish, and other wares. It was a perfect place to take pictures with all the bright colors, a creative patchwork of texture and aromas. This was nothing like the stores back home where aisles were neatly organized with cleverly marketed packaging, and signs directing the shopper to the proper location of items.

Suddenly through the crowds of people, Tom caught a glimpse of dreadlocks. With sounds of locals bartering and dickering over items all around him, Tom watched the Rastafarian. He was passing silently through the crowd like a cloud in the sky unaware of Tom raising his camera until he heard the click. Tom's desire to take the picture had propelled him to do the unthinkable. All his cultural training for the trip went out the window. No sooner had he taken the picture, than he saw the face of the Rastafarian turn and look directly at him. The man's eyes darkened, smoldering with anger. Tom dropped his camera, the safety strap around his neck saving it from hitting the ground. The next thing Tom saw was angry dreadlocks sprung toward him like a deer startled in the woods. Tom didn't wait for introductions or apologies. With the now furious ranting of the Rastafarian filling the air of the market, Tom did what any young student away from his suburban home would do: he ran. His adrenaline kicked in and he shot out of the market like a bullet.

Scampering down a side street and in between buildings and huts, Tom managed to lose his pursuer. His heart felt as if it was ready to pound out of his chest, but he smiled as he thought about the picture. He didn't realize at the time how ethnocentric he was by deciding that it was foolishness for the Rastafarian to think it evil to have his picture taken. Anyone knew it was just a picture and nothing else.

God would keep working with Tom, teaching him how to be culturally sensitive by learning to respect different ways of doing things, regardless of how ridiculous it seemed to his western mind. Each culture has its own worldview; God's instructions through the Apostle Paul remind us that we are to be all things to all people, as long as it is not in direct violation to the scriptures. Over the years Tom would learn how to contextualize the basic principles of scripture and even styles of music in order to bridge the Gospel of Jesus Christ to others. He would learn that while keeping true to the message, the packaging of this message might vary in how it looks. For Tom, letting go of ethnocentricity also meant letting go of the white Jesus—the Minnesota pew with organ music playing, and the suit and tie. Jamaica had been the first layer of the onion of his ethnocentric worldview to peel back. The next would be in the heart of Minneapolis and eventually across the ocean to a land that was waiting for someone to come with the life-giving message of living water. Somehow, God was going to take a clean-cut, tall, white, Scandinavian suburban man and send him to a people of dark skin who had been taught all their lives to worship not one god, but millions of gods. If Tom had only known then where he would end up going with the Gospel message of eternal life through Jesus Christ, he would have instinctively reached for a clean washcloth.

Chapter Eight

A Sad Farewell

It was a cold winter day and Vicki was trudging the one block to school. She couldn't wait until she could get a car and drive to high school like some of her classmates did. Her blonde shoulder-length hair was carefully styled with a side part. The late 1960's look of smooth straight hair, had gently flipped-up ends kept in place with a generous amount of hair spray. She had turned sixteen last March and was looking forward to turning seventeen and almost being an adult. Vicki's dad had left for another trip to Detroit. He had kissed her the night before like he always did and told her to keep up the good grades in school and help her mother.

Vicki had noticed something about him. "Dad, you're getting more gray hair!"

"I suppose I have one or two. I am fifty-four, ya know."

"Fifty-four? That is so ancient! Do you need a cane? Did they even have electricity when you were born?"

Vicki smiled as she kept trudging along the winter street.

When Vicki got home from school that day her mother told her to pack an overnight bag, "Vicki, you are going to Aunt Pearl's house for a few days."

"During the school week? What's wrong, Mom? What is it?"

"I'm sorry, honey, but your dad is in the hospital in Detroit. He's had a heart attack, but he's in stable condition. Gretchen and I are flying down there. Your brother-in-law, Dick, is going to drive us to the airport."

She normally enjoyed being at her aunt's house. Playing with Aunt Pearl's three daughters had filled that void of being an only child after her two sisters, Linda and Gretchen, had married. One cousin was the same age and they were still close, even as teens approaching graduation from high school.

Vicki waited at her Aunt Pearl's house for news about her dad. When someone told her the news of her dad's sudden death, she felt her body go numb. As she stood listening and watching the others, the room began to shift. Suddenly she was in a tunnel. Her hearing had changed, the lighting had changed, everything was fuzzy. Then it came. The grief, the anger. Its embers smoldered until she was consumed by the force of it all. No more football games on TV with her dad. No more of his teasing and tickling. She would even miss his instructions to her before going out of town about listening to Mom and keeping up the good grades.

The day of the funeral was bitter cold. Grandma and Grandpa Wolden walked into Mt. Olivet Lutheran Church, the pain of losing their son etched on their faces. Vicki sat on the pew next to her mother. Her two older sisters, who normally looked so attractive with their blonde hair and beautiful satin skin, now looked pale with hollow eyes. On February 1, 1968, her father died while on business in Detroit at age fifty-four. At sixteen that was hard to figure out.

The family gathered at home after the funeral, some sitting in the living room and some in the kitchen. Vicki sat watching, listening, and questioning...

Why?

Why did this happen?

Why God?

Why did you take my dad away from Mom and me?

With the force of a hurricane, the angry question ripped open her heart of pain and Vicki let it out for all to hear. "I'm never going to church again!" She stomped down the hallway with tears breaking from her eyes like sheets of rain. The door slammed behind her leaving a room full of blank faces. Someone called after her. Another voice said to let her alone to cry in privacy.

After all the relatives left, Vicki and her mom began to stumble through life. She went back to high school. Many students avoided her. Who could she talk to? Did she want to talk to anyone? Certainly not God. Her resentment grew. Her mom wasn't a healthy woman. She had the beginning of rheumatoid arthritis. Didn't God know this? Well, she would take care of her mom and she would do the best job she could. And another thing she would do is find a job and start buying her own clothes. A stubborn rebellion was born in her that day. And it felt good. Finally she was getting somewhere. She would tuck her dad's death away in a neat little drawer and be her mom's biggest ally.

Vicki's sister, Linda, who lived in Florida, invited them down for Easter that year. It was their first holiday without Dad. Who would carve the Easter ham? Linda's husband, Don, tried to be a big brother for Vicki. In the years to come both Don and Dick would become like fathers to Vicki, looking after her and loving her as best they could.

As Neil Armstrong took his first step onto the moon July 20, 1969, two young people in Minnesota were navigating through their teen years to adulthood, while a young married woman in India was being persecuted for her newfound faith.

Vicki Wolden was now a young woman of eighteen. Her graduation from high school came and went. Everyone in the family tried to make it special, but it wasn't the same without Dad and they all knew it.

Tom Elie had just turned seventeen and was looking forward to his last year of high school. The whole world was before him, and he was itching to get started at whatever lay ahead.

One day in the future, Lakshamakka's path would cross with these two teens in a way none of them could imagine. She would symbolize what many others in India were waiting for—the chance to hear the message of hope. The chance to have a church building. The chance to drink fresh water from a clean well, free from rules of caste restrictions. Yes, the eternal legacy of a quiet echo was beginning to sound. But there would be a few more years before the destiny of that echo would unfold.

The Gospel According to Scrooge
Music and Lyrics by John Worre & Tom Elie
Memories
Recorded on location at Jesus People Church

Part Two

Jesus People

Chapter Nine

One Million or One

India before 1969

A small village with no electricity and no transportation facilities, Sirivaram's nearest bus stop was a six-kilometer walk. Lakshamakka lived in Sirivaram and at age thirteen had become a married woman. He seemed a good man. He was twelve years older than Lakshamakka and was a relative on her mother's side of the family. Many men and their mothers were cruel to the new daughter-in-laws, demanding large dowries. If these demands were not met then beatings would begin and sometimes "accidents" would happen with kerosene and the cooking stove. Her parents had tried to do their best to arrange a good match for her. Her new husband was very spiritual; at least she could say that much for Sunkanna. He was a Hindu priest at the goddess "Peddakka" temple. She would try her best to make Sunkanna proud of her as his wife. Perhaps she could become more spiritual herself. With her water pot on her head, Lakshamakka headed back to the village from the low-caste well. When she got there, she found that a crowd had gathered around an elderly man with kindness in his eyes, holding a small book in his hands. As she passed by she heard a few words in her language of

Telegu. "This God is not a god who is distant and far-off—but close. If you will draw near to him, he will draw near to you. He is not a million, but one–the One True God."

Men, women, and children were politely listening while cows roamed the streets looking for something to eat. One dusty black cow found a shady spot on the side of a large clay home and settled in for a nap. Lakshamakka continued with her water container into the house. As she peered through the window, she saw that her husband, who had been part of the crowd, was now coming back to the house. He saw the questions on her face and told her about the old man. "His name is Samuel, a name from the holy book of the Christian God. He walks to many villages talking about this Christian God and reading words that he says come from the Christian God's own mouth. He has come many times now. Sometimes we talk and I ask him questions."

India 1969

Lakshamakka lifted her head watching a cloud pass over the silvery moon. She was a mother of three now. The cool night air felt good after another day of the scorching Indian sun. As she closed her eyes, words in her Telegu language began to form softly on her lips. The peaceful evening contrasted sharply with her mood, the anguish in her face intensifying to match her clenched hands. She pressed her hands against herself, as if blocking the doors of her heart, to prevent hope from pouring out like the floods in the monsoon season. Doubt was crouching ready to take the place of hope. What did she have from the Spirit of the One True God? Yes, it was faith. A little word with mountainous consequences. Falling to her knees, the whisper of Abba Father in Telegu calmed her face and quieted her soul. She and her husband had been asked, no, rather escorted out of their village for speaking that name again as the only One True Name. For three days they had lived in the neighboring village after angry men had come in the dark and tried to burn the home of a believer. Lakshamakka and her husband had been with the few who had gathered to worship and pray to the Christian God.

Her newfound faith in Jesus Christ had cost her reputation, but what did she care? The burden of appeasing thousands of gods only to come back after death and have to appease them all over again was gone. She was free—free to worship the One True God who was close to her now, closer than any other of her thousand gods who only demanded, oppressed, frightened, and tormented her soul. They were distant; Jesus Christ was near.

"I feel your presence even in the midst of this," she whispered in Telegu. Great faith welled up in her. Peace was her companion. Yes, she would follow Jesus to her grave and until then she would pray.

She and her husband, Sunkanna, had begun to believe the words of the old man Samuel. Often they would get together with him after the others left and he would read more words from the Christian holy book. Then one day it was as if a light came on in both of their hearts and chased the darkness away. A door opened up and they understood what Samuel had gently yet boldly explained for months. They had both prayed with Samuel asking the Christian God to forgive their sins and become their One True God. Lakshamakka smiled as she thought of that day.

"You have a new spiritual life!" Samuel had told them with brown eyes that twinkled with joy.

Lakshamakka relished the memory as she spontaneously ran her small brown hands over her rounded stomach. A new life was growing inside of her. Covering her head once more with the ornately decorated pallev of her saree, she kept praying. A tiny fierce thought, filled with the same faith of many who had gone before her, welled up inside of her. She would ask for the impossible: her unborn child to believe and a place of worship for those who called upon His Name for salvation to gather together. Lakshamakka smiled, her tear-filled eyes opened with joy.

One year later all had changed. Yesaiah, her fourth child, was a healthy baby boy. The villagers were impressed with the large herd of goats they now had, which enabled them a few luxuries: three meals a day and a house made with stones and wooden beams. Sunkanna had taken the Christian name of Matthaiah and was very respected in the village. His elder brother was observing how much the Christian God was blessing their lives, not only with material blessings, but also with a peace that was a mystery to him. Soon Matthaiah's elder brother became the first of several in the village to put their trust in the One True God.

Chapter Ten

Souls Harbor

By the time Tom was a senior in high school he became the president of his church youth group Christ's Ambassadors. His knack for administration and leadership were apparent to those around Tom and he seemed to enjoy the challenge of all the activities he was immersed in. He would try to make the after church family dinner as much as possible, but with the youth group and school activities, he wasn't around the house much anymore.

On Friday nights music blared from the radio as Tom cruised down Lake Street. It was the place to show off whatever vehicle you had and see what everyone else was driving. The route consisted of going between two Porky's restaurants, where young drivers could pull in and get a root beer and hamburger while keeping a sharp eye out for street rods pulling in and out like a parade. Tom had bought his second car when he was eighteen, a 1968 Olds Cutlass sport two-door with a good engine and three-speed with a whiney transmission sound. He was proud of his pale yellow two-door coupe Cutlass with black interior, and it would become his all-time favorite car. It looked sporty going down Lake Street from the east side Porky's to the west side Porky's. After buying the Cutlass, Tom decided he wanted a "thrush" muffler and had a friend from church who owned a service station install it. The mechanic's wry comment was, "I'll never understand why people take a perfectly good muffler out and put in one that sounds like it has holes in it."

It was a life-long love affair between Tom and cars, a hobby of sorts, for a man who wasn't keen on hunting and fishing like other Minnesota outdoor types. He enjoyed learning all he could about cars: the year of manufacturing (or make), engine power, and overall design. Eventually, Tom began buying slightly damaged cars, contracting the body and engine work out, and then selling it for profit. Not mechanically inclined or liking greasy hands, he didn't tinker with the engines much.

The 8-track player stopped the music of Tom's favorite group, the "Carpenters," while changing to another track. Tom kept on singing till it picked up again. "These harmonies are so incredible," he said. Tom liked singing the different harmonies, from the soprano to the alto and then to the background backup voices. "Another great vocalist is John Davidson."

"Hey, Tom, let's see what the top forty is this week," one of his riding buddies suggested.

"Okay." Tom switched on the radio just as the announcer of WDGY gave the lead-in for the Top Forty countdown of the week. As eighteen-year-old Tom and his buddies cruised Lake Street, the sounds of the 70's filtered through the car mingling with the sound of the engine and young men's idle talk. Every once in a while a favorite would come on and Tom would crank up the volume and you could hear a choir of guys belting out the Beatles, The Monkees, The Mamas and The Papas, and whatever else came across the airwaves.

"Don't sleep in the subway..." Tom was singing along with Petula Clark. His friends continued discussing their favorite music.

"Another song I like is MacArthur's Park," Tom said. "It's the orchestral arrangement that makes that song so good. I have no idea what it's all about, but I think the chord progressions are so fabulous. It must be something to write music like that and then record it in the studio."

With Tom's natural bent toward naivety, he either wasn't totally grasping all the lyrics of modern music, or simply didn't have enough street smarts to know there were underlying meanings in some of the songs being played. Music was just music to Tom and he enjoyed all types. He never saw a conflict with the music and his Christian values. He loved the Lord with all his heart and there weren't any contemporary Christian artists for his age. It was perfectly acceptable to many believers to sing hymns and traditional spirituals at church and listen to secular music on the radio. Pop music remained his favorite style as some stations started to focus exclusively on the harder rock songs associated with the drug culture of the 60's and 70's. It was a time in American culture when values were getting stretched and tested, but for mainstream America radio and TV, it was still fairly wholesome. All that was soon to change and Tom would be confronted with the realities of street people and drugs, exposing him to a way of life he hadn't an inkling existed in his protected suburban life. Not in his wildest dreams did Tom think his love for both Christian and pop music would one day merge and he would land right in the forefront of a movement of contemporary worship. It would be a new sound for a new generation.

It all started at Souls Harbor, a church in downtown Minneapolis, when Tom had been invited to sing with a group known as "Lost and Found." While he sang, Tom prayed for those who were looking for answers. As his eyes roved throughout the packed-out audience seated in the beautiful former Lyceum Theater, he saw many hungry and thirsty faces who seemed to be looking for answers. So many young faces. He felt new vitality course through his body. This was where the action was.

Not long after this, one of Tom's friends, Steve Carlson, had heard about some young people who were serious about sharing the Gospel with other young people right on the streets of downtown Minneapolis. "Tom, you should come down with me to Park House. It's a place where a bunch of kids live who really love the Lord. They have meetings on Tuesday nights."

"Okay, let's go," Tom said, and made plans with Steve to go to the next Tuesday night meeting.

When they got there, Tom looked over all the people in the room. They looked as if they had just returned from Woodstock. Most of the guys wore blue jeans and had long hair like his sisters. In contrast, Tom had a clean-shaven short haircut and was wearing his signature outfit: a collared shirt tucked into polyester pants with a basic belt. He was the epitome of the suburbanite who lived across the tracks in a safe and sterile environment. Suddenly Tom realized he had more in common with these hippie-type people than with his clean-cut suburban peers. The people at Park House had passion, real passion for the Lord that reflected in their eyes and on their faces as they worshiped. His heart nearly exploded with joy, thanking God for hearing the deep desire of his heart: to find people his own age who really wanted to follow God seriously. Tom's worldview concerning outward appearances and what made someone acceptable in the Lord's eyes began to change that night.

Someone was strumming a tune in E minor on his guitar and the young hippies began to sing the simple melody of *They'll Know We Are Christians By Our Love*, by Peter Scholtes, starting with first line of *We are one in the Spirit, we are one in the Lord....* After the chorus they began the next verse: *We will work with each other, we will work side by side*...and ending with the final line of the chorus...*yeah, they'll know we are Christians by our love.*

These kids from the wrong side of the tracks knew what sin was and also knew its consequences. They knew what separation from God was really all about. Some of the kids from Tom's youth group seemed to put God off to the side, striving for popularity by how they dressed or by what achievements they had accomplished through good grades or sports. At times, they reminded Tom of white-washed tombs—having a form of godliness, but denying the power of Jesus as Master and Lord of their lives. For some it seemed Jesus was merely "fire insurance," a safety net, if you will, from the heat of hell. The good life in suburbia had given many of the kids a false sense of spiritual security that led to a spiritually passive lifestyle. Not wanting to be judgmental toward his peers, Tom reasoned that some of it was just plain immaturity and some would outgrow this and make Christ their own later as adults. That night at Park House, Tom knew he needed these new rough-around-the-edges disciples of Christ. His thirst and hunger told him he was at the right well and the water was sweet, holding a lot of promise for the future. He felt more complete than ever before. Not only was he determined to work with these Jesus hippies, he would live with them, too.

When Tom broke the news to his parents, he was not ready for the look of shock on their faces. Al was processing all that Tom was telling him, but Ruth couldn't help blurting out, "You want to live at a place called Park House?"

Tom proceeded, "Park House is just the opportunity I've been looking for to minister to people. It's a five-bedroom house with a basement located on Park Avenue. The idea is to invite new believers who are struggling with the basics of life to live there surrounded by mature believers. By living there I can be more effective in helping these people. Their lives are being transformed and they need people willing to live there and show them how to live for God on a day-to-day basis."

Tom continued explaining, "Mom and Dad, I realize how much I've learned from both of you that I take for granted. Most of these kids never had the upbringing I did and they need life modeled before them just like I needed it from you." Tom searched their faces. Their approval meant so much to him.

Al had listened thoughtfully and Tom could see the familiar look of encouragement etching its way along the lines of his father's face. "Well Tom, you have our support if you feel that it's the right thing to do." It was funny how many times Tom had looked to his father for guidance and counsel and never realized that his father was getting older. Their relationship was moving towards adult friendship.

Ruth relented with a nod, but her mind was swirling. How could her boy, a boy from the suburbs, who didn't know the first thing about drugs, go in there and help them?

Tom concluded with, "I have prayed about it and I feel in my spirit that it's what I'm supposed to do." Suddenly, before their very eyes, Al and Ruth saw their son transformed into the evangelist he had always desired to be since writing to Billy Graham. It just looked different than how they thought it would.

The day came for the move to Park House and Ruth found herself wandering up to Tom's room. She sat on his bed. Tom had all his belongings boxed up ready to go after he got back from running one final errand. Ruth let her fingers run over Tom's Bible. Its edges were well worn. In silence she sat and stared at nothing in particular. And then it came. A tidal wave of emotion grew from deep within her being and she began to cry to her Father in heaven, "God, you have to show me something that will give me peace about Tom going. I'm frightened!"

And then the dam of restraint broke altogether and Ruth sobbed freely, tears streaking her face. Finally, letting out a huge sigh, she touched the edges of Tom's well-worn Bible again and found herself opening it up to the Book of Psalms. With fingers slightly trembling, she began to read the words in front of her from Psalm 121.

First she read out loud the seventh and eighth verses: "The Lord shall preserve thee from all evil; he shall preserve thy soul. The Lord shall preserve thy going out and thy coming in from this time forth, and even for evermore." Then she read the first two verses: "I will lift up mine eyes unto the hills, from whence cometh my help. My help cometh from the Lord, which made heaven and earth."

Suddenly her burden of fear was lifted. How good was her God that he would visit her to reassure her with peace. How great was his kindness toward her that he would care to help a mother let go of her first bird leaving the nest. From that day on Ruth had a measure of peace that never left her and would always be a comfort to her.

On a hot summer night in 1971, Al and Ruth drove down to Park House to see how Tom was doing. As they approached the door of the men's Park House they could hear talking and laughter. The smell of food frying wafted out through an open screen window of the five-bedroom house. Someone greeted them at the door and told them Tom was in the kitchen. Much to their surprise Tom had an apron on and was flipping hamburgers like a pro.

"Oh, hi, Mom and Dad!" Tom flashed them a grin and turned back to watch the hamburgers.

Ruth's mouth opened slightly. Tom had never cooked anything at home—not even breakfast food. In their home, chores were assigned to their traditional roles with respect to gender. Now here was Tom cooking dinner for a bunch of ex-drug addicts and loving every minute of it. Tom showed his parents around and introduced them to all the guys living there. Ruth and Al looked past the long hair and tattered blue jeans and into the faces of souls saved from the ravages of sin. A few had decided to cut their hair short, but they still had their hippie clothes on. Others kept their hair long in line with the current fad of what some referred to as the "Jesus look" of the late 1960's. Al and Ruth left Park House with peace in their hearts.

After Tom had moved into Park House, his spiritual maturity quickly became recognizable to many. Everyone could tell he was from a well-mannered hard-working family, something they had only seen on Leave It to Beaver TV shows, which created a class separation. But Tom's humble attitude won them over, and after a short while they felt a kindred spirit with him. No matter their difference, a common cause bonded them together for many years to come: reaching the lost souls of the Twin Cities for Christ. If they only knew what God was about to do with this ragtag group, it would have, in hippie terms, "blown their little minds apart."

Chapter Eleven

A Second Birth

Vicki graduated from high school and wondered what to do with her life. Should she try going to the University of Minnesota like a lot of her friends were doing? Her life didn't seem to have much pizzazz to it. Was this all there was after high school? Her sister, Linda, who lived in Florida, needed help with a brood of little ones. Feeling restless and needing an excuse for a diversion, Vicki decided to say yes to her sister's request for assistance.

Georgine, one of Vicki's closest friends, invited Vicki over for pizza before she left for Florida. Georgine's mom was in the kitchen and began discussing religion. Wanting to be polite, Vicki listened as she explained the concept of entering into a transforming relationship with God by being born again. "This term 'born again' is actually found in the fourth book of the New Testament known as the Gospel of John. One night Jesus had a midnight conversation with a prominent religious leader, Nicodemus. In fact, Jesus came right out and told him that if he wasn't born again he would not have eternal life. Confused, Nicodemus asked Jesus to explain what this meant. So Jesus explained that not only are we born once physically, but that there is a spirit part of us that needs to come alive in order to have fellowship with God."

Then she quoted the scripture from John 3:16, "'For God so loved the world, that he gave his only begotten Son, that whosoever believeth in him should not perish, but have everlasting life.'"

On the way home from Georgine's, Vicki thought about God and decided she was too young to serve him right now. Maybe when she was older, but for now she had her life to live. It was fine for Georgine's mom, she seemed genuinely happy, but Vicki was ready to do her own thing now that she was finally done with high school.

The palm-tree-lined streets of Florida greeted Vicki each day as she shuttled kids back and forth from school activities and ran other errands for her sister Linda. The hot steamy summer was an adjustment for the Minnesota native, but it was a new adventure being a nanny. On the weekends she would help her sister with cleaning. Her nephews and niece loved having the extra attention. "Auntie Vicki, would you read me a book?"

Eventually Vicki found a job at a local restaurant that served breakfast and dinner.

It was a quiet night, which was unusual, because there were not a lot of family-type restaurants in the area, mostly nightclubs. Consequently, a steady stream of customers came in regardless of the time or day of the week. But tonight a family with two small children was seated in the back room in Vicki's serving section. After Vicki's initial greeting, she asked for a beverage order and they responded with, "You have an accent!"

"Well, I'm from Minnesota, but I don't think I have an accent."

The couple laughed and said, "Oh, yes, you do!"

With so few customers, Vicki found herself making small talk with the couple. They were so warm and friendly she couldn't help but enjoy being around them. As the conversation proceeded, it turned toward spiritual matters and they began discussing religious topics. The couple stayed for about two hours ordering dessert and spending time with Vicki, who began to open up to them. "You know, I've had a lot of questions. I've gotten away from going to church and I feel like I need to get back to church."

The couple encouraged Vicki by telling her that it was probably God who was putting these thoughts in her heart. "He is drawing you to *Him* because *He* loves you." Before the couple left they handed her a small brochure about Christian faith. "Here, Vicki, this is a tract filled with information you may find interesting. Our names, phone number, and address are on the back. Please call us if you have any more questions. We would enjoy helping you in any way we can."

The days passed and Vicki forgot about her interesting encounter with the family at the restaurant. It was the end of August and she needed to get back home to Mom, whose health condition with the rheumatoid arthritis was difficult to handle without help.

Back in Minnesota, Vicki unpacked her suitcase and sat on her bed cleaning out her purse. She pulled out the Christian tract the young couple had given her and read it over. All the things they had said came back to her mind about entering into a relationship with God that was personal rather than distant or vague. A relationship that was based on repentance of sins, love instead of fear, and forgiveness in place of maintaining a performance chart of religious duties. The word "grace" summed it up. By faith in Jesus Christ, a person was saved by grace and the desire to live the right way would follow, like water springing from a well. Vicki whispered to herself, "Oh boy, I'm away from God." She could feel the separation between her and God and wondered what to do about it.

After tucking her suitcase away in storage, Vicki called her closest friend on the phone, "I'm back. Let's get together!"

Georgine invited her over and greeted her at the door with a giant hug. While they were chatting, Georgine's mom passed by with a basket of laundry. After listening about Vicki's time in Florida, Georgine's mom began talking about religion again, but this time Vicki's heart stirred. Much of what she was hearing sounded similar to what the couple in the restaurant had told her. Georgine's mom gave her a book about the Holy Spirit. Vicki had never thought much about the Holy Spirit except when reciting the liturgy in church. It just seemed to be tagged on to the liturgy that began with the Father, Son, and then conclude with an automatic Holy Ghost. She didn't ever really consider the function of the Holy Ghost other than he or it was invisible. She was confused. But she knew one thing for sure, there was a choice being set before her: either to follow God in a serious way, or put him at a distance where he was viewed with respect, but was not the central focus of her life.

One day Georgine's mom came into the kitchen while the girls were fixing a snack and said, "You girls have to come to this revival meeting!" Before Vicki knew it, she was agreeing to go hear someone named Brian Rudd speak at a place called Souls Harbor. Her curiosity was getting the best of her. She had to find some answers and thought maybe going to the church service might help.

"Mr. Rudd is holding revival meetings at Souls Harbor in the evening, which is the church that meets in the Lyceum Theater in downtown Minneapolis. During the day he is holding school assemblies and inviting students from public schools to come to the meetings."

Vicki was surprised to see the busloads of kids coming from the local high schools. What was going on here? They worked their way through the crowd and managed to get three seats together. The music started and people began to stand and sing songs Vicki had never heard before. And they sang with all their hearts. They were respectful, yet more buoyant, maybe joyful was the word, than she had seen except at Christmastime. She didn't notice the young man helping with the music, who was wearing a polo shirt neatly tucked into his polyester pants and his brown hair groomed short—but she would someday.

Vicki recognized a familiar hymn, but most of the songs were new to her. Another thing was strange to her: no liturgy. No saying and repeating the same thing as she had done for years. But all was set aside as Brian Rudd took the stage in his wide-lapelled suit with his curly hair and flashing smile. His accent gave him away; he wasn't a local boy.

As he began to share his testimony of how God had saved him from a life of crime, anger, and sin, Vicki felt something break in her. All the resentment she had held onto since her dad had died was melting. Suddenly she became thirsty—thirsty for whatever this young man was talking about. A living God who was not far off—but close. A God who loved her so much that he was willing to let someone dear to him suffer a cruel death on a cross to pay for the sins of the world. And when God the Father raised Jesus from the dead, it was proof that Jesus really was the Son of God, given in exchange for eternal death. A soul could have eternal life, and it could start right here, right now on planet earth. The wellspring of salvation was something that started as soon as a person was willing to humble themselves and admit they had sinned and needed cleaning up in order to stand before the creator of heaven and earth on judgment day. Now many believed you could clean yourself up by being good or going to church, maybe even taking a religion class could help. But did this really cleanse sin? Weren't you just a nicer sinner? Perhaps a better-smelling sinner, but aren't you just a rotten sinner underneath it all?

Vicki didn't know what to do. Her heart was pounding. She was realizing for the first time in her life that although she believed God existed and Jesus had died on the cross, her faith had been based on the good things she had done, which was just enough to balance out the bad things. And she had been doing plenty of those bad things since her dad had died. Suddenly she wanted to change her life, to start over on a fresh slate with God. Could she turn a different direction, do what the speaker was asking, repent? Could she make God personal in her life as the Lord of her life, or keep him in a compartment to draw out on Sundays, holidays, and emergencies. Did God Almighty really want her to call on the name of Jesus for salvation, and make *Him* her own?

As soon as Mr. Rudd called for those who wanted to come down to the front and pray with him, Vicki bolted out of her seat like a rocket. Many followed after her filling the entire front section. She had never even seen what evangelists refer to as an "altar call" except when she watched Billy Graham on TV, but she didn't care. The burden was too great. It had to go, and God wanted to take it from her. Tears streamed down her face as she repeated the prayer to ask forgiveness and ask Jesus to come and be first in her life. She called on his name and she knew she was saved. Saved from eternal separation from God, saved from a life of anger and sin. Never again would she have to wonder about going to heaven, it wasn't totally up to her. God's Holy Spirit would lead the way and counsel her. She just needed to trust and follow Jesus. It was faith, simple faith. Her head swirled with new thoughts as they rode home from the meeting. She couldn't wait to go again and again. Souls Harbor was like a well for her. She would learn as she began to read her Bible that once a person has been born again as Jesus spoke to Nicodemus in the Gospel of John, they thirst for living "spiritual" water.

Vicki's mom was happy for her interest in religion until she learned about her plans to move into Park House. "What is this Park House all about? It sounds weird, like some cult commune one reads about in the paper."

Vicki tried to explain that it was a place for young people who wanted to grow in their Christian faith to live and grow together. One house was set up for women and one house was set up for men. It would be a life-changing decision for Vicki in ways she never dreamed of.

Chapter Twelve

Park House

Tom's new friends at Park House soon learned that Tom was the Bible guru and answer man for any questions they might have. Even in the middle of the night people would come to him wanting to discuss a doctrinal question or to pray with them. He saw how parched their souls were after living in a dry and barren wasteland. A popular rock song with the words "teenage waste land" was so accurate in describing the wearied condition of the new generation. The anti-establishment worldview philosophy adopted by many people in search of true meaning ended up in a bankrupted soul. The promises of peace and love through drugs and casual sex were a lie. Even a popular soft drink promised the real thing if you just drank the beverage. Soon, though, many would be saying that Jesus was the real thing.

That September, when Vicki moved into Park House, she contributed to the community by keeping the women's Park House running smoothly. Instead of working for employment, she helped with cleaning, shopping, and preparing meals for over forty people. Oftentimes she would help cook breakfast for both the men and women's Park House and the men would walk over and get their fill of pancakes. Added to these duties was driving the community van from Park House to run errands and providing transportation for people. In between all of this, Vicki was absorbing the Word of God through Bible studies that were a part of the everyday life at Park House. There was often good conversation with God when she was alone, or about God with others. As she began getting to know the other young people who lived there, her faith kept growing. She soon learned that this was called Christian fellowship. Finally, Vicki Wolden had that sense of belonging, and knew she was where she was supposed to be.

The revival meetings at Souls Harbor with Brian Rudd lasted over six weeks and many young people gave their lives to Jesus Christ. The effect was a complete transformation for many. In order to facilitate all the new interest in becoming serious believers in Christ, Bible studies were set up. Christian youth with years of Bible study were asked to help nurture these young followers of God. Tom was part of this group and felt fulfilled in helping and being where the action was. He had never seen so many people give their lives to Christ since his trip to Jamaica!

In addition to Bible studies, teams were formed to share the Gospel with total strangers.

"Okay, let's go," Tom said, after the threesome had finished praying that God would bless their time on the streets of Minneapolis and lead them to the right people. Down on Lake Street, Hennepin Avenue, and Nicollet Avenue or in Loring Park, Tom and his two friends would share God's message of love and freedom from sin with as many hippies and drug addicts as they could. Soon people were calling the threesome the "God Squad."

Many young people would talk with the God Squad and other teams. Then they would visit the young people's Bible study and be transformed by God's power. Some of these visitors even moved into

Park House and learned a new way to live. After getting back on track with God, these former drug addicts would tell others what God had done for them and more people would be invited to church, and so the momentum continued. Discipleship programs were developed and new converts were evaluated before being selected for coming to live at Park House for further training. There they had a regimented schedule of worship time, Bible teaching, study time, and even a basic work ethic. Then it was back out to the streets to let the light of God shine to those still in darkness.

Soon the Bible study, a mixture of seasoned Christians and new converts off the streets, began thinking about starting a church—a church to reach the new generation lost in drugs or self-absorption. The sexual revolution with no boundaries and the new mantra: "If it feels good do it!" wasn't proving to be the answer for the hippie generation. This would be a church that would be a light to the city of Minneapolis. In the early 70's, the term "Jesus People" was coined to describe the nation-wide revival. As the Jesus People movement swept through America, it became the unifying symbol of the young people in the Bible study at Park House.

On the heels of the Souls Harbor's revival meetings with Brian Rudd, the Tuesday night Bible study that Tom had been invited to had grown from a handful of people to a group of one-hundred young people. Young men and women were sitting everywhere, reading the Word, hungry for God. There was a stream of people going downstairs to be prayed for and then coming back up. Out of this organic supernatural move of God came a need for these hippies, college students, and ex-druggies to have their own identity. Already recognized as the leaders of the group, Dennis Worre and Roger Vann became the co-pastors in December of 1971. From this would emerge a community filled with a divine thrust that would be known as Jesus People Church. It would never become a denomination, but its influence would be felt across the nation as the life of this church unfolded with Tom right in the middle of it all.

During this time Vicki's older sister, Linda, had asked her to come to Florida over the holidays. It had been two months since she had given her life to God through faith in Jesus Christ. Her relationship with God had blossomed as she studied the Bible and spent time with other Christians at church and at home. She felt deeply satisfied and complete with her new worldview of having a relationship with God rather than merely religion. Soon she just referred to him as the Lord and he was part of her daily life, interwoven with her thoughts and conversation. She might pray more formally or she might talk to him like a trusted friend. She was his and he was hers. It seemed that the picture the New Testament used of the bride and groom was a perfect analogy because it captured her newfound feelings for the Lord.

As she packed her bags, she thought of the couple who had taken the time to talk with her about the Lord. She now knew that it had been a God appointment, and there were others too, including Georgine's mom. It was amazing how God had put all the pieces together for her good. To be sure, Brian Rudd had been the preacher who had asked her to come forward for the life-changing prayer. He had been in on the final harvest, but other people had done their part too. What if they had been afraid or decided that kind of thing was for professional clergy? At the thought of this, a renewed interest to share and witness about God's loving plan of salvation through Jesus Christ was kindled in her heart. She wanted to always be a light for him, some way, somehow. She might not be an up-front person like Brian Rudd, still she could talk to people and she did always like singing in choirs at school and at church. Maybe with a group it wouldn't be so bad standing up in front of people. After all, the message was about God's love, not about her. Well, one thing she knew for sure, as she dug through her wallet and pulled out a well-worn little brochure, once she got to Florida she was going to call the people's names on the back of the Christian tract and tell them everything that had happened since that night in the restaurant.

Tom had been out with the God Squad again and been able to share his faith with several people. When he got back to Park House, he pulled out the new Bible his parents had given him for his nineteenth birthday. He thought back over the past six months to when he had first moved away from home and all that had happened since then. After high school Tom had gone to the University of Minnesota, but that didn't seem to fit; so he had picked up a brochure on becoming a radio broadcaster. He had announced to his parents, "I've decided to go to Brown Institute and become a Christian radio announcer. I want to be a Christian influence somehow and I think broadcasting would be a good tool for getting out the message of God's love to millions of people. Besides you can make big bucks at it."

However, since that discussion with his parents, the revival at Souls Harbor had come and suddenly his aspirations as a radio broadcaster and making the big bucks didn't seem so important. He did complete the program and look for a job in broadcasting, but his greatest desire was helping people find life in Jesus Christ. He ministered day and night helping out wherever he could, explaining the scriptures to new believers, showing them how to have good work habits. He also helped with music, singing along with the guitar player at Park House, or accompanying on the piano at Souls Harbor. Suddenly, all those years of piano lessons and practice seemed worth it. Here was a real way he could serve God using a talent he had not only worked hard for, but also enjoyed more than ever. Finally, Tom Elie had found where he belonged: in the midst of a tidal wave of lost souls finding peace with God.

Chapter Thirteen

Lake Street 1972

One winter night in 1972, after the members of Jesus People Church had finished praying at Park House, Co-Pastors Dennis and Roger had some exciting news to share. Two young men in their twenties, Roger Vann and Dennis Worre, were new believers with a passion to reach others with the Gospel of Jesus Christ. Roger was of average height with a full build and light features, while Dennis was a head shorter, the same full build and darker features. In answer to his mother's payers, Dennis had finally surrendered his life to Christ in a dramatic way and even began attending the Bible study Mrs. Worre was leading. Then he had gotten a phone call, "Dennis, it's me, Roger. What's new?"

Dennis told him what God had done in his life and invited Roger to the Bible study. Roger couldn't believe the change in Dennis and was curious to see what all the commotion was about. After Roger began going to the Bible study, in came Jesus and out went the drugs. He was free and began telling people his story of redemption.

Now that the small Tuesday night gathering at Park House had grown to 100 people, it was time for a larger place to meet together. They had been scouting out several options and had narrowed the search down to a church building located at 2917-15th Avenue South. The new church raised $10,000 by finding 100 people to give $100 for the down payment.

The church shared a parking lot with an x-rated movie theater on the corner of Lake Street and 15th Avenue. The traditional red-brown brick structure had stained-glass windows, topped off with a steeple. The pipe organ completed the 250-300 seating capacity sanctuary covered with dark wood and matching wooden pews.

As Tom listened to Dennis and Roger talk about the building, his interest was piqued. They had become more than mere acquaintances; they were now co-laborers in the harvest of souls. Their passion for souls matched Tom's and he could feel the momentum of new believers being added regularly to the group. Usually the group worshiped with a guitar, but now that they were buying a building, Tom suggested that perhaps they could get a piano and expand in the area of music.

One of the co-pastors said, "Yeah, that's right. You play piano. Okay, let's get a piano." Tom could see that some type of organization was needed with regard to the music. Because Roger and Dennis were busy with preaching, taking turns every other Sunday, and discipling new believers, they didn't have the time or the technical training for developing the music aspect of the new church.

Being a team player, Tom saw a way to benefit the whole team while supporting Roger and Dennis in what they were doing. So one night after another meeting at Park House, he approached both of them with an idea. "Roger and Dennis, I would like to talk about something with you."

"Sure, man, what is it?" one of them said. He was wearing a wide-collared shirt with sharp points made of a loud 1970's fabric.

Tom was wearing polyester pants, a tucked-in polo shirt with a sensible belt, as he replied in his proper suburban English, "I have been thinking that it would help things to run more smoothly if someone were in charge of the music ministry. The church is getting to the point where it would be beneficial to have a Minister of Music. I have a lot of ideas and practical experience, and I would like to volunteer for the position."

Both Dennis and Roger liked Tom's idea. They often teased him about his clean-cut Leave It to Beaver naivety, but they also respected him and admired his sincerity and love for people.

"Cool man. Do it," Roger said. He had full sideburns, a thick mustache, and his light wavy sandy-colored hair touched the back of his shirt collar.

Dennis, who was a carbon copy with brown hair, immediately made the announcement. "Hey, everybody, Tom Elie is running the show for music now, okay?"

It seemed good to everyone else who heard about it and soon Tom was busy organizing and planning music that would be drawing hearts to the Lord.

The new owners went to work dividing unused areas into staff offices and a fellowship hall for gatherings. Jesus People Church was based on community, and the fellowship hall would help them live life together. The time came for the first service at their new facility. The excitement of the people that morning was intoxicating. Smiles and joyful laughter filled the sanctuary. The contrast of casual dress and 70's hairstyles against the traditional architectural style of the brick church didn't seem to occur to anybody. They were a real bona fide church now with a building.

"Wow, this is such a cool place!"

"Look at the ceiling. It's way up there…man!"

People filed in and finally settled in for the first official Sunday morning service of Jesus People Church.

The building smelled of history. There was a lingering atmosphere;

a foundation of many worship services in the older building that had sought the presence of the Lord. But there the conventional tradition ended. For one thing, the ushers were often barefoot. Most people would come in the side door from the parking lot and head up the steps into the sanctuary so they had no grand entrance, but that was their style. This was a church based on relationships, not stylish first impressions.

During that first service, Tom looked up to heaven and closed his eyes as he played the upright piano. It felt so good to be playing a real piano in a real building. The acoustics were not too bad because the majority of the sanctuary was wood with red carpet. He lifted up his heart of gratefulness to the Lord and was soon lost in worship. During the preaching of the message Tom silently prayed for people. He knew that new people had come this morning and were searching for the truth. After the sermon he got up to play the piano for the altar call excited to see what God would do this morning. He didn't have long to wait.

As soon as Dennis and Roger had given the first call to come forward to the front to receive Christ, a young man got out of the pew, and walked forward on the red carpet. He was barefoot, wearing cut-off jeans with a frayed hem. His hair was parted down the middle and hung down a little past his shoulders. His face was like one bent on a search-and-rescue mission. Others followed. The first young man to come forward that Sunday morning was soon known as Pete. He kept growing as a Christian by moving into Park House and craved in-depth studies like a newborn baby cries for milk. Eventually, Pete moved on to doctrinal studies and intellectual works by theologians. He became an integral part of Jesus People Church serving where he could. Pete had a way of connecting with people and challenging them to serve God without using shame or guilt. One night during a service God prompted Pete to ask an older man if he was ready to go forward. Dennis Worre's father said yes, and the two men made the walk to the altar together.

As the volunteer Minister of Music, Tom began forming a worship team of vocalists and musicians. He searched for as much talent as he could find, willing to work with beginners if he could see a natural musical gift in them. Then one day he decided the vocalist team should have a name. How about the JP Singers? Somehow, being hippies and all, Jesus People Church was too long for this casual community, so at first the name got shortened to Jesus People, and then to simply JP. That stuck and after a while only newcomers said the longer version. Tom would introduce a new song to the JP Singers on Tuesday night with, "We're going to do this song on Sunday by memory."

The vocalists were compliant and if they did groan it was quietly inside. There was no sheet music or music stands on the stage for the vocalists. Tom was a go-getter and had total confidence that this was a group of great, talented singers who could do just about anything they set their mind to do. He didn't seem to notice that he could at times be demanding to the point of annoying people. He just thought of it as stretching people outside of their box.

Looking back, Tom would wince a bit at his insensitivity to those serving with him. Tom expected a lot from his singers and he got a lot from them. They would bring their tape players, snap in their audio cassettes, wait as the worship band would run through the song a few times, and then they would practice and record. On Sunday they would all come with the words and musical parts memorized. They didn't learn a new song every week, but many weeks they did.

Tom had finished training for radio broadcasting, but hadn't landed a job making big bucks yet, so he worked driving truck, delivering batteries and tires. One day, though, his training would come in handy when JP started doing radio shows. In the meantime, Tom started getting ideas of taking the JP Singers and the worship band on the road someday. Going over music, selecting songs, and putting together arrangements for the JP Singers took up most of his free time, not to mention witnessing and discipling new believers. Tom knew he was being called of God to go into full-time ministry and kept praying about it.

Finally, Tom asked Roger and Dennis to meet with him. "I want to quit my job and do ministry full time," he said.

Roger and Dennis looked at each other and then back to Tom. They both knew he was right but money was tight. "We can't afford to pay you much."

"That's okay. Living at Park House keeps the rent low." He didn't have much for bills and being single he could get by pretty cheaply. If there was one thing he was good at—it was being frugal.

Tom looked at himself in the mirror. He was now the Minister of Music overseeing the music ministry at JP and making $50 a week. After he combed his sandy brown hair over across his forehead and down past the top of his ears he worked on his sideburns. They were down to the bottom of his ears now. His mustache was getting thicker since he first started growing it four years ago at age sixteen. Then he let out a sigh, "It looks like a caterpillar."

George and Kathy Ridge were both involved in the JP Singers. George, who was shorter than Tom had a lean build, a full mustache and thinning hair on top. After looking Tom over during their first practice together, he leaned over to his pretty wife with softly curled brown hair, and whispered, "He looks like a kid."

"Oh, George," she laughed, "that's because he's only nineteen."

George wasn't sure, but he thought Tom was trying to grow a mustache so he could appear to look older. Afterward, George came up to Tom to go over a few things for the coming Sunday. When Tom had first met him, George only knew how to play two songs on the organ: "Greensleeves" (a traditional Celtic-sounding tune) and "Born Free" (from the popular movie about lions being released back into the wild). Yet, somehow, it all seemed spiritual. If George played "Born Free" for the offertory, then he would switch to "Greensleeves" for the next time. It didn't matter that George had only two songs in his repertoire because Tom believed in giving people opportunities to serve. And George did have a good singing voice, so he often led the praise and worship while Tom, directing from the piano, did more of the musical specials, concentrating on the technical side of the music arrangements, working with the musicians and vocalists on harmonies. Tom enjoyed being around George Ridge; he had a good sense of humor and was always ready to help out with whatever needed to be done. Often George would do a little segue between the songs, tying them together with scripture verses or even objects that he could use for a spiritual analogy, much like Jesus had done; such as the bread, the vine, or a seed. A couple of times, though, George's creativity got to the best of him and he would come up with spiritualized stories about a butterfly or even a grapefruit!

Al and Ruth, Tom's parents, couldn't help but visit Jesus People Church as often as possible. Exciting things were happening. It was like a true revival they had read about. People were getting saved every week and more were being added to their numbers, just like in the Book of Acts. And here was their son right in the middle of it!

Their youngest daughter, Beth, now six years old, with brown hair and freckles splashed across her perky face, came along too. Her heart was like Tom's, always looking for ways to help people find Christ. Once she had asked her Mom for a small New Testament to give to a classmate after she prayed with the boy to receive Jesus as his Savior.

When Beth had gone with her parents to Tom's new church off of Lake Street, she had been so proud of her older brother. On the way home she thought about all she had seen at Jesus People Church. Even the name was cool. A lot of young people went there and they were so excited about the Lord. Another thing she noticed was the way they dressed. At her church everyone dressed formally as though they were going to a wedding. At Jesus People Church everyone dressed in casual clothes, usually wearing blue jeans. The boys wore their hair longer. People came as they were. Beth liked this new way of doing church. Wasn't Jesus like that in the Gospels? He didn't expect people to clean up their act first, but took them as they were. Why, even Jesus wore sandals and dressed like a common everyday person. She couldn't wait to go again.

Chapter Fourteen

Two Hearts, One Head

After Tom had moved into the discipleship home located on Park Avenue in Minneapolis, he began the morning ritual of walking over to the women's building for breakfast. However, this breakfast was far from ordinary.

She intrigued him, even her simplest movements, as she flipped pancakes. And a plan began to form in Tom's mind. After his meal Tom walked up, introduced himself, and thanked her for the pancakes. "They sure were good," he repeated. It wasn't the most intelligent thing he had ever said, but it kept things moving.

Her bright smile melted him on the spot, "Why, thank you, Tom."

He was encouraged to venture further, "Say…Vicki, I was just thinking that…well, I've formed this singing group, the JP Singers, and if you like to sing you might want to join?"

"I might be interested," Vicki replied casually. Her blond hair had darkened since high school to a warm brown that fell softly around her delicate feminine features. Struck by her beauty, he also sensed there was something more about her.

She interrupted his thoughts, "I've always enjoyed singing and now that I'm learning all these new Christian songs I enjoy singing even more. What does the group do exactly?"

"Well, I'm not totally sure at this point. It's still in the developing stage." Tom couldn't help but notice she had hazel eyes, beautiful eyes. "We're going to…"

Had he mentioned something about forming a group with an evangelistic thrust, maybe over-the-road concerts?

Even though they were crossing paths on a daily basis, a year had passed since the morning breakfast at the women's Park House kitchen without Tom asking Vicki out for an official date. At first Vicki didn't think Tom was different from the rest of the guys at Jesus People Church. Occasionally, while out for a bite to eat with a group or walking by themselves back and forth from area shops to Park House, they found each other's humor funny when others didn't. Although a few of their friends were beginning to wonder if they might become a couple, neither Tom or Vicki saw that they were becoming more than close friends.

By now Vicki had shared with Tom how she had been asked to Souls Harbor by Georgine's mother and details about the restaurant people in Florida. She had confided in him how tragic it was when her father had died and how angry she had been at God. She even opened up about her mother's rheumatoid arthritis and the extra care it required as the disease caused greater suffering each year. Tom was drawn to Vicki's compassionate heart toward people. Her loss and hardship growing up had taught her to love people and take them as they came. His youngest sister, Beth, enjoyed being around Vicki too, because Vicki had a way of making everyone feel included. Her ability to openly love people filled the need he had in this area.

From his upbringing, Tom had inner strength and security. He had been taught to love people, but he was naïve to people's pain. In contrast, Vicki loved others with patience and empathy. He had to work at it sometimes; with Vicki it was spontaneous.

She also had a deep passion for God. And it drew him to her like a magnet. Tom knew he had a call to serve in the ministry, which would require a life partner who had the qualities Vicki possessed. But did she have a call on her life for the ministry as well? Before he surrendered his heart completely to Vicki, he had to make sure he knew for certain. A marriage mismatched in this area would be a colossal mistake for both of them. He respected Vicki too much to hurt her by asking her to follow his calling and his dreams. She had to have her own calling from God to the ministry.

Sometimes for a break Tom would go for a walk around one of the city lakes and either pray or just let his thoughts ramble and untwist from all the business of ministry. On some of those days, he asked Vicki to go along.

Vicki liked being around Tom even though in some ways they were complete opposites. Tom could be so serious and she was bubbly and lighthearted. Her face was like a mirror reflection of her heart. If she was happy her face lit up; if she was upset her eyes said so with tears. Tom, on the other hand, although given to humor, was definitely the stoic. Sometimes he admired Vicki for being so open and free about expressing herself. "Lighten up, Tom Elie!" she would say, "You are way too serious sometimes."

Yet she admired Tom for his dedication to his spiritual life and his confidence in leadership. He could challenge people to exceed past their own expectations. She could also see that this was the kind of man who would honor his wife by being devoted to her for a lifetime. No matter how they were trying to keep the door of romance shut, afraid of how complicated love could get, their hearts kept pushing it open.

One day after working on some arrangements for an upcoming service, Tom once again decided to go for a stroll around a city lake.

Naturally, he called Vicki and asked her to go with him. "Sure," she responded, "I can be ready in a few minutes." After brushing her hair and making sure her outfit was just right, Vickie heard the sound of Tom's car pulling up. Not wanting him to waste time walking up the sidewalk, she opened the door, gave a wave, and slipped on her platform shoes. As she approached his car she opened the car door of the blue Chevy Vega and smiled. Tom's pulse quickened, "Hi, Vicki, all set?"

"All set," said Vicki, slipping into the black vinyl bucket seat. Tom stepped on the clutch pedal and shifted into first, and then second gear. It was a compact car designed in answer to the energy crisis of the 1970's, and Tom enjoyed jetting around the cities in it.

"Thanks for asking me to come; it's always fun to ride in a sporty car. Usually, I'm in one of the Park House vans or I take a bus," said Vicki.

They chatted and made small talk until they got to Lake Calhoun, a city lake surrounded by upper-class homes.

After parking, they began walking side-by-side enjoying the fresh autumn air. For a moment there was silence and Tom realized that it didn't bother either one of them. They were comfortable enough with each other to enjoy quietness together. He was over a head taller than Vicki and could see her soft brown hair bounce with every step. The sun brought out her golden highlights that seemed as brilliant as the turning leaves reflecting in the water next to them.

It was in that moment Tom finally knew he was having deeper feelings for Vicki than friendship. He wanted their relationship on a different level, but wasn't quite sure how to broach the subject. If she didn't feel the same toward him, he risked alienating her and ruining their friendship altogether. Then what would he do? Why hadn't he realized this before today? Confusion settled into his entire being. He was a calculating person, living in a world of order. How had this happened to him?

For someone who could masterfully play the piano in front of hundreds of people, lead the worship team service after service, and talk to complete strangers about Jesus Christ, Tom suddenly found himself drowning in stage fright. His parents had taught him everything he needed to know to be responsible and to follow the Lord; but whose parents sat down at the dinner table and said, 'Tonight we're going to talk about how to ask a girl if she loves you…'?

He was a train wreck going at full steam with no brakes. Tom knew he couldn't hold in his feelings for Vicki any longer, it would almost be like lying to her. He felt out of control, but he would come up with a plan. He'd better be quick, they were at the car and Vicki was waiting, with a smile, for him to unlock the car door. Tom glanced at her quickly and returned her smile. Oh, those eyes! he thought to himself.

As soon as they had settled into the bucket seats, Tom said, "Can I ask you a question?"

Vicki was used to Tom discussing all kinds of topics with her. They talked about everything under the sun.

"Sure," she replied, totally unaware of what was on Tom's mind.

Tom blurted out, "Can I kiss you?"

Immediately he realized his mistake when Vicki's eyes got large and her face looked like she was watching a horror movie.

"NO!"

She said it with such force that Tom felt his six-foot frame shrink to about six inches. Then there was silence. Cold, hard, long silence. Frustration began kindling a fire in the pit of his stomach that made him angry with himself for putting them both in an awkward situation. He started the car and purposely drove off slowly trying to control his emotions. On the drive back neither one said a word. What a lousy world, he thought to himself, and decided that he was even a little mad at Vicki, although he didn't know why for sure.

Vicki didn't know what to do either. He had shocked her. No warming up with a little bit of small talk about relationships, romance, nothing. Just, will you kiss me! What did he expect her to do? She knew she was getting more and more fond of him, but good grief! Couldn't a girl have a little warning?

Vicki sneaked a look at Tom out of the corner of her eye. He seemed under control for someone who had just been rejected. She started feeling a bit sorry for him; her response had been curt, but she had been taken completely by surprise. She was too shocked by the whole thing to even think; she had just reacted. Finally, after what seemed an eternity of silence in the car together, Tom dropped her off at Park House.

Walking into the building Vicki thought about their relationship and knew that she cared deeply about Tom, but what would happen now? She certainly hadn't given him much hope by her abrupt answer.

It didn't take Tom long to get over his embarrassment and ask, "Vicki, could we have a talk together somewhere after music practice tonight?"

"All right," Vicki answered, trying to give Tom some encouragement with her tone of voice. She felt too shy to say anything else at the moment.

Tom drove the Vega to Powderhorn Park and turned off the engine. He thanked her for coming, especially after how foolishly he had acted a few days before. He tried to articulate his feelings as best he could for her and then Tom looked at Vicki with questioning eyes and asked, "I wonder if you would reconsider?"

Vickie's face blushed a bit and she said, "Oh, yes."

Tom leaned over and kissed the girl of his dreams.

Changes were taking place for Tom, both on the inside and outside. One day the young couple slipped away from Park House to do a little shopping together. After consulting with Vicki as his personal fashion assistant, Tom stepped up to the counter of the clothing store and laid a pair of blue jeans on the counter. He was twenty years old and buying his first pair of jeans. Back at Park House he slipped on the rigid pant legs and walked to the bathroom to comb his hair. The stiff cotton of the dark indigo jeans rubbed together, swishing as he walked. Staring into the mirror, Tom combed his brown hair over to one side and checked his side burns. His hair was touching a little past his ears, and his bangs would fall down to his eyebrows from time to time. He emerged from the bathroom a true guy of the 70's.

Out in the commons area Vicki was chatting with people as they came and went, when Tom came around the corner. She couldn't help but smile a little, knowing Tom had been a double knit kind of guy up to this point. She was a hippie and more open to new fashions and trends than Tom. A few of their friends noticed too. "Hey, Tom, nice threads."

"Thanks," Tom replied, his trademark smile taking the teasing in stride. He had to laugh a little at himself as well.

A few months after their first kiss, Vicki left for Florida to spend the holidays with her sister and family. Because the phone rates for long distance were so expensive, Tom and Vicki exchanged letters constantly. Anticipating another letter, Vicki ran down to the mailbox in her short-sleeved top and jeans. Once again there was a letter from Tom addressed to *Miss Vicki Wolden*. She tore it open before going into the house where peering eyes might tease her with questions. It started off with Tom's usual greeting and current events around Jesus People Church.

Then Tom wrote a line or two about their relationship:

Maybe we should date other people just to make sure.

Vicki went along with Tom's suggestion and wrote back:

Tom, I completely understand what you're saying. Maybe it would make sense for us to date other people.

When Tom got Vicki's reply, he thought about her walking around a lake with someone else and quickly changed his mind. Soon he began planning a trip to Florida. Steve, the friend who had invited him to go to Souls Harbor, was registered for flight school in Florida. They could drive down together and Tom could fly back with Vicki.

Vicki's sister, Linda, and her husband, Don, welcomed the opportunity to meet Tom and check out this young man interested in their Vicki. After being introduced, Vicki's niece shyly said hello, and soon the boys were tumbling around with Tom, while Don asked if he wanted to go water skiing.

"In December? This I've got to see!"

Away they went and Tom was skimming over the waters of the Florida Intercoastal Waterway on skis. Vicki could tell Linda and Don approved of him; the day would always be a happy memory for her.

As they flew home together, they knew they were falling deeply in love with each other. Yet neither one wanted to let marriage just happen, they needed to seek the Lord seriously. Tom looked toward the future with Vicki and knew he wanted her to be a part of it, but he still was unsure about the finality of marriage. Why couldn't the Lord just write down a message on paper and let you read it plain as day, like the cartoon tuna fish commercial, where the note comes down on a fish hook with a written message for Charlie the Tuna?

Tom kept praying and by February he had the confidence that he had found the right life companion emotionally and spiritually. Yet another plan formulated in his mind. He certainly didn't want another awkward situation, so he prepped Vicki with several discussions of their possible future together in the ministry. They also spent time praying together about their callings in life. Vicki had stayed overnight at her Mom's house to help her, so Tom called her and casually asked, "Can I come over and get you? I just want to talk to you about something."

As they drove over to Lake Street making small talk, Tom could hardly wait to ask her the big question. The clear crisp winter day, bright and beautiful, matched Vicki's smile.

After walking into Jesus People Church, Tom suggested, "Let's go into the prayer room." Tom looked into Vicki's upturned face searching her eyes. They were both about to step off the edge of familiar ground.

Tom gently took Vicki's hands into his own. He knew with all his heart she was the right one. It seemed so easy now to ask her that the words simply fell from his lips with joy: "Vicki, I was wondering if you would marry me?"

"Yes," she beamed, not letting one second slip by.

Their lips met, two hearts merged, united under One Head: Jesus Christ.

Vicki's mom, Ruth Marie, knew something significant had happened when Vicki came back to the apartment holding hands with Tom.

Ruth Marie gave her formal consent to the marriage; however, there was a growing concern inside of her. Tom was a fine catch for her daughter, but now her relationship with Vicki would change so much. After Tom left, Vicki sat down with her mom for a while. "Mom, is there anything you would like me to do for you before I go back to Park House?"

"No dear. I'm just fine," she answered in a noble tone, trying to hide her anxiety from Vicki.

"Well, Mom, what do you think about Tom and me getting married?"

Ruth Marie felt threatened by Tom's relationship with Vicki. With her husband dying so suddenly, she would have been so lonely without her Vicki. And with her rheumatoid arthritis getting worse she had grown dependent on Vicki for help. Even during Vicki's turbulent teen years, there was someone else at home. The move to Park House had been hard enough, and now marriage. This cycle of life was taking a lot out of her. "Are you sure, Vicki?"

"Mom, what is it?"

"Oh, I don't know," she said, voicing her own indecision, "it just seems like you two are rushing things a bit. That's all."

"Mom, he's the right one. He'll become part of our family too, just like Linda and Gretchen's husbands did," Vicki comforted.

Chapter Fifteen

A Time to Laugh

Vicki was a little nervous meeting everyone at the engagement party at Ruth and Al's home, but she didn't say anything to Tom about it. As Tom began to introduce her to the people she hadn't met before, they came to a couple who were the same age as Tom's parents. "Pete and Betty, this is Vicki Wolden. Vicki, this is Pete and Betty Peterson. They have been friends of our family for as many years as I can remember."

"Yes, we knew Tom when he was in diapers. As a toddler, he used to get so excited whenever company would come over," Betty said, giving the historical information with a laugh.

Vicki shook their hands as she smiled, "Hello, it's nice to meet you both."

She noticed how warm their smiles were and Betty's chocolate brown eyes seemed to dance with joy complementing her carefully-coiffed brunette hair. Pete was shorter than Tom and had light blue eyes that were wise and humble. Vicki felt accepted by them immediately. Betty began chatting with her and soon they were laughing about all kinds of things. On the way home in the car Vicki, commented to Tom about the Petersons. "Oh, Tom, that Peterson couple was such a cute pair. And to think your parents have known them since the early 1950's. What a gift to have such life-long friends."

"Yeah, their kids, Jill and Jeff, feel more like cousins to me," said Tom. "We have even vacationed together over the years. This summer if we stay at my aunt and uncle's camp near Alexandria, you should come. It's a lot of fun and it's such a beautiful resort. The lake isn't large, but it's a good fishing lake."

"Sure, it sounds like fun," replied Vicki.

Six months after their first kiss, Tom and Vicki were in the midst of marriage arrangements when a proposal came about for Jesus People to begin a Christian discipleship camp. The church was buying raw land two hours north of the Twin Cities to be used as a retreat center. The idea was to be able to send new believers to a place where basic training in theology and life skills could be taught in an atmosphere away from the distractions of city life. They were doing an Acre for Jesus to raise the funds, so the idea was if eighty-six people were to buy an acre at $450 per acre, the total sum of $38,700 would not have to be financed with a loan. The name of the camp would be Shepherd's Inn and construction teams would build the earthly housing, while pastoral teams would work on the spiritual temples.

Tom was sitting at the piano listening to the proposal while Vicki was worshipping at the back of the church. He felt impressed that they use their wedding money to purchase an acre for $450, yet part of him was hesitant to suggest to Vicki that they should spend their wedding savings with the wedding just around the corner. Tom made his way back to Vicki and asked her, "Are you sensing anything? Is God saying anything to you?"

Vicki replied, "I think we should use our wedding money to buy an acre."

That was the bulk of the young couple's wedding fund with only a month or two to go before the wedding. Together they prayed and said, "Lord, we know you're going to take care of this."

So off the ledge they stepped into faith and did as many have before—they took a risk and put their trust in the Lord. They didn't feel manipulated or challenged inappropriately by the leadership, it was just simple faith. God was asking them to partner with him, and they wanted to respond to the invitation to bless others. So they did it.

Tom wanted to make good on his invitation to Vicki for a trip to the family cabin, so he asked his parents about it. Their reply was instant, "Of course, it would be wonderful to have her come to the cabin." It was the first time Tom's parents really got to know Vicki. She had been at the house some before that, but they didn't feel like they knew her that well. At the resort there was a pond between the two cabins the Elie's had for the weekend. Vicki stayed in the girl's cabin with Barbara and Beth. A young slender girl, Beth really liked Vicki, and on occasion Vicki would even brush her sandy brown hair. One afternoon Beth walked by Vicki's room and heard Vicki talking to someone. As Beth glanced into the room, she stood there for a moment listening, and then quickly left the cabin. Later she relayed to Al and Ruth, "I didn't mean to eavesdrop, but I walked past Vicki's room and couldn't help but listen to Vicki thanking the Lord for the wonderful family, the Elie family, whom she had met."

The report touched Al and Ruth's hearts. "This so impresses me," Ruth said, "because it's more than a mere compliment to us. It means that Vicki has the gift of appreciation."

The Petersons were also at the resort and Vicki and Betty often found themselves in deep conversations about many things. Betty's eyes lit up as she talked with Vicki. They both enjoyed laughing and soon a friendship developed between them that would last many years. After one such conversation, Vicki's eyes teared up, "Betty, I feel like I'm with my mom when we have these kinds of conversations."

Vicki was having a wonderful time with Tom, and the beautiful setting in the woods with all the cabins nestled close to the pristine lake was as refreshing to Vicki, as the social interaction. On Saturday afternoon, Vicki took extra time getting herself dressed and fixing her hair. Tom's cousin was getting married near the area, so everyone had made the weekend a part of a summer vacation.

When Betty saw Vicki walk out of the cabin, she couldn't help but tell her how nice she looked, "Oh, Vicki, you look so cute. Your hair is so beautiful; you must have put a lot of work into it."

"Why, thank you, Betty. My hair is so fine that I have to leave my rollers in until just before I leave home and then I spray on nearly half a can of hair spray. I don't think a semi-truck could ruin it today!"

Vicki and Betty were laughing when Tom strolled up to Vicki, "Hey, Vicki, do you want to go for a quick boat ride before we leave for the wedding?"

Tom glanced at his watch. "We still have an hour."

Vicki quickly agreed and off they went down the dock toward the lightweight fishing boat. The motor wasn't on the back so Tom just used the oars and began rowing toward the center of the lake. It was a beautiful day and the sun glistened magnificently off the water. Back on the shore, people were gathering for the drive to the wedding. Al and Ruth joined Betty and Pete in the grassy shade and watched the young couple in the boat.

"What a nice couple they make," someone commented.

"And what a romantic picture," said another with a sigh.

Betty looked over at her dear friend, "Ruth, she is such a lovely girl inside and out."

Ruth nodded approvingly, "Yes, she sure is, Betty."

Just then they all noticed Tom standing up in the boat and rocking the boat from side to side. Ruth let out a little gasp. "What is he doing? That boat could tip over!"

Al chuckled, "Oh, he's all right. He's just giving Vicki a little tease. You know what they say 'boys always tease the girls they like.'"

No sooner had the words left Al's mouth when Tom picked up his fiancée and flipped her right over the side of boat. A head surfaced on the water bobbing like an apple. Laughter could be heard across the ripples. Vicki's contagious laughter sang across the water like joy bells.

Ruth's face was in mortal shock. "Thomas Gregory Elie!" was about all she could sputter.

By now a larger crowd, drawn by the commotion, had formed on the shore to see what would follow. Vicki crawled into the boat like a wet rat. Then Tom rowed back toward shore, tied up at the dock, and helped Vicki out like a gentleman. Ruth began scolding Tom as she soon as she had him in earshot, but Tom just kept smiling. Vicki came up to Tom and began shaking her long hair at him like a dog would do after it had frolicked in the water. Betty's eyes sparkled as she watched Vicki trot off toward the cabin for a fresh change of clothes. A trail of water marked where she walked. Al didn't know which was more fun to watch, Tom's antics or Ruth's reaction to it all.

After Ruth calmed down, Betty spoke up, "You know, Ruth, this was a good test for Vicki's character. She could have been furious with Tom by pouting and crying, but she came up laughing. Married life throws a lot of curves at you and a person needs to have a sense of humor."

Pete added his two cents. "She's a keeper, all right. Betty would have murdered me if I had tried that."

"No, I wouldn't have," retorted Betty, "I would have drowned first!"

Ruth acquiesced and switched into a more pragmatic gear. "True enough, but now those of us that can, need to help that poor girl get cleaned up for the wedding. It will be a true miracle if she makes it in time."

Operation-Get-Vicki-Ready ensued with several arms and hands resembling a human octopus helping put her hair in rollers and plugging in the bonnet-type hair dryer. These were the days before blow dryers and curling irons so Vicki had to sit and "bake" for a while. Her outfit for the wedding was assembled. Finally, out of the cabin bounced a young adventuresome girl ready for the event. Everyone scurried to the vehicles and off they went to the wedding. Along the way, Tom slipped his arm around Vicki. Their eyes met as two people do when they have passed from friends to sweethearts.

Tom had been seeking the Lord for the right wife. He knew that his call to be in the ministry required a certain type of life partner. But what was he looking for? Love could be so confusing. Even though they were engaged, he had held onto one last tiny doubt. Now it was gone. Tossing Vicki over the side of the boat just to see what her reaction would be wasn't exactly a scientific method, or even a spiritual way of seeking the Lord for guidance, but in his heart Tom knew Vicki would always be the love of his life.

Don Manning, Vicki's brother-in-law from Florida, heard the musical cue and knew from the rehearsal that it was time. "Well, are you two lovely ladies ready?"

"Yes!" Vicki and her mother said at once, laughing. Don and Ruth Marie flanked the bride on either side and began escorting her toward her future.

When Vicki stepped around the corner, ready to walk down the aisle, she was surprised to see how full the church was. Tom's boyhood church, Bloomington Assembly, could only accommodate 500 people at the most, so the pews were crowded with many friends and relatives. Tom waited for his bride in his rented white tux offset by a pastel blue shirt ruffled down the front. He thought Vicki looked gorgeous in the simple pretty dress she had borrowed. Instead of the white dress being the center of beauty, the bride was. His bride. Because family meant so much to both of them, they decided to have the wedding party primarily of relatives. Blending the past with the future, the ceremony was officiated by Tom's longtime family pastor, Arvid Kingsriter, the husband of Tom's piano teacher, along with co-pastors of Jesus People Church, Roger and Dennis. George Ridge and a few other JP guys served as groomsmen.

The June wedding was perfect for salads and homemade cranberry and banana breads that friends and relatives had helped to prepare. It truly was a community event shared in the context of Christian fellowship, a tremendous witness to the guests who were not familiar with Jesus People Church. People saw it was more than a group of young people trying to do church with a new twist, but rather a community of believers who loved one another.

Before leaving for their honeymoon, Tom and Vicki opened their many wedding gifts and counted the cash gifts they received. "Thank you, Lord!" they said in unison when they discovered the cash gift total of over $1,500. The $450 Acre for Jesus had been more than replenished! In the future they would need to trust God for larger amounts and situations the size of mountains, but this first baby step in releasing what they had into the hands of their Heavenly Father had taught them a powerful lesson in trusting God. They would always look back warmly at how God gave them the courage to give away their first little nest egg for his Kingdom and the joy of seeing the Lord provide in a different way. They had a week of bliss at a small rented cabin in the north woods of Minnesota with a perfect week of sunshine making them feel married not only on paper, but in their hearts.

Chapter Sixteen

And the Beat Goes On

Upon returning from their honeymoon, Mr. and Mrs. Elie were both thrust back into the hectic schedule of ministry. Tom had been making $50 a week as Minister of Music along with room and board at Park House. Now that he was married and moving out he received a huge raise, a fifty percent increase in his salary. So now with $75 a week Tom was thinking through his budget for housing, food, utilities, car expenses...it didn't look too good, but God would provide... wouldn't he? Tom felt a twinge of anxiety knot up in his stomach. Vicki had a good job at the bank so that would help with the expenses until they started a family. They had shopped around for houses and settled on a fixer-upper home in Minneapolis. They took out a loan against the Chevy Vega for $500 and used it as a down payment on their first mortgage of $15,000. Their monthly payment would be $144 a month. At first, Tom had been so excited about getting married and buying a house that he hadn't worried about his financial situation. After their honeymoon they settled into married life, and at age twenty-one, Tom found himself overwhelmed with all the responsibilities of a married adult. Groceries alone were costing them $15 a week. "How are we going to afford that? It's going to kill us!" Tom lamented.

In addition to all the home repairs, the monthly mortgage payment, and everyday living expenses, he had his student loan of $30 per month from Brown Institute for learning radio broadcasting!

His stomach churned again as he mulled over all the expenses. Tom turned to the Lord in prayer and got alone with him, which was a natural reaction after years of seeking the Lord. "Lord, I thank you that you've brought me to JP. I know I'm right where you want me to be, but things are so tight financially, I feel like there's no breathing room."

Tom continued in prayer for a while and waited on the Lord. Then something wonderful happened. Tom felt the Lord speaking to his heart very distinctly: *Do not look to the church to sign your paycheck. I am your Provider. I sign your paycheck. Don't look to the pastors. Don't look to men or organizations.*

A weight lifted off him. He had an overwhelming assurance that the same God who had called him for such a time as this to Jesus People Church for a great harvest of souls, was the same God who would provide for his physical needs. This seed of faith for provision was planted in his heart and became an anchor that held him steady through many years. From then on, instead of wishing he had just a little more money each month, Tom kept looking to the Lord for guidance. In three years, the house market jumped with inflation and their first little castle, a small two-story home at 4020 Lyndale Avenue South, sold for nearly double the price they paid for it.

The new couple settled into a routine and looked forward to Monday nights when they could have their one "home night" together. First they would carry the laundry one and half blocks to wash, dry, and fold, ready for another busy week of ministry. After that they were free to watch their favorite TV shows. In those days, television sets were expensive so they had waited and saved for a TV rather buying it on credit. Tom plugged in the colored console TV and turned it on waiting for the tubes to warm up. He adjusted the portable antenna. "I just have to get these rabbit ears right."

Sounds from the Mary Tyler More show were coming in, but the picture was still fuzzy. "Should we try a little tin foil? My mom and dad use to do that with their TV," suggested Vicki.

Finally the picture came in clearly. "I think we're okay. Not a bad deal for 100 bucks is it?"

It was a used TV, but it had a nice large screen with stereo speakers covered in brown and gold cloth netting encased in a beautiful wood cabinet. Tom sat back in a chair and admired their wise purchase. He checked his watch. "Almost time for the Rookies," he said, getting up to find the correct channel and adjust the sound dial. "How's this sound? Is it loud enough?"

Vicki was stretched out on the couch. "It's just fine, honey."

Tom sat back down. After the theme song for the police show, the station switched to a commercial announcing the beginning of Monday night football with announcer Howard Cosell. "Hey, look, football on my night off!" exclaimed Tom. "I hope the Vikings will be playing Monday nights."

"They better get their defense in shape for the season or it won't even be worth watching," commented Vicki.

"Coach Bud Grant will whip those purple boys into shape. And don't forget who their quarterback is," Tom said.

"Tarkenton can throw all the passes he wants, but if the defensive line is lacking what difference does it make?" Vicki responded.

Tom looked at his wife with appreciation, "Vicki, you really have this football thing down, don't you?"

"One of my favorite memories of my dad is watching all the sports games with him and listening to him explain everything to me. I guess it will help if we have any boys in the family that are into playing sports."

Tom and Vicki enjoyed their Monday nights together. It gave them the Sabbath rest they needed to regain energy for the rest of the week and the long schedule on Sundays. One of their greatest challenges as a couple was to carve out free time from a vocation, with demanding hours any time of the day or night. Over the years they would see others who didn't practice balance in their lives leave the ministry hurt and disillusioned.

Money for the retreat center called Shepherd's Inn had been raised right before Tom and Vicki's wedding, and now work was commencing on the project. It was, in Minnesota vernacular, up north at the lake, in the woods of Finlayson, Minnesota, a two-hour drive from the Twin Cities.

"Hey, Tom!" Dennis was shouting above the din of the bustling crowd at JP. He motioned for Tom to come over. "Tom, I want you to meet my brother, John and his wife, Patti."

"So you're the mystery couple who are going to run the camp up north." Tom shook their hands warmly and his trademark smile flashed across his face. "It's nice to meet you both. My wife, Vicki, is here somewhere..." Tom's head swiveled around looking here and there.

John's eye's shone as he watched Tom's tall figure turn into a lookout tower for his wife. Dennis glanced over at John and lowered his voice, "Well, I see that you like him, don't you?"

"Yeah, I do," replied John. "He reminds me of the verses in the first chapter of John where Jesus takes a look at Nathaniel and says, 'in him there is no guile, nothing false.' "

Dennis nodded, "Yep, that's Tom. What you see is what you get. He's the most sincere person I've ever met."

Tom was oblivious to their conversation. "There she is. Vicki, can you come over here?"

Vicki came over smiling, her shorter frame was closer to Dennis' height than Tom's. Tom slipped his arm around Vicki's shoulder, "This is my wife, Vicki." Tom continued, "Vicki, this is Dennis's brother and his wife, John and Patti. They are the couple who are moving here from Michigan to run Shepherd's Inn."

"Nice to meet you," Vicki smiled, "Are you older or younger than Dennis?"

The two Worre brothers laughed. Dennis nodded toward his brother, "John, here, will collect social security two years before I will."

The young couple, John and Patty Worre, would be the directors and build a home on the land. Over the next ten years Shepherd's Inn would offer discipleship weekend retreats in the beautiful north woods where people were able to leave the city and its distractions behind. There were so many people getting saved, that the church finally bought a used Greyhound bus to offer people a free ride for a weekend to the camp, giving people the opportunity to become more rooted in Christ. The basics of prayer, studying scriptures, water baptism, fasting, and tithing, were taught. Oftentimes teaching about the Holy Spirit would cause many to desire more of God's Holy Spirit and they would pray for Jesus to baptize them with the Spirit, as in the Book of Acts.

People could receive prayer for issues in their lives, which brought inner healing to those struggling with bitterness, fear, and the inability to trust God and others. Old addictions were broken and people were set free to be a new creation in Christ. Confessing their sins to God, and to each other, many were set free from the darkness these bondages had brought. Oftentimes the worship services would last late into the night.

As Tom and Vicki would participate in the services and walk the grounds of the eighty-six-acre camp, they marveled at what God was doing in the lives of these people. Their small contribution of $450 had made a difference for others and would echo in eternity.

During this time, Tom and the JP Singers not only did morning services but also started touring as well. They began taking road trips through Duluth and up along the north shore, following Lake Superior along scenic Highway 61. While in Granite Falls, a few of the JP Singers had trouble singing during an outdoor concert because they were accidentally sucking in tiny flying insects. One of the JP Singers, George Ridge, couldn't resist the humor of the situation. "Hey, we got a little extra protein in our diet!"

Then the big road trip to the East Coast came along. Before leaving, George looked over the used coach bus. "It looks like death warmed over!" he said to his wife, Kathy.

"But we don't have any other vehicle," she lamented.

"Come on everybody! We can do this!" Tom's enthusiasm was contagious and soon they were all rolling along the freeway singing, praying, and laughing.

Tom sat down next to his bride, Vicki. It was springtime and they were heading to Atlantic City and hopefully back. It was their first year of marriage and life couldn't be better. However, there were challenges for Tom along the way.

In one city, they were all standing around waiting for the pastor to come and open the church so they could begin moving the sound equipment and instruments inside.

"I'll try to contact the pastor on a pay phone," offered Tom. "He said he would be here to let us in. Maybe there was a misunderstanding about the time."

When Tom got back from calling the pastor, he couldn't believe his eyes, "What are you guys doing?"

"Well, we found out we have a policeman in the group and he picked the lock to the church, so we unloaded and started to set up the equipment."

"Well, you're going to have to reload everything before the pastor gets here. We can't pick locks at churches!"

A few people moaned, but Tom's character would not allow the JP Singers to break into a church and possibly offend their host pastor in the process.

In another city in Iowa, several of the JP Singers were staying in campers parked in the church parking lot that church folks had provided. With the tour winding down, Tom decided to have a little fun. The next morning he got up at the crack of dawn and stepped outside his camper with a trumpet. Strains of revelry filled the air and heads started popping out of doors and windows with sleepy eyes trying to focus. Laughter erupted at the sight of Tom standing outside his camper in a bathrobe and black socks playing revelry on the pastor's brother's trumpet.

The coach bus made it all the way to the east coast and back to Minnesota and then died a week later.

Every dream for ministry seemed possible, so this group of go-getters tackled a radio program on KNOF. Finally, Tom's radio broadcasting training paid off, even if it wasn't in big bucks. They built a small sound booth downstairs in the church and called their program "Come Together." Hearts were touched as people all over the Twin Cities listened to the program. These were big steps of faith for the band of believers—with more in the future.

Chapter Seventeen

Great is the Lord, and Greatly to be Praised

Another crowded service had begun at Jesus People Church and Tom was playing the piano. He asked the Holy Sprit to come and lead them all into courts of praise, and into the inner courts of worship, drawing them closer to the throne room of God. How grateful he felt to be born at this time and season when all worshipers could come into the Lord's presence because of the death of Jesus on the cross. As Tom continued to play and the JP Singers sang, people began to clap their hands and tap their feet with smiles of joy on their faces. After a few rousing choruses, Tom began to play softer songs filled with lyrics of adoration to the King of Kings, such as "He is Lord." Then he modulated into "As the Deer," by Martin J. Nystrom. The first paragraph so aptly captured the tone of service:

As the deer panteth for the water,
So my soul longeth after you.
You alone are my heart's desire
And I long to worship you.

People began to lift their hands up to heaven as an embrace of God's love and all that he had done for them. After that, they moved on to a modern-day Psalm, "Great is the Lord" written by a thin wiry Holy Ghost preacher from Texas, Robert Ewing:

Great is the Lord and greatly to be praised.
In the city of our God, in the mountain of His holiness
Beautiful for situation, the joy of the whole earth,
Is Mount Zion, on the sides of the north, the city of the great King.

Based on Psalm 48:1, the last line was always accelerated. According to Robert Ewing's explanation, "the desire to see the Lord would cause the believer to break into a run, once his or her eyes caught site of the glorious city."

Many lyrics were based on actual scripture, which helped a person memorize scripture more easily. And if you didn't know the words? No problem. Just open up your Bible to the portion of scripture being sung and follow along. In addition to scripture songs, choruses were so simple that a person could learn the entire song after singing a couple of times through. Some people thought these new chorus songs were lacking in the richness that the hymns of former generations had. Yet, for people coming off the street, it was the perfect way for them to begin worshipping Jesus. It was childlike faith— simple and heartfelt.

Tom continued to play, drawing people into a deeper place of adoration, until they no longer were conscious of the musicians, but their focus was totally on the Lord alone.

Tom knew he was spending more time away from home than he should, but the church was growing so fast because people were constantly getting saved. Always open with his heart to Vicki, he spoke of his concerns. He knew she was a people person and loved helping in any way she could at the church: still there seemed to be a missing ingredient in their new life. "Vicki, I've been thinking.

Because I am the Minister of Music, I often am the first one there to set up and the last one to leave after tear down. It really doesn't leave much time for companionship for you, and I certainly don't expect you to wait around for me all the time. Maybe we should start a family. I mean you'll have someone to pour your love into besides me. I can just picture you as a wonderful loving mother."

Several months passed, and about the time Vicki was very pregnant, George and Kathy Ridge, who had joined the JP Singers, went on a trip with Tom and Vicki to the Wisconsin Dells recreational area. Although they were having a good time, Vicki and Kathy were both pregnant and tired easily. Navigating a walking path, Tom and George took the foursome up a steep hill to see the beautiful scenic view that was promised on the sign.

Vicki was panting, "I don't know if I can make it."

Kathy felt the same way, "I know what you mean. The baby is taking up more room every day and it's getting harder to catch my breath."

Tom and George, "the explorers," kept cheering the women on. "Come on, girls, you can do it!"

"Oh George!" Kathy exclaimed, "If you say that one more time…"

Vicki could only laugh at her husband. He was always encouraging the JP Singers to give testimonies or hit a note that was impossible to sing. Even if a person had laryngitis Tom would say his mantra: "You can do this!"

Eighteen months after exchanging vows, Troy was born on December 14, 1974. They had been concerned when Vicki hadn't felt any movement until she was five months along. Vicki had gone into the clinic every week waiting to hear a heartbeat; waiting to feel a hint of movement, but there was none. Finally, one day she felt a little flutter and hoped it was the new life in her telling them everything was fine. The doctor was encouraging also. "I think I hear a faint heartbeat, Mrs. Elie. You've got a quiet one in there all right."

Vicki felt a wave of relief flooding over her. "Thank you, Lord!" She couldn't wait until Tom got home to tell him everything was all right. But now as she sat in the hospital holding her little bundle in her arms, ready to go home, the doctor came in with unpleasant news, "Hello, Mr. and Mrs. Elie. I'm sorry, but the lights haven't cobated the jaundice enough, so your little guy will need to stay a few extra days here. There are too many health risks associated with jaundice. I'm sorry, but you can't take your baby home with you today."

Vicki's eyes brimmed up with tears, but she nodded to the doctor her acceptance of his verdict. Every day she would travel back to the hospital and nurse Troy. She talked and sang to him and caressed his soft beautiful skin. Then every day she would leave in tears trying to be brave, but it was just too hard to dam up her emotions.

"Is my baby ever coming home with me?" she cried out to herself and to the Lord. Tom was beside himself not knowing exactly how to comfort Vicki. This was all new to him, too. Finally, after ten days Vicki was able to bring Troy home. Mom and baby rested up for a few days and then began going out for short trips. Soon they were going everywhere together. Her "little bud," as she was fond of calling him, gave new meaning to her life.

The new building with the fellowship hall provided more opportunities for people to get acquainted with newcomers. Tom and Vicki were making small talk with another couple, Phil and Ruthie Osterhus, when Tom brought up the usual question, "So, Phil, what do you do for a living?"

"I'm a police officer with the Minneapolis Police Department," answered Phil.

"Oh really? I always kind of wanted to be police officer. I think because I've had a desire to help people in some way that also involved adventure, it was on my list of 'what to be' along with an FBI agent and an evangelist."

Phil laughed, "That's quite a combination: police officer, FBI agent, and an evangelist. Hey, why don't you come along with me sometime on one of my shifts? They have a program where we bring observers along. You can ride in the patrol car with me."

Tom got excited. "Sure, I'll come along."

It was dark when they climbed into the squad car. Phil and his partner rode in the front while Tom rode in the back. Tom began looking around the interior of the squad car. In order to see all the equipment on the front dash, he had to peer through a criss-crossed wire screen that separated the back from the front. Because Tom had never ridden in the back seat of a squad car, he eagerly listened while Phil explained what some of the equipment was for. Everything was quiet and routine for a few hours, until a call came from the radio dispatcher to investigate a suspected window-peeper prowling around Lake Street. Phil and his partner began a systematic drive through the neighborhood, scanning for anything suspicious. Suddenly, Phil's partner called out, "There, down that alley—I saw someone walking."

Phil backed up the vehicle and proceeded down the alley. A person glanced over his shoulder, but kept walking as the squad car pulled up alongside of him. Tom was trying to get a good look at the guy while Phil was making small talk with the stranger. Abruptly the man bolted and ran back the way he had come.

Phil's partner opened his door, and before the chase began on foot, he yelled, "Left, at the end of the alley!"

Phil threw off his seatbelt, shifted the car out of forward, and pursued his partner and the suspect. Tom turned around in his seat and watched Phil disappear around the corner. The next thing Tom noticed was motion. Something was moving.

"It's the car!" Tom whirled around. His fingers grabbed the wire seat divider as his eyes searched for the gearshift. It wasn't in park.

Tom let out a quiet scream, "It's in reverse! Phil, you put it in reverse!"

Frantically, Tom searched for the handle of the passenger door in the dark when he remembered with a sinking feeling, "There are no handles. I can't get out!"

Now the car was moving a little faster and all Tom could do was watch it helplessly roll down the alley to whatever fate was his. Here he was in some dark lonely alley in a bad part of town at 3 a.m. locked up in a rolling squad car. Visions of signing the release papers came back to him. Would he ever see Vicki and his new little son Troy? Before all was lost the car rolled into a pile of garbage cans and came to a gentle stop. In what seemed like hours to Tom, Phil and his partner came back.

And they weren't alone.

Tom was relieved to see them until they opened the rear passenger door and guided the uncooperative suspect into the back seat. When Phil pulled the car around to leave the alley, the man leaned right into Tom. Tom thought the man was trying to cozy up to him and let out an undecipherable sound.

Noticing Tom's face, Phil smiled, "Don't worry, Tom, he's cuffed."

On the way to the police station, Tom decided he had made the right decision to serve the Lord in full-time ministry.

Beth was drawn to Vicki's positive attention and was often invited over to the newlywed's home. Even as an eight-year-old, Beth enjoyed helping them with remodeling projects. After Troy was born she helped Vicki with Troy and a special bond grew between the auntie and nephew that carried through the years, making them feel more like brother and sister. At JP, Beth would help with Troy while Vicki was singing. Sometimes Beth just followed Tom around and would listen to all the interaction of the staff as they discussed plans for upcoming services. She was proud of her older brother even when the staff leaders would tease him, "Hey Tom, we would give anything for your upbringing, but man, you have no clue what life is about."

"Yeah, Tom, you are one naive guy."

Through the years, Beth watched Tom's character grow as a result of being a part of the JP leadership team. There were so many people from different backgrounds, which helped him gain perspective on other people's lives and how God can transform them. Tom was losing his tunnel vision a little more each day.

Vicki grabbed her purse on the way out the door to the grocery store. Tom was in charge of baby Troy while she did some shopping. "I just fed him about fifteen minutes ago so he should be fine until I get back."

"How long do you think it will take?"

"Only a couple of hours," replied Vicki.

"Okay, because I have an extra music practice with the musicians later this afternoon."

"I'll be back before that," Vicki assured him.

"All right," said Tom, "I'll hold down the fort with Troy until you get back."

After Vicki left, Tom peeked in on Troy. He still got a thrill every time he laid eyes on the little guy. This dad stuff was great. Tom looked over the music he needed to use for the afternoon rehearsal for a while, until he heard a small cry. Tom went to the door of Troy's room and peeked in again.

"Hi there, Troy! Are you waking up to see your dad?"

Tom was delighted until he held Troy in his arms, "Oh boy... something happened while you were sleeping."

Tom couldn't believe the odor coming from Troy's cute little body. He glanced at his watch to see how long it would take before

Vicki would get home. He hoped she wouldn't be too long. The smell coming from Troy's diaper was really starting to get to him. And Troy didn't look too happy about the situation, either.

Tom decided to lay Troy down on a blanket on the floor like he had seen Vicki do. "Let's see if I can find you a nice toy to play with."

Maybe if he distanced himself a bit it would help with the smell. To his relief he heard the car pull up.

He practically ran to the door, "Hi, honey, need any help with the groceries?"

As soon as Vicki was in the kitchen Tom was heading for the car. "Troy's in the living room on a blanket. I think he needs his diaper changed."

Tom went happily to the car to gather in all the groceries for his wife, enjoying the fresh air.

Tom was awakened out of a deep sleep from ringing sounds somewhere in the distance. He could hear Vicki's voice mingled with the sound of the ringing. "Tom, it's the phone!" Tom sat up and started for the phone. His alarm clock told him he should still be sleeping for another hour or two.

"Hello?" he managed.

"Tom, this is Phil. I just apprehended a burglary in progress at the church." Phil, who had given Tom the ride of his life in the police car, had joined the music ministry, along with his wife, Ruthie, as vocalists.

"What do you mean?" The cobwebs cleared out of Tom's mind and he was now alert.

"Well," explained Phil, "I woke up about 3 a.m. this morning and thought the Lord was telling me 'Get down to the church.' I wasn't sure what to do. I've never had this kind of experience before, but I felt this intense need to 'Get down to the church' so I got my clothes on and drove down there. After I got out of the car, I looked around and found that the side entrance door adjacent to the parking lot was open. So I went in to investigate. First I looked toward the offices and didn't notice anything so I decided to check out the sanctuary. I pushed the door open to the sanctuary just a crack and that's when I saw some guy fumbling with the stage equipment. I gave him a shout and he took off like a bullet."

Tom couldn't believe it. "So he got away?"

"No," Phil continued, "I chased him down the alley and caught him trying to climb over a fence. And then when I apprehended the guy, I frisked him and…and…," Phil began to laugh and couldn't get the rest of the sentence out.

Phil was always chasing someone down an alley. "What, Phil? What's so funny about some guy robbing the church of its sound equipment?"

"Well, Tom," Phil was now desperately trying to keep his composure, "you had to be there to appreciate this. Here is this guy with pockets full of stolen microphones…and he is so shocked by being caught by a real live police officer that he wet his pants!"

From the bedroom Vicki could hear Tom laughing hysterically while pulling a kitchen chair out from the table to sit on. Vicki couldn't figure it out. "What is so funny that someone had to call my husband in the early hours of the morning and have a laugh about it?"

Ruth and Al had started going down to JP and naturally ended up talking about it with Betty and Pete, their dear friends for many years. Often their daughter, Jill Peterson, would tag along with Beth and her parents. "Mom and Dad, can't you please try it out just once? Al and Ruth like it and they're as old as both of you."

Pete replied, "Oh, we're not that old, Jill. You act as if we're museum relics."

Betty smiled, but added seriously, "You know what, Pete? When I hear Ruth and Al describe the worship at that Jesus People Church,

I just feel hungry for something more of God's Spirit."

Pete looked surprised, "What's wrong with our church, Betty?"

"Nothing. It's a wonderful church. But there is something going on at Jesus People. Didn't you hear what Al and Ruth were saying at dinner the other night? They have people getting saved every service. Something's going on at that place that is akin to a revival and I for one want to see what's going on."

The next Sunday Pete drove Jill and Betty down to Jesus People Church. They selected seats toward the back and settled in for the service. When the music began, everyone stood spontaneously.

"Oh, look, Pete, there's Tom at the piano," said Betty. Soon she was lost in worship. When people began to clap, she clapped her hands with a joyful heart. When people started raising their hands up to the Lord in worship, Betty naturally followed and closed her eyes in heavenly bliss. She couldn't ever remember feeling God's presence so strong. It wasn't hype—it was beautiful.

Pete broke into her happy place with the Lord, "They can't all be sincere about this, can they?" Then a few minutes later he mumbled about something else he thought was weird.

Finally, Betty looked up at him with brown eyes filled with righteous irritation. "Will you let me alone to worship? These people have been saved from a lot. They are so appreciative to the Lord they're just showing thankfulness and gratitude. And I want to too; I'm so hungry for this."

Betty closed her eyes and continued to worship, leaving Pete to himself. After a few more visits to JP, Pete realized people were sincere. Consequently, when he began to consider all that the Lord had done for him, he couldn't help but clap his hands in thanksgiving and raise his arms in adoration. Somehow, it seemed so natural. Years later, Betty and Pete would find that this new expressive way of worship would be commonplace in their home church, as well as other churches across the Twin Cities and the nation. God's Holy Spirit was calling this generation of worshipers to be free to worship him in new ways as it had been done thousands of years ago by other "God-seekers," such as King David. In the book of Psalms he wrote that people should rejoice in God, clapping their hands, and praising him with loud-sounding symbols.

As Tom sat at the piano and worshiped the Lord with all his heart, he had no idea that he was part of church history. Jesus People Church was a prototype of what the future would look like for worship in the 21st century. It was one of the several start-up models for other churches to catch the spiritual fire for passionate worship. There would be no turning back no matter what happened to Jesus People Church in the future. God had used this church and its people, including Tom and Vicki, in a defining way in church history.

Chapter Eighteen

Nicollet

For almost four years Jesus People Church had been located at 2917-15th Avenue South and Lake Street. But now the space was overcrowded with new converts and others who had found renewed passion for serving Christ. It was time for a new building, so Tom went with Roger and Dennis on a scouting trip, while the co-pastors navigated. "Okay, what street should I turn on?"

"It says 24th and Nicollet, so if we're on Hennepin it looks like we need to turn east? Take a right here and it should be down just a block or two."

"Either way, if we just get on Nicollet we'll find it eventually."

Turning onto Nicollet, they spotted the tall white pillars in front of the building that was for sale, "Can you believe it? It's the old Christian Science building! What a trip it would be to have this building."

"Yeah, man, it's like the devil got it all ready, and then the devil got kicked out. Far out for Jesus!"

"I really dig the pillars, man, let's see what the place looks like inside." Never in their wildest dreams did they picture themselves as pastors of such a large church.

"Oh my, this is quite stately looking," said Tom, as he followed

Dennis and Roger into the building. They just looked over their shoulders at Tom and smiled. Tom stepped into the spacious foyer and walked through the doors into a large meeting room. The floor sloped towards the front. It definitely had a more modern feel to it than their current location.

"There seems to be a lot of wasted space in this building. I guess we'll be putting in more office rooms and another fellowship hall."

Construction teams were formed to put in staff offices and a whole entire floor for the fellowship hall where people could mingle, have dinners, or conduct classes, with easy access to the lobby. Twenty-five steps on either side of the foyer led up to the second floor sanctuary that could now accommodate over 800 people per service. Eventually, 2,000 people would be passing through the massive white pillars each week. Bulletins and flyers were printed listing the services on Sunday at 9 and 11 a.m., 5 and 7 p.m., and Wednesday at 7 p.m.

And the harvest continued. One young man, Larry, kept watching from his restaurant window across the street from JP as young people went back and forth with Bibles in their hands. Drawn by the Holy Spirit, he walked past the white pillars and into the service. During his first curious visit he gave his life to the Lord, and eventually Larry asked Tom to perform his wedding ceremony.

At the Nicollet location, Tom started experimenting with musicals. The first musical was a Bill Gaither production called *ALLELUIA!* Tom had to laugh when he read over the music score. Here was a contemporary out-of-the-box church on the cutting edge of trends for church music, and they select for their first musical a conservative traditional genre along the lines of Barry Manilow. Not exactly coolness. Tom assembled the JP Singers and others interested in helping vocally with this new adventure.

"Okay, let's try that part one more time. Watch the timing. Some of you are coming in on the first beat of the measure while some of you are coming in on the second beat."

"Well, which beat is the right beat?" someone asked.

"It should sound like this. I'll do it slowly first with the correct tempo. Count in your head while I sing." Tom kept going over the song until they had it right.

In the next room, Styrofoam shavings were floating everywhere as people cut out giant sized three-foot letters for the word "alleluia." After painting the letters, they were hung from the ceiling over the stage area.

Tom's experiment of inviting friends to a musical event had an overwhelmingly positive response.

After *ALLELUIA!* Tom worked on Easter and Christmas productions and other musical concerts at which people shared testimonies or anecdotes between the songs. JP was fast becoming known for its quality concerts that also had an inspirational message. People were coming to faith and taking the claims of Jesus Christ seriously.

At home during dinner, Tom was eager to share his latest idea with Vicki.

"What about doing an actual musical? A play production with actual actors, using the songs to move along the story?" Tom bounced the idea off of Vicki.

"You mean with a real stage, props, and costumes?"

"Not only that," he said, "but we could have a dinner before the play."

"Would that be possible at church? The sanctuary floor slopes and the fellowship room wouldn't work either."

"Maybe some other venue would be better. Some people just don't want to set foot inside a church building, but a nice restaurant setting would be more comfortable for them. We need to meet them halfway. We can't always expect unbelievers to attend a church to find God."

"I agree, but what's the play going to be about?"

"I don't know quite yet, but I've got some ideas swirling around in my head."

Vicki burst out laughing, "I bet you do, Tom Elie! You have more ideas than you know what to do with!"

Tom began writing down his ideas and listening to other ideas from Pastor Dennis. Soon he had a theme: *Christmas 1976*. The Hopkins House, a hotel with a beautiful restaurant, agreed to rent out the banquet room and let them create their own stage complete with wall flats that they could move as the scenes changed. Someone came forward to help with the costumes, designing Old-English attire. Tom finished up the details of the script, which had only a few lines for the purpose of transitioning from one song to the next. The excitement was contagious and word spread about the upcoming *Christmas 1976* dinner play at the Hopkins House.

The overflowing crowds and the response of the audience to the Gospel message convinced Tom that a new era of communicating the Gospel had arrived. Drama and musicals in theater-like settings were being used by God to bring in the harvest of souls. When he got to the regular weekly staff meeting everyone was talking about the people who were impacted spiritually by the performance.

"I think we should try a different venue."

"Where?"

"The Chanhassen Dinner Theater," Tom replied. "It's the Cadillac of dinner theaters, well known throughout the Twin Cities."

Everyone stared at him.

"They have several theater dining areas under one roof. We could use their smallest eating and stage area. If we brought in a well-known Christian artist or two and had it in that type of setting, people would know that they were in for a quality night of performance, instead of some church basement thing. It would be a festive Christmas Gospel show for people to celebrate the season."

Tom began working with a team, writing a script and composing some of their own music, as well as using traditional Christmas standards. *Christmas 1977* would be a variety show featuring the singing couple, Amos and Sue Dodge. They were a nice addition to the JP Singers, who were by now becoming a very professional-sounding group.

Souls were added to the kingdom.

After three years, the question was asked, "What should we do next?"

Some of the staff at JP put their heads together and rewrote the Dickens classic, *The Christmas Carol*. Staff member, Jim Schumacher, was the main writer of the script, and Tom and John Worre wrote the music. Buddy Van Loon, the visitation pastor, poked his head in Tom's office one day, "Tom, I have a great title for your new adaptation of the *Christmas Carol*. Why not call it *The Gospel According to Scrooge*?"

"You mean like a spinoff from that comic strip?"

"Right, the one Schulz did called *The Gospel According to Peanuts* but not using his story line, just tweaking the title to go with the theme of the Dickens story and the Gospel of Jesus Christ."

Over the years everyone at JP began calling the production *Scrooge*. They did four Monday nights of *Scrooge* in the Chanhassen Dinner Theater. One year they did the show for free at the Minneapolis Institute of Arts Children's Theater, which was unheard of to offer a free show at that venue.

In the midst of special events, JP had all kinds of people with different lifestyles coming to the church. Some were hippie types, others were wayward street people looking for a place to rest, and others were just plain curious about this nontraditional church.

Sometimes people would get very vocal about their opinions of the service and there would be outbursts. The ushers were not trained for such disturbances and didn't know quite what to do, so they usually did nothing. But Tom didn't think these outbursts should be ignored. Often Tom would slide off the piano bench after worship was finished and escort the person out if they didn't calm down. He had a sneaking suspicion the devil could very well be sending people in just to get some attention for himself. Tom knew from reading the Gospels that the presence of Jesus often stirred up demonic tensions within people, and they got so agitated they couldn't sit quiet. People would get saved today. People did every service. God's power was at work and the powers of darkness couldn't handle it.

One time, just as Tom was finishing worship, a lady stood up and started speaking in tongues very loudly. Tom didn't recognize her and figured she was a visitor. He looked her over and began assessing the situation. She was tall, average weight, and had good voice projection. He figured she must come have come from a good old-fashioned black gospel background because she was really belting out the tongues. This was not altogether unusual for JP, since they were a charismatic church, however, the lady went on and on and on.

Tom felt a growing uneasiness inside. Something wasn't right. He was sure the lady meant well, but as Paul had written in 1 Corinthians, the gift of tongues was for the edification and encouragement of believers and it was to be done decently and in an orderly fashion. This did not seem orderly to Tom. He hesitated, thinking the situation over. On and on she went. Finally, Tom looked toward the ushers. They had that same confused look on their faces again, so Tom slid off the piano bench and walked up the center aisle and politely told the lady, "Please stop."

She kept on. Again Tom said, "Stop."

No response. Just a flow of uninterruptible words kept coming from her lips. Tom tried one more time, "Ma'am, if you don't stop, I'm going to have to personally escort you out of here."

She wouldn't stop. Tom positioned himself behind her, put his arms around her stomach, and began to drag her out into the center aisle. The floor was slanted uphill toward the main doors, so he decided it would be more effective to drag her downhill toward the front past the stage, and out the side door. Everybody was watching anyway, so it didn't really matter which way he took her. As Tom dragged her toward the front, he began thinking about how he was going to squeeze both of them between the huge column and the drum set. There was only about ten or twelve inches.

Unbeknownst to him, she had come with a whole row of people and they had gotten up and followed Tom down the center aisle like a parade. Tom kept working toward the side door. If only he could reach that side door, it would all be over with and the service could continue. Finally, after they got through the side door, he tried to set the lady down on the floor, but instead, she flopped on the floor like a fish. Out of breath, Tom knelt down on one knee and leaned over the lady thinking that maybe he should pray for her.

All of a sudden something caught the corner of his eye. It was a shoe with a pant leg, and then lots of legs. Tom looked up and found himself surrounded by eight or nine tall healthy…strong-looking… black men. And he didn't recognize one of them as a regular attendee. No one had come to assist him—not another living soul from JP was around. Not even one lonely gutless usher was peeking around the corner.

They were staring down at Tom with serious faces. Tom felt his insides get ice cold with fear. He had been making friends with a lot of different people of various ethnic backgrounds since joining JP, but he was still a white boy from the suburbs who had heard many stories about black gangs in the big cites, such as Chicago and New

York. Was this his last day on earth? He waited for the first blow.

"Thanks," came a voice.

Then another, "Yeah, thanks, man, we didn't know what to do."

Another chimed in saying, "We're all here for a company convention and she asked us to come here for the Sunday service. We don't even know her all that well." By now the lady was sitting up and Tom was breathing a sigh of relief. They all shook hands and Tom invited them to come back if they were ever in town again. They helped the lady out the door and Tom wandered through the lobby until he found the drinking fountain. As he bent over to sip the cool water, he could feel his legs trembling. He thought about his stereotypes of black people. He was learning a lot about people at this church. When Tom came around the corner into the main lobby, he heard someone shout, "Hey, it's Tom the bouncer!" Others heard and soon everyone was calling him that.

Eventually, the ushers organized themselves into an efficient capable unit (even wearing shoes!) and were able to handle any situation that arose. After another packed service of 700-800 people, Tom heard the ushers talking intensely in a group about a situation that had happened during the service. "What's going on?" Tom asked the group.

"Oh, we had an interesting 'worshiper' here this service, Tom," said one of the ushers while others laughed,

"Oh yeah? What happened? I didn't notice anything."

One man spoke up and explained, "That's because the guy was in the very back standing behind everybody so very few noticed, which was good because he started taking his clothes off one piece at a time until he got down to his underwear!"

Tom's mouth dropped open, "What did you do?"

Another fellow joined in, "I found a blanket and we wrapped it around him, picked him up, and carried him out like a cocooned caterpillar."

Tom left the ushers to their discussion to look for Vicki. "Hi, honey," he said after he found her. She had Troy on her hip, who stretched out his hands toward Tom.

"Hi, big fella! How's my boy?"

After finding out what Tom wanted for lunch, Vicki left Troy with him while she went to a nearby restaurant to pick up some food. Tom visited with the last few people to leave the second morning service, and when Vicki returned they made their way upstairs to the sound booth. It had carpeting on the floor with a couple of couches and was the only place that was quiet. Here they could eat lunch as a family and rest for a while before the two evening services. With two Sunday morning services and two evening services, it was too much running around with little Troy to get him home, fed, down for a nap, and then back again for pre-service rehearsals. Because Tom was the Minister of Music, they were usually the first to arrive and the last to leave for every service or event. Vicki looked over at Troy as he slept on the blanket she had laid on the floor. She and Tom each lay down on a green upholstered couch and rested for two hours before the two evening services. It gave them a chance to talk a bit and connect during the busy schedule they had every Sunday.

By now the community of JP had seen thousands of people come to faith in Jesus Christ. There just wasn't a service where someone did not give their life to Jesus Christ. People were coming to Christ even when the sermon was on tithing a portion of one's income to the work of God's kingdom. When either Dennis or Roger finished preaching they would launch into an appeal to invite people to follow Christ while Tom continued to pray as he played the piano. He never got tired of seeing people repent and give their lives to Christ. The weight of sin was being lifted off their souls. Soon they would taste the abundant life of serving God, but it wasn't without cost. These new believers would have challenges along the way, but they would not regret surrendering their lives to the Good Master. *Lord Jesus protect these new believers. Help them to grow strong in you. Help them to learn who you are. Help that new seed of faith in their heart to be protected from the enemy so that weeds of doubts and the cares of this life don't choke out their faith in you. Thank you for this harvest of souls, Lord.*

It was time for a new idea. How about putting together a two-night Easter production at Orchestra Hall? Tom gave his proposal to the JP staff. "Let's make it two nights of free music at Easter."

"Free? Nobody does free concerts at the Orchestra Hall. Why that's unheard of! It's a brand new facility."

"Well, people are going to hear about it and they are going to come and be blessed." Tom was not discouraged by the raised eyebrows. He was used to trusting God for new and different ways to communicate his love to people. Tom was getting excited just thinking about how fun it would be to sit in that music hall and see the people pour in—people who probably would not otherwise have the opportunity to sit in a professional concert hall like this.

Tom rented the hall and hired Minnesota Orchestra musicians, along with his best volunteer musicians, to accompany the JP Singers. For two nights the packed-out audience responded overwhelmingly to the large combined orchestra and vocalists. Tom sat at the piano leading the whole production. Excitement built up inside Tom until he thought he would be the next man to land on the moon. The momentum continued.

The next venue would be the Minneapolis Auditorium. "How much seating is in that place?"

"Around 7,500."

"What are we going to do?"

"Let's bring in Barry McGuire from Eve of Destruction. He's a Christian now."

"Well, how is this all going to work?"

A musical was planned with Barry called *The Witness*. He would be the lead singer with the JP Singers as the backup group.

Barry came in a week before, to practice with Tom and the JP Singers. It happened that Barry's good friend, Keith Green, the late singer and composer, was in town doing a concert the week before JP had scheduled their event.

"Tom, let's go see Keith at the Minneapolis Auditorium."

So they went backstage to find him before the concert.

Barry asked around, "Where's Keith?"

"Oh, he's in the bathroom," someone told them.

They found him alone in the men's bathroom kneeling, crying out to God for his presence to fill the auditorium that night. Tom was touched by this man, alone on the cold tile floor, crying out to God in prayer: *This is a man of prayer, a man whose heart is really after the Lord.*

Keith looked up, a smile broke across his face, surrounded by a brown mass of curls. "Hey, brother! What a surprise! God is good!" The two Christian artists embraced and then Barry introduced Keith and Tom to each other.

"Why don't you guys join me while I finish praying."

The three men joined together for a great time of prayer and then Keith brought Barry out on the platform later on during the concert as a "surprise guest."

Barry put in a plug for the next Friday night. "Same night, same time, same place. Same good time with God. Bring your friends! Let's pack the house!"

And they did. The Minneapolis Auditorium was packed out with around 7,000 people. And more souls were added to the harvest.

After that, all engines were full steam ahead. "What should we do next?"

"Let's ask David Wilkerson to come and speak," Tom suggested. "I'll put together some good quality music specials along with some praise and worship songs. People can invite their friends."

And more souls were added.

After moving into their second house, their second boy, Ryan, was born on September 8, 1978. Vicki was especially grateful for the new little one because of a miscarriage she'd had after Troy. It had been one of the most painful things Vicki had ever been through. Ryan brought so much healing to her heart. Tom was relieved to see Vicki comforted by their second son. It was a wonderful time in his life. He had much to be thankful for: a beautiful wife, and two boys to tumble and wrestle with someday. His family was a pleasant escape from all the demands of ministry.

The relocation to Nicollet Avenue had made room for 800 regular attendees. JP had gone from a guitar hippie church to doing drama productions like *Scrooge*. During this time the JP Singers recorded two albums. And most of all, people were getting saved at every service, which was Tom's true heartbeat.

The question was not IF but HOW many souls would be saved.

As the church matured, people were getting married and having families, and more wealthy influential-type people came. Jesus People Church became quite well respected and began to have a good reputation among the other churches, which expanded its influence worldwide.

Would the momentum continue?

Chapter Nineteen

Hennepin Avenue

Leaning back in his office chair at JP, Tom glanced over the advertisement in the newspaper. The large bold headline read, "Attention Twin Cities, Jesus People Church is looking to move to its next location; we want you to be a part of it." The copy in smaller font described the fundraiser event as a musical extravaganza, including popular local and national guest artists: Andrew Culverwell, Amos and Sue Dodge, The Gamble Folk, and Tim Shepherd, to name a few, along with the JP Singers and musicians.

Tom reflected on the past events since JP had moved to the Nicollet location and gave thanks. *Lord, you are so faithful. I am amazed at your generosity towards us. Thank you for all the souls who have been harvested for your kingdom these past years here at Nicollet. I ask, Lord of the Harvest, that you would empower us by your Holy Spirit to continue to labor in your fields.*

By now Jesus People was a well-oiled machine when it came to events. However, Tom would not take the Lord's favor for granted. Prayer was still a major part in the overall planning. And it would not be thrown in as a final "Oh, and by the way, Lord, please bless our plans."

Intercession was going on, not only to enable them to purchase the State Theater property, but also for the ministry that would take place. People like Randy Morrison, the future pastor of Speak the Word Church, were dedicated to laying the foundation for the next phase of JP in prayer. He was one example of many pastors who would come from JP to lead a church of their own someday.

The night of the fundraiser had come and 7,000 people flooded into the Minneapolis Auditorium excited about Jesus People Church and its positive impact on the community. Funds were raised and the purchase of the State Theater was completed. Renovation was underway and a moving date was scheduled. Hennepin Avenue, also known as Hooker Hennepin, because of its notorious nightlife, would soon have a lighthouse in the middle of the darkness. Instead of finding twenty acres out in a white suburban community, Jesus People would continue as an inner city church. A Salvation Station needed to be located where the people were who needed it most: the lost, the hurting, and the oppressed—those whom Jesus sought out. The religious community did not need a doctor. Jesus had once told the Pharisees: Why go where the healthy are, when the sick are in need of a doctor? Maybe they were the rejects of society, but they were not rejects of the Lord of Harvest.

And yet, even those from upper class neighborhoods would be drawn in by the Light. All the success they had achieved by hard work and honest living was not satisfying after all. What was missing? Could it be that inside the vacuum of materialism there really was a longing to know a living God? Was there something more than the religious duty of attending church weekly, singing in the choir, or being an usher? Spiritual hunger was everywhere in the Twin Cities, regardless of socioeconomic status or ethnic background. Jesus People Church was a spiritual melting pot where one simply came as they were and worshipped as one community.

John and Patti Worre, the directors of JP's northern retreat center, Shepherd's Inn, moved down to the Twin Cities in order to help prepare for the move to the State Theater. As business administrator, it was John's job to initially develop the theater space and renovate it. He was a man of average height, used to building projects and hard work, with the same brown hair and eyes as his brother, Dennis. Tom watched with anticipation as the work crew began to knock holes through walls. They had to take what had been stores and offices and integrate them into the theater space for Sunday School rooms, offices, and storage. The whole block was being altered. The State Theater location was perfect because the hallmark of JP ministry was drama and music. Tom began dreaming of all the possibilities. "To have a real stage, a real theater is great."

John, who was wearing carpenter clothes and a tool belt, agreed. "It will be a blessing to have all the props and equipment here for different productions." He glanced at his watch, "Well, back to dust and drywall."

"And after that services and souls!"

As the State Theater site developed to peak performance the attendance for services Sunday mornings grew to 2,500 utilizing the 2,100-seat auditorium. People were constantly getting saved and giving their lives to Christ. Even on Sunday and Wednesday evenings, attendance was strong and people were making the walk to the front to declare publicly that they wanted to follow Jesus.

Al and Ruth were still coming for the second service and would see the crowds pour out of the first service praising God. Some people were drying their eyes. People that they knew personally would comment, "Oh, you won't believe it today. It was just fabulous!"

This was not just another routine church service to ease a guilty conscience. Prominent people came hungry for God, knowing that wealth did not truly satisfy. Through these grateful hearts, generous donations poured in to support the many ministries of JP.

Tom's main ministries included: overseeing the play *Scrooge*, praise and worship, some choirs, a mini-orchestra, and a new trio formed with Tom, John Worre, and Jane Thompson, called Spirit and Truth. People often remarked how their voices blended beautifully together. Over the years, John would recount that of all the people he had ever sung with, there was never anything like singing with Tom and Jane. "We didn't ever think about working at it. It just flowed, everything just fit. We would listen to a song once, pick out who was going to do melody or harmony, and that was it. After singing it through a few times we were ready to go."

Tom wrote a lot of the music for the productions, along with John Worre. He also wrote many worship songs and was always looking for new music to try. Public venues were still used for special events, and Tom often found himself immersed in the project.

"Let's do a night of music."

Tom and some other staff members began tossing around ideas.

"Let's call it *The Jesus 1980 Concert* and rent the Met Sports Center for it," Tom said, adding, "We need big names."

"Like who?"

"How about Barry McGuire and The Imperials?"

It was a big step of faith for Tom, but Co-Pastors Dennis and Roger had encouraged all the staff and leadership to let God lead in big ways. At one staff meeting Dennis had said, "There are many GOOD ideas. What we need, however, are GOD's ideas."

This thought stuck with Tom for years, helping him to remember that anything was possible if it was God's idea.

Both Vicki and Patti were part of the JP Singers and began getting to know each other better through practicing together. Both women were the same height, a head shorter than their husbands. Patti's short blonde hair, accented with a splash of freckles, seemed to fit her vivacious personality. Eventually, she became director of the women's ministries at JP and did counseling and mentoring with Vicki and some of the other pastors' wives. Patti, who had known Tom only slightly while she was at Shepherd's Inn, commented on Tom's ability to pull together events like *The Jesus 1980 Concert*, saying, "He is very unusual in that he is visionary and administrative."

"Yes," Vicki added, "he likes planning and coordinating events. He gets that from Ruth, his mother, and his sister, Beth, is the same way."

The combination of Tom's musical giftedness, his ability to come up with new ideas, work through the details, and build teams, helped him to be successful. Add to this, riding the wave of excitement during the preparation, surfing on the adrenalin in the anticipation of it, and then finally the night of performance. At times all this energy would bubble to the surface with comments like: "We're going to pull it off!"

Vicki walked down the hallway to the church nursery carrying three-year-old Ryan on her hip. "No, Mommy, no," his little voice protested. Vicki got to the door of the nursery and tried to pass Ryan over the half split door into the nursery worker's arms. Vicki didn't recognize her, but knew some of the other workers who were further inside watching over the other toddlers.

Ryan started in again, "Don't leave me, don't leave me, I don't want to be here!" Big tears rolled down his sweet round face. Vicki tried to soothe him, "It's okay, sweetie. You'll have fun playing with your friends and all the toys."

The nursery worker took one look at the situation and saw two hours of trouble. "Ma'am, you can't leave this crying baby with me."

Vickie offered an explanation, "I don't think we've met yet. I'm Vicki Elie, Tom Elie's wife and this is our son, Ryan. I assure you he will be just fine in five minutes. I'm not the one he misses. Ryan likes to be by his daddy's side helping him to direct the music and the plays. But he can't be a helper today."

Relief spread to the nursery worker's face and she took the challenge of helping Ryan work through the situation. "Okay, Ryan, I need some help today. Could you please help me?" Ryan eyed the lady over.

Vicki could hear him crying as she walked down the hall but she knew he would be in fine a few minutes. She would have to hurry if she was going to make it in time to join the JP Singers for the first song of the service.

Later after service Vicki swung by the nursery to pick up Ryan and learned he had quickly settled down.

John Worre ambled into his busy household amongst kids here and there. He could hear Emily singing somewhere. Something smelled good in the kitchen, "Look Patti, Tom was gracious enough to help me with the arrangement of these songs that I've wanted to score professionally. He really knows the technical side of music." John showed Patti and gave her a kiss. "It's so satisfying to finally get this down on paper properly. I really enjoy working with Tom because he enjoys watching others succeed."

Patti went back to stirring dinner on the stove, her blonde hair settling around her face in layers. "I'm happy for you, John," she said. "And you're right about Tom. I've noticed the same thing. It's so refreshing because music people have some of the biggest egos in the world. He doesn't see color, gender, or age. He only sees people with potential and wants to help them." She was an energetic woman who could read people as easily as reading food labels.

"He's really a good guy to work with. I've worked with a lot of people over the years and Tom is just a class act. He's always steady, always positive. If anything, he's so positive that he's a bit naive. I don't think he's had a lot of experience outside his church and family. It's like he's a really smart guy, but not street-wise at all, even after mentoring hippies since the beginning of JP—what...eight years now?"

"Yeah, he's got that wide-eyed innocence about him."

"When we get into staff discussions he sometimes has a puzzled look, wondering why everyone doesn't act or think like he does."

"It's too bad more of us weren't raised in that kind of environment. The world needs families with that kind of foundation." Patti went back to stirring dinner while thundering sounds of little feet approached.

Caleb, their youngest of six kids, came running around the corner, "I'm hungry! Is it time to eat yet?"

When Tom got home that night all the kids were in bed sleeping for the night. He could hear his wife doing something in the kitchen. They embraced, both enjoying the moment. After asking him how the night had gone at JP, Vicki began her planned discussion with Tom. She knew his heart was in the right place, but like a lot of men, she also knew he was tempted toward working too much. "Tom, I think Troy feels like you are not at home, even when you are home."

Tom was open to listening to Vicki when it concerned their relationship or the family. He knew that Vicki was the keeper of the home and had discernment for what was going on there. After assessing the situation, they both agreed to purposely set family time together as a priority. They began calling Monday nights Family Night, carving out a night at home or going somewhere together as a family. This worked well, except for September through December, when rehearsal and performances for *Scrooge* were held on Monday nights. There was a lot of work involved in *Scrooge* during this time, day and night. But even then they tried to implement more of a team approach in doing ministry. Troy was part of the children's cast and as Ryan grew he would follow his dad around "helping" him.

Chapter Twenty

Scrooge

The original version of *Scrooge,* written by Charles Dickens, was adapted by Jim Schumacher, one of the JP staff members, to include a stronger Christian message. At first the play was performed using the original musical score, written by Leslie Briscusse, but as JP began to copyright and tape the production, they had to come up with their own music. So that forced the writing team, Tom Elie and John Worre, to come up with their own score. It was magical how Tom and John could sit down and have the time of their lives coming up with the score for the play. One would write the lyrics, the other would write the music. Then the lyricist would become the composer and so it would go—back and forth. Eventually, a film production with a Hollywood actor, Dean Jones, as the narrator, was in the works. John Worre wrote the extra part for the narrator in between scenes, allowing for TV commercial breaks.

One song that was fun for Tom and John to write and was probably their tightest collaboration, musically speaking, was the theme song for *Scrooge,* "Ring the Bells." It started out the beginning of the production and was a high-quality medley of several traditional carols. A phrase from one, a half verse from another, a half of a line here and there, modulating up and down the scale, combining solo parts, duets, and chorus groups. The day Tom and John sat down to work on the opening song, they had books and music spread out all over. Going over the different songs, they began to hum and then sing a few lines. It was like being on a musical adventure together. They weren't even sure where they were going to end up, but by the end of day it was finished and they both were satisfied with what they had.

"Did we really work today, John?" Tom asked with a smile, as they gathered up all the papers.

"I'm not sure," John responded. "It felt more like being out on recess instead of in school!"

Days like this refreshed Tom and kept him motivated to make *The Gospel According to Scrooge* the best production possible. This would be a high-quality drama that would help people understand what Christmas was all about in story form as Jesus had done.

Troy Elie and Caleb Worre, John and Patti's son, were chasing each other around the set. They were buddies and spent all their time at church together, as families of pastors often do. A few adults saw the boys pass by and someone yelled out. "Hey, there's the next generation of Elie and Worre music and drama team!" The boys ran down the steps to join some of their other young friends. Another comment was, "Just think what those two will accomplish after being around all the talents and achievements of their fathers."

Troy glanced back over his shoulder. A frown crossed his face for a moment and then he caught up to Caleb. He didn't like that feeling of pressure he felt sometimes as a pastor's kid.

As with most productions, there were always last minute glitches getting all the props, staging, and costumes ready for opening night. Before the play started, adults were running here and there shouting questions and answers, while children were playing with their friends and climbing on set furniture. Vicki and Troy were part of the townspeople and the beginning scenes had gone well. Now Vicki would have to make a costume change for the Fezzewig's Ball scene. It was a beautiful choreographed traditional English dance scene that was high-spirited, with formal dancing gowns for the women to wear. The costume people had just finished sewing in the hoops for all the ladies' skirts, except for one.

"Are you sure this will hold?" Vicki asked, after slipping on the satiny pastel blue ballroom gown. It complemented her sparkling hazel eyes and soft brown hair. A few ladies with pins in their mouths attacked her with the efficiency of a paramedic team, while the stage crew rolled out the flats and props for the next scene.

"Places everyone!" the stage manager whispered as loudly as possible.

"Are you sure this is going to hold?" Vicki asked again.

"Yeah, yeah, it'll be fine. Now scoot, before you miss your place. We'll sew it up later."

Vicki cautiously strode out onto the stage. She loved the feel of the gown swishing about her. The music started and off she went. They had all worked hard to learn the fast-paced steps and look in sync with one another. Her foot kept coming down on one side of the skirt, but she managed to keep in step with everyone else. As they swirled and turned, Vicki found herself in the back row of the dancers. She was just starting to enjoy the moment when disaster struck. In one fell swoop, her skirt-hoop floated to the floor circling her like a hula-hoop.

Vicki's survival instinct kicked in. She danced out and away from the hoop stage right and hid in the shadows until the scene was over. "That was a close call," Vicki exclaimed out loud to herself. "Thank goodness I had a slip on underneath."

After the dance scene finished, Vicki humbly received the fallen hoop skirt from a prop person and went in search of the seamstress.

Practice for *Scrooge* would begin in September. Oftentimes rehearsals for the *Scrooge* production would last until 1:00 a.m. A young and energetic group, no one seemed to mind getting up early the next morning to start a new day of work. People thrived on the camaraderie, knowing there was an end purpose to this that was greater than themselves. Eternity would be filled with people who came to this production and made a life changing decision to follow Jesus Christ. God was in this. He was going to change people's lives and they wanted to be part of it. It was crazy, thinking about God using a play such as the *Gospel According to Scrooge* to reach thousands of people. But that is exactly what happened. It was a different era. It was a season of change in the use of tools and mediums of art in the whole process of evangelistic endeavors. Those who clung to former methods might see some fruit for their harvest, but bumper crops were coming in by new and different means. And different didn't necessarily mean it was wrong. If God decided to open up the heavens with choirs of angels and do a concert for the lowly shepherds when Jesus was born, why couldn't he use a group of energetic humans on stage declaring his glory to people in the 20th century?

The success of *Scrooge* gave fuel for new ideas and a new production. One day Tom and John were sitting around the staff conference table, talking with Dennis and Roger. "Tom," said Dennis, "I'm thinking about doing a sermon series on the Holy Spirit and I've been thinking maybe we could put together some kind of teaching with music. Is there anything out there like this that you know of?"

"You mean like a musical about the Holy Spirit? No, I don't think there is, maybe a few songs here and there."

Dennis continued to inquire. "But nothing that speaks about

who and what the Holy Spirit is all about?"

Tom shook his head. He looked over to John, who shrugged his shoulders and added, "I did a few simple choruses at Shepherd's Inn when we taught on the Holy Spirit at the discipleship camps. But I wouldn't say they were heavy on doctrine or explaining about the gifts and fruit of the Holy Spirit."

"That's just it," Dennis continued, "there's a lot of music about God the Father and his Son, Jesus Christ, but not much about the third person of the trinity, the Holy Spirit. What if we did a musical about the Holy Spirit based on scripture? It would be like a mini teaching series in one evening. At the end, we could have an altar call for those who want to receive a greater infilling of the Spirit. Most often churches keep quiet on this powerful part of the Christian life. Here the Counselor was sent for our benefit, something most Old Testament people never had, and what do we do with this power? Hide it under a bushel basket. It was the Holy Spirit who gave Peter the guts to proclaim 'Jesus Christ is Lord' on the streets publicly."

"And the power to heal, too." Roger was getting excited about this idea. "You're right, man. There's a lot of emphasis on the gift of salvation. And rightly so, but what about the gift of the Holy Spirit?"

Tom joined in, "We were taught quite a bit about the Holy Spirit at our church when I was growing up because it was the Assemblies of God. But I know a lot of denominations do little more than give a nod of existence to the Holy Spirit let alone the power and function of the Holy Spirit to be a witness for Christ. And certainly not about the gifts of the Spirit, or growth of the fruit of the Spirit in a Christian's life."

Dennis added his thoughts, "Some understandably are afraid of the gifts because they seem too mystical for our intellectual western mind to understand. So what we can't explain and contain in linear thinking terms, we don't want to deal with."

They all agreed that they should pray about this kind of musical—yes, there was something of God it. Tom and John began collaborating with Dennis and production began for the musical about the Holy Spirit: *The Wind Is Alive*, written by John Worre and performed by Tom Elie and the Jesus People Singers. It began being performed not only at JP, but also at other churches and public venues. People responded in droves to the invitation to receive a greater infilling of the Holy Spirit.

In the midst of all of this, another son was added to the family nest. His brothers and parents proudly showed off Jonathan at church. Troy and Ryan looked over their new little brother, Jonathan Ralph Elie. He had arrived a few days before Ryan's third birthday, on September 5, 1981. A few people were teasing Ryan about getting a new brother for his birthday.

Patti was rushing by with a couple of her kids to drop off at the nursery and stopped for a peek. "What a beautiful baby!"

"Why thank you. He is so good and hardly ever cries," Vicki beamed with thankfulness at the little bundle.

"That must be a blessing with two older children at home to care for and Tom gone so much."

"Yes, it is. God is good, and life is good. It seems like the busiest time of my life, but it is also one of the happiest."

"Do you think you'll stop at three?"

"I don't know...we'll see," Vicki kissed Jonathan's soft pink skin while he slept peacefully in her arms.

Vicki took a little time off from the JP Singers and then went back to her busy schedule of home and church life. Soon Troy and Ryan would both be in school and that meant school tuition would somehow have to be part of the Elie home budget. "Tom I have been thinking, if we still want to go the private school route, I could clean houses a couple of days a week when the two older boys are in school."

Tom had asked everyone in the JP Singers to list the three things they enjoyed most in life. Then at church he read over the responses people had written on the 3x5 cards. They were anonymous; however, Tom immediately recognized his wife's handwriting. One of her favorite things was worshipping the Lord. Tom thought about Vicki's commitment to the JP Singers all these years since he had asked her to join. Not only did she have a lovely soprano voice, her worship was genuine. Right at that moment he determined they would always be in some kind of musical ministry together. He had seen how some couples drifted apart doing the work of the Lord each in their own sphere. He also wanted to honor Vicki's desire to sing and worship the Lord with all that was within her soul.

Often Tom could hear the intercessors, as he would go back and forth between services. People would gather before every service, play production, concert, or event, and pray for God's favor to be poured out and for souls to be added to God's kingdom. One of the intercessors, Randy Morrison, would be in the prayer room crying out to God for the release of bondages and physical healings. Tom tried to join them as much as possible in the midst of getting music ready and doing last minute practices. Nonetheless, he was thankful for the men and women who sacrificed their time to do the hidden part of the service that fueled the more visible part. It bolstered his faith, knowing that however the Lord would lead in the music and worship that day, Tom could confidently follow the Holy Sprit's leading. And more important than this—the Gospel would penetrate hearts and people would be added to the Lord's harvest of souls.

It was time for another staff meeting and another fresh idea. "We should do an Easter musical," Tom suggested. "I still remember visiting the "Passion Play" in Eureka Springs, Arkansas. To this day, I can vividly recall the performance and how awestruck I was at the ending when Christ rises from the dead and ascends into heaven."

A few seemed interested and a few raised brows with eyes of doubt mingled with the dread of hard work. By now they all knew what it took to pull off a professional production of this magnitude. Tom flashed his encouraging smile, "We can do this! Think of all the souls that will be reached at this time of the year when people's hearts are sensitive to the story of Easter."

Again, all the cast, directors, and crew, joined together to make it a communication tool for the Gospel. They had hardly finished their Christmas production, taking only a few weeks off, when they began rehearsals for the upcoming Easter production. As spring neared, everyone pitched in and activity accelerated. It looked like a frenzy of ants, scurrying here and there, yelling directions and asking for help. Others were off to run errands or grab their kids and bring them back for evening practices. On weekends, the church building was pulsating with life as every space was used for the Easter production. The special effects crew was going over the best way to raise Jesus up from the stage to ascend to the heavenlies of the State Theater.

"We need a counterweight on the rigging that will be ample enough to pull Jesus up in a smoother fashion than just having a few guys pulling on the ropes behind stage."

The men looked over the harness that Jesus would wear under his robes and then began looking at the lightweight aircraft wire someone had brought. One of the men began attaching the wire, and casually asked, "Well, who wants to be our test pilot and fly up to the ceiling?"

"What are we going to use for a counterweight? We don't have enough space backstage to lift Jesus all the way up, and simply pulling on the wire sends Jesus up in small jerks."

"I have an idea," someone replied. "Now, who is going to be Jesus today?"

Tom walked by the men gathered around the harness and over to his musical score. A few more tweaks and it would be ready for the upcoming dress rehearsal. Excitement built up inside of him as he thought about all the weeks of preparation, and now the opening night was drawing near. He knew every division of the cast and crew had competent leaders so he didn't have to involve himself in every aspect of the production, as he had in the earlier days of *Scrooge*.

The opening night of the *Passion Play* came and went without a hitch. Everyone was into the routine of the performance schedule and people in the audience were responding to the Gospel. Prayer teams were asking for the power of the Holy Spirit to come during each performance.

During one of the performances, Ryan wanted to sit by his dad and shadowed Tom wherever he went. At four, Ryan could have been very mischievous and goofed around; instead, he was intensely absorbed in whatever his dad was doing and took it all very seriously. Tom had been working on the *Passion Play* and chose the classical "Hallelujah Chorus" as the grand finale. When Tom stood up for the final number, Ryan couldn't help but follow Tom and stood right next to him pretending to direct the choir.

However, one night toward the end of the play, something didn't seem quite right. As Jesus was supposed to ascend, some distracting voices could be heard behind the stage. Then Tom noticed Jesus was taking a little longer than usual to ascend into heaven. So he signaled the musicians and singers to be ready just in case he had to add a few more bars of instrumental.

After the altar call, as Tom walked backstage, he heard all kinds of chatter.

"What's going on?" he asked.

"Oh man, did we have a close one!" A man's face was filled with relief.

"What do you mean? What happened?"

"Well, the two guys who jump down the stairwell to counterweight the ascension of Jesus, didn't realize that the harness hadn't been hooked up in time. So they were ready to take the big plunge when at the last second someone yelled out 'NO! STOP! The wires aren't attached to Jesus!'"

Tom felt his face go white. "You mean, all this time two guys have been jumping from the top of the stairwell, holding onto the ends of lightweight aircraft wires?" Tom thought about the two-story open stairwell with a hard concrete floor at the bottom.

"Yeah, that's why sometimes Jesus would ascend just a little crooked. If one guy jumped a second sooner or fell faster, then one side of Jesus would ascend a little faster."

Someone else added, "That's still better than that one performance when you could see Jesus' feet dangling until they shut the curtain."

"Talk about anti-climatic," someone else chimed in.

Tom walked away shaking his head. All of their striving to be professional and have credibility in the eyes of the Twin Cities, and now this piece of humble pie. Surely God must need a sense of humor and a lot of patience when working with humans.

Winter winds blew down Hennepin Avenue searching people's coats and hats for a way to penetrate their armor of clothing. Inside the State Theater, Tom watched the people stream forward to the stage. They were well into their December schedule of sixteen performances of *Scrooge*. Over the past five years of *Scrooge* performances, there had been about a dozen or maybe two dozen people go forward each night, but tonight they kept coming and coming. His heart burst with the sight of it all. Finally, the front swelled to nearly seventy people and now it was time to lead them in the prayer of salvation and commitment to Jesus Christ. The cast and crew stood by watching and praying. All the practices, all the work on the sets and gathering of props, all the technical challenges, were worth it. For in this room eternal destinies were being transformed. New life was starting right in this State Theater on Hennepin Avenue. Tom was almost beyond words. Giving a simple thanks to God was all he could manage at the moment. The intense joy he felt wasn't like any earthly pleasure he had ever experienced. It was without guile or wrong motives. It was pure and satisfying to the deep regions of his soul. Approximately 30,000 people had viewed the performance this season and hopefully next year, in 1983, there would be even more people.

Chapter Twenty One

A Time to Let Go

It was time. God was cleaning house. Because of his love for various staff members who needed to clean up their act, and for the good of the Christian community, God allowed things that had been done in secret to be now discussed in public. It would be years and decades before some would recover from the hurt and disappointment of their leaders' failures. Others were able to navigate through the maze of grief, loss, and pain more quickly, and then finally, to acceptance and forgiveness. Many would have their faith shaken to the very core and would reexamine their belief system, asking themselves, "Why do I believe the way I do; and what do I really believe in, after all is said and done?"

Many people felt as though they were going through a family divorce. The leadership team had split up and other staff members were leaving.

"How could they abandon us like this?"

"We trusted them."

"Weren't they our leaders?"

Many wondered what the future would look like.

These men were human, dust formed into clay vessels. Clay pots crack. Sometimes they crack into a million pieces without the hope of ever being put back together again.

One key pastor had left in 1982 to start his own church and JP had felt the sting of his departure. Rumors surfaced that it had not been a clean break because of personal problems. A short time later, things crumbled and JP would never be the same. After the pastor's departure, Tom and Vicki sensed a change for them coming until the process screeched to a halt. Another key pastor at JP had had a personal failure that took a while to unfold. After that came to light, Tom and Vicki decided to stay a little longer and try to help the church recover and move forward.

It was 1983 and the winds of change were in the January air. Three large churches had called Tom for a position of Minister of Music. He was in such turmoil; he just couldn't make a decision. Tom and Vicki prayed about what to do. Should they leave Jesus People Church and begin another ministry somewhere else? This was all they had known for the past twelve years. Fond memories they would cherish forever with relationships forged through community tugged at their hearts. But things at JP were shifting. Tom felt a distance between himself and the other leaders. Could this be God nudging them along out of the nest to something new?

Tom decided he'd better go talk with the staff at JP. "I'm thinking about leaving and doing something different. I've been praying about it and I have a few ideas. I don't know what it is yet, but I feel like God is leading me to go on to something else."

One staff member began to fidget a bit, "Are you sure, Tom? I mean…what are we going to do?" They continued to discuss the situation, which ended with a request, "Tom, could you give us some time to think and pray about it?"

The staff was trying to hold it together. Forgiveness was requested, but the story kept having a life of its own. People took sides concerning the pastor in question.

"He should stay, be supported."

"He should have been dismissed and let someone else come in and take over, at least for a while."

Advisors were brought in to help salvage the situation, but in the end it was fruitless. Jesus People Church was an independent church so there was no concrete governmental structure to come in objectively and sort things out. People left by the hundreds.

Tom discussed the situation with his parents at his house in Plymouth.

Ruth was shocked, "How could this have happened?"

Tom's face was strained with emotion, "That's what people keep asking. That's what we're all asking. I honestly don't know how it all happened," Tom sighed. "Even though I have worked with these people for years, I really didn't see it coming."

Ruth inquired, "Well, are people assuming you knew what was going on?"

"Some question how much I knew and for how long. But I didn't try to cover up for anybody."

Al drew close to Tom, "We believe you, son. Can we pray for you?"

Beth couldn't believe her ears. How could the leadership at JP have done this? It shattered her trust. She felt she had known them so well. As Tom's sister, she had had the chance to rub elbows with the pastors on many occasions. It didn't seem possible. She had to talk to her brother. "I'm glad I'm going away to college. I can't believe they could fall into sin like that. And then to top it off, people are blaming you for not reporting it sooner when you didn't know it was happening, either."

Tom looked at his sister, her face full of pain and anger, "Beth, listen to me. I know it's hard and I'm sorry you have to go through this, but give God a chance to work in your heart. You need to ask God to forgive them for what they did."

Beth shot him a look of confusion. "What? They are taking down the whole church with them!"

Tom began again, "Forgiving leaders is hard when they fail. I'm not saying that all of this is okay, but unforgiveness is a poison. You have to give it to God or it will become your master. It's hard for me, too. We can pray for each other, okay?"

Finally, Beth yielded a little and her eyes began to tear up. She knew Tom was right. It would be a long road ahead with new twists and turns. In time, as Beth looked back, she often wondered if there was pride and jealousy among other things that crept into the leadership at JP because it was such a successful church. People could get puffed up in knowing that God was working in tremendous ways spiritually. They sometimes attached affections on exciting "God things" rather than on God.

At the Elie home in Plymouth, after tucking their youngest son in bed for the night, Vicki sat down next to Tom on the couch in the living room. She let out a sigh. Lately, all this thinking about the situation at JP was giving her regular tension headaches. "I'm concerned about Troy. This is going to be so hard on him. I'm not sure how he's going take all the changes."

Tom looked over at Vicki. She was his best friend, his trusted ally. Not only did she support him, she often helped him to see a different perspective on situations that he overlooked. He slipped his arm around her, "I'm not quite sure how much to tell Troy. I know we have to tell him something. But how much is appropriate for a nine year old? I don't ever remember anything like this happening when I was a kid."

The couple sat for a few minutes in the quietness of the moment, drawing strength from each other's presence.

The remaining staff continued to work through the situation. Vicki and Patti were determined not to engage in gossip, but they did exchange their own struggles briefly. Patti's face was etched in pain, "Sometimes I have to decide how much emotional energy I want to spend today deciding if this person is right or wrong?"

Vicki sighed, "I know, it's so draining. I wake up in the morning and it's the first thing that fills my mind like a dark cloud before a rainstorm. Some days I feel like it's suffocating me."

They were parting as friends, each to their own new path in the road.

Pete and Betty Peterson's daughter, Jill, who Tom considered more of a cousin than a family friend, was also having a hard time with the break-up of JP. Betty tried to remind her, "Jill, God has to work through very ordinary people. You will work through it eventually. You younger people seem to be affected more than us older ones. We know from experience that this is how life is sometimes. God does not promise us that life will be perfect. But He does promise to be with us until the end. And then we will be with him in eternity."

JP was more than a church for its regular attending members; it was a beacon for other people and churches. How true that scripture is in 1 Corinthians, chapter 12:26, where Paul writes using the metaphor of the human body when speaking about the church: "If one part suffers, every part suffers with it; if one part is honored, every part rejoices with it." (NIV) Yet God would remain in the midst of these people who had gathered under the banner of his Son Jesus. They would still be his people. As the children of Israel had journeyed and lived in exile, so the community of JP would feel the hardships of exile. But a remnant would be gathered up and protected through the years. At times it would not be evident with the natural eye. The scattering of the JP family would have some amazing and far-reaching effects resulting in the extension of God's kingdom. It was time for a major multiplication of what God had done at JP. It was time for little beacons of hope to be placed all over the Twin Cities and the nation.

After all, failed leaders were nothing new. Time after time in the Bible, God worked with failed leaders. After Moses killed an Egyptian, he waited forty years in a desert for God's second calling. The Apostle Paul arrested and executed Christians using the legal court system. After Paul's encounter with Jesus on the road to Damascus, he went back to Tarsus to wait ten years until he was asked to come back to Jerusalem by Peter and the other leaders. David and Samson were forced to deal with sexual indiscretions. Yet in the end, God redeemed them all. Some were propelled into greater ministry and for others life would end with one last blaze of glory for God. They died knowing that the Blood Covenant was more powerful than their past failures.

At JP a lot of people tried their best to pray and love each other through the situation, but for others the gossip was so bad it seemed demonic. In the middle of all this were Tom and Vicki and their family. It was the biggest test they had faced yet. Their dreams of the ministry crashed to the floor. Now it was time to start letting God pick the shards out of their heart. But it was so incredibly hard to not let protective scars form. Fear of being hurt like this again crept close to them like a dark cold mist.

The youth group and younger kids in grade school had the classic reaction that children of divorced families have. They felt like somehow it was their fault. Could they have somehow prevented all this from happening? The older children of the church leaders' families felt the sharpest end of the spear. Many turned away from

God in response to their anger and bitter disappointment with the church. This was their church, too, not just the adults. A spiritual hurricane devastated their homes, destroying people along its path of destruction.

Troy went into a depression. His whole world, his entire identity was wrapped up in his church life. Every time the door was open, the Elie kids were there. The ache in his heart was too great to bear. He saw now that his self-worth was wrapped up in what he did, what his parents did, and how people perceived him. Troy became a man that day. His boyhood innocence was stripped away. The harsh reality of adult life assaulted him with such force that he nearly lost his grip. As far as he was concerned the future held nothing. There was one good thing, though. Now he wouldn't have to live in his dad's shadow of greatness anymore and be a pastor's kid with the magnifying glass on him.

Patti walked into the office area. It was in disarray. File drawers were open; garbage bins were full. While going from office to office, she saw Bob Buchanan, who had played the part of Ebenezer Scrooge and was also part of the leadership team at JP.

"What's going on here?" Patti asked with disbelief, spreading her arms out toward the paper tornado.

"I'm cleaning it all out," said Bob.

"Do you mean you're throwing out the history of JP?" Patti started looking through the office trash bins. They were filled with old sermon tapes, photos, music books, posters for events, and videos—all kinds of things.

"I want a clean break. It's time to move on. We have a new location in Eagan," Bob pragmatically explained. "All of this is like a dead weight."

Patti felt her heart beat faster and her face flush, "Yes, it is a new season for JP but we still should honor the past. There was a foundation laid that people prayed and sacrificed for. That was no small thing."

Bob looked up for a moment. "Patti, I think it's best if we have a fresh new start. The JP logo is like a tainted well now."

Patti didn't say anything more. Bob had it in his heart to lead and pastor the remnant of JP when others had turned down the position of senior pastor. He would have to lead as he thought best.

For days, anger kept building in Patti's heart, as she would make trips back to the JP offices to rescue some memorabilia from the offices and the dumpster out behind the building.

Videotapes of *Scrooge* and other plays lay jumbled next to garbage bags filled with rotting food. *Lord, help me to fight this bitterness. I know not everyone is as sentimental as I am, but it was no small thing what happened. A lot of lives were changed for the good through JP. This church was an instrument of yours to touch people in this area and beyond.* She wondered where she would store all of this stuff and what she would ever do with it. No matter, it was like rescuing a child from a flood. She couldn't let it drown and fade from existence.

Her mind was a swirl of thoughts. *First of all, it's bad enough for people to have a sin this great, but it's just as bad to destroy people over it instead of trying to restore them. Isn't that God's business: restoration? Aren't we all just the sick getting well? The perfect ones are in heaven. But we just don't let people fail. No, you can't fail.*

Patti's eyes moistened into pools of tears. She and John would continue on in ministry for as long as God called them. It was not an easy road, but it was part of their journey. "God is in the valley as much as on the mountain top."

As she drove home, a spark of hope flickered, some words from Ecclesiastes came into her mind, "mourning may endure for the night, but joy comes in the morning." It would be a long night for JP but a day of great joy would come again.

Hippie ushers with no shoes. That was JP and its era. An entrepreneur church, with a pioneering spirit, that could not be under the bridle of any denomination. The church was ahead of its time in the ways of ministering, however, by not providing accountability it failed to provide adequate protection for its leaders.

After twelve years of being Minister of Music at JP Tom had not been an itinerate evangelist as he had envisioned when he first saw Lowell Lundstrom pull up in their church parking lot. And he hadn't done crusades like Billy Graham. His passion for souls was the same as those two men, though it looked different. Through musicals, drama, and worship, Tom had seen many people give their lives to Christ. Now a new road lay ahead for him, Vicki, and their three sons. It was both intimidating and exciting. Would he ever become an evangelist in the way he had always dreamed?

Part Three

Northeast

Chapter Twenty Two

Staying the Course

India during the 1980's

Lakshamakka folded most of the six yards of red silky material back and forth like a fan. After tucking the folded material into her slip dress, she quickly arranged the pallev with its several yards of embroidered gold trim and began her morning ritual of walking to the low-caste well.

When she arrived home to cook the breakfast rice, Yesaiah came into their home hungry, as usual. "Mother, is the rice done yet?"

His fifteen-year-old frame filled the doorway by height, but certainly not from weight. His belt looped around him almost twice to accommodate his slender waist. His tucked-in shirt helped to fill out his dark trousers one more notch on the over-wrapped belt. He was looking more like his father every day. His round face and black hairline that framed his face and ears, was like a carbon copy of his father Matthaiah.

"Be patient, my son," she replied in Telegu, "it is almost ready." Lakshamakka noticed something about him. "What is it about you today that is different?" she asked.

Yesaiah smiled with brown joyful eyes, "I will tell you when Father returns for breakfast after tending the goats."

Lakshamakka let him have his way.

After Matthaiah had prayed over breakfast, Yesaiah could not contain himself any more, "Last night I became a Christian!"

Matthaiah exchanged a happy glance with his wife, "So, my son, how did it come that you have put your trust in the One True God, Jesus Christ?"

With a flood of words, Yesaiah explained all that had been going on in his mind since he had heard about the One True God. At first, it had been confusing that one God could be better than one million others combined. Then there was the social pressure to remain Hindu like many of his friends, but the words of Samuel and his parents kept coming back to him. And Uncle had shared with him how the burden of reincarnation had been lifted from his shoulders.

"I also observed that the Christians had a life that seemed abundant in many ways. There was something there that rupees or a large herd of goats could not buy. Then I thought of the choice between serving a Master who is like a Father and Shepherd to me: loving and yet not spoiling me for my own good. One who would find a way to remove all my bad karma. Or the other choice: many other gods—angry, far-off, always needing appeasement, and never satisfied with all our labors and rituals."

Yesaiah's dark eyebrows pinched together in a frown for a moment and then he continued on. "Removing the karma from myself seemed an impossible task. I could never be sure, because it was up to me to get the job done. But Jesus Christ has already gotten the job done."

Lakshamakka and Matthaiah listened attentively as Yesaiah told his story. Matthaiah's eyes danced with joy, and yet, he wanted to make sure his son understood the Truth, Life and the Way. He cleared his throat with a cough, "My son, do you acknowledge that there are not many paths to the God of the universe and that this is a deception of the enemy to make the shed blood of Jesus Christ weak?"

"Yes, Father, if you simply add Jesus to your mantle of other gods, how can that be? Does mother mix dirt and water when she boils the rice?"

Over time, Lakshamakka watched her son grow taller in many ways. He was more patient with others. He desired to learn to read and write so he could study the Holy Book. Then one morning Matthaiah came home early from tending the goats. Although the heat of the day was still hours away, he was coughing again and wiping his brow. "I need to lie down for a few minutes."

"Can I bring you anything?" Lakshamakka asked.

"Yes, a cup of water would be good."

"I have just finished getting this pot from the well. It will be fresh," she replied.

"Thank you." Matthaiah accepted the water with gratefulness and laid his head back down to rest.

Lakshamakka studied her husband for a moment, "You have been working too much again. Perhaps Yesaiah and the other children should do more."

"They do a lot, I cannot sit at home," he responded.

Lakshamakka would not say more. She did not like to think that her husband's cough wasn't going away and that he seemed to fatigue easier. Nor did she want to recognize that his pants were hanging looser and his belt was wrapping around his waist like Yesaiah and the other young boys in the village.

Later that night, Christians in the village stopped by to pray for Matthaiah. He did not get out of bed for several days. When he finally arose all were overjoyed until he had a relapse.

Before he died, he asked for Yesaiah, "Son, I want you to know something."

"What is it, Father?"

Matthaiah's breathing was labored but he pressed on. "Remember the preacher, Samuel, who told our family the way to find the One True God?"

Yesaiah turned his head from side to side in the Indian fashion of saying yes. He could not speak for fear of crying.

Matthaiah began coughing uncontrollably and then rested a moment before explaining, "On Samuels' deathbed he had a prophecy from God—a message from God about you."

Yesaiah waited, watching his father's chest rise and fall with strained breaths.

"Son, he said that you would be a trained pastor one day."

Lakshamakka had been listening from a distance. Tears streamed down her face. She was in excruciating pain watching her husband suffer so much. Even so, she had hope deep inside her pain. He had told her he would be waiting for her on the other side and then they would be together forever. And they would worship the One who had called them out of darkness—face to face without a veil.

Later that year, Lakshamakka watched Yesaiah climb into the transport bus. The dust lingered in the air as the vehicle disappeared down the dirt road. After Matthaiah had died from tuberculosis, Yesaiah had heard about the Bible school started by Rev. G. Peters. Lakshamakka had been afraid to let her young son, still in his teens, travel twenty-seven kilometers to the school for one year. He had never been far from their village. First her husband was gone and now Yesaiah. Yet she knew this was the Call of God on his life and she would support him.

Lakshamakka strode past the rubble that had been the church for two years until the heavy rains came. They had worked so hard bringing stones from the fields and cutting branches from the wild. Many had cheerfully mixed water with dirt to make cement that would hold the stones together. For two years they had enjoyed coming together as a Christian community to worship on Sundays. Then all had changed.

The Hindus in the village wondered why the Christian God would do this to such good people. First, the death of Matthaiah, the first believer in the village, then the church was destroyed, and now Matthaiah's son going so far away to learn more about the Christian God who let these terrible things happen. It didn't make sense. Lakshamakka knew their thoughts and heard the talk whispered around the village. She hadn't gone deaf since her husband had died. However, she knew that trials came to Christians, as was written in the New Testament. Her faith would not depend on everything going well in her life. Her faith was about following Jesus Christ. It was hard right now, but He was with her, even in this. She would keep praying for her children and for her neighbors—and for a church building. She remembered Matthaiah telling them that they would all be together in God's heavenly home someday and all their tears would be wiped away. That there was a time to live and a time to die. That he had tried his best to show them all how to live and now he would do his best to show them all how to die—with unswerving faith in the One True God who had set him free. She would honor his memory by showing others how to live until her time came to join her husband.

Chapter Twenty Three

Let the Praise Begin

Tom stood out on the balcony overlooking their Plymouth backyard, watching the breeze playfully make its way through the autumn-colored trees. Three months had passed since he had resigned from Jesus People Church as the Minister of Music. The sun was setting, its last rays bursting silver and gold around the edges of the clouds. It was the end of a day and the end of a chapter. Through circumstances beyond their control, all that was familiar had been ripped away.

I want you to start a church.

Tom spoke out, "Lord, I don't really want to start a church. I want to travel and be an evangelist."

I want you to start a church.

"But churches don't win souls all that much. You know JP was the exception to the rule."

This church will be different. This church will be an evangelistic center.

Tom thought back to when he was a teenager helping to pass out flyers in Hibbing announcing the beginning of a new church in the northern part of Minnesota, known as the Iron Range. He knew that Clarence St. John's church had grown from zero to eight hundred people. *And* it wasn't from people swapping churches. It was primarily newly-saved people. It could be done. A ray of hope stole into Tom's heart. The church in Hibbing truly was an evangelistic center. Tom felt faith rise up inside of him "If Clarence St. John can do it, I can too." Then he added, "With God's help, anything is possible."

Prior to this conversation with the Lord, Tom and Vicki had tried to tell the boys right away that they were leaving JP. After a family dinner and playing a game together, Tom and Vicki started their evening call, "Time to get ready for bed, boys! Get your pajamas on!"

They had just finished family devotions and were gathered together in the living room. Tom and Vicki looked at Troy and Ryan with heavy hearts. Two-year-old, Jon, had been tucked into bed for the night. Tom glanced over at Vicki for a moment, and then explained to the two boys that he wouldn't be working at JP anymore, which also meant they wouldn't be going to church there anymore.

Nine-year-old Troy burst into tears, "But why do we have to leave?"

Ryan, a few years younger, and always ready for the next adventure, just listened, watching.

Vicki began to tear up, "I'm sorry, honey."

Tom tried to smooth things over, "Changes are hard, son. But this is what we have to do."

Troy persisted, "But why do we have to leave JP?"

"It's just one of those things that happens in life, Troy."

Vicki gathered Troy in her arms. He was getting taller, but she could still get him on her lap. Her face touched his soft brown hair. "It's hard for Dad and me too. It's getting late, you better get your teeth brushed and get some sleep. We can talk more about it later."

Later that night, Ryan lay in his bed listening to Troy cry. Mom had come into their room to say good night in her sweet voice and tucked them both into bed with a kiss. A few minutes after she had left, Troy started crying again. Ryan knew that lights out meant no talking, but he was worried about Troy. He could hear Mom and Dad's muffled voices in the other room. In his softest whispering voice possible, he called out, "Troy."

Rolling away from the wall and onto his side, Troy said, "What?"

"Sh-sh! Mom and Dad will hear."

"So what? I don't care." But then Troy thought better of it and lowered his voice, "What do you want?"

"What's wrong…why are you crying so much?"

"Are you that dumb? Cuz I won't see my friends anymore, that's why!"

"Oh." And then Ryan asked the question Troy had asked his parents earlier, "Why is Dad leaving the church?"

"I don't know for sure, but everyone's been talking a lot lately when they think none of us kids is around. Something happened. Someone did something wrong."

Ryan sat up on his elbow, wide-eyed in the dark bedroom, "Was it Dad?"

"No. Don't you know anything?"

"Well, who then?"

"Just go to sleep. I'm tired."

"Okay, Troy, good night."

"Night." Troy wasn't all that tired, but he wanted to think through the situation. What had he and his friends done to set everyone off like this? They had gotten in trouble before, but all the parents seemed to agree on a solution or rather a 'punishment suitable for the crime,' as they would explain it, and then it would be over. What had happened?

Vicki didn't realize it until later but the feelings they were all going through was like a divorce. A family had been split up. A job had been lost. A community was gone. Would the pain ever leave? The only joy in her life right now was her children and the surprise. She would tell Tom and the boys tomorrow night at the dinner table, if she could wait that long. At least Tom would be around for dinner more.

Finally the news was out, "I'm pregnant!"

On May 30, 1984, Darren was born, 9 months after Tom and Vicki left JP. "Another healthy son, a blessing from heaven." Tom had said to Vicki at the hospital.

Before Darren's entrance into the world, though, God was also birthing other things in Tom and Vicki's world. With the phone tucked into his shoulder Tom flipped open the calendar Vicki kept in the kitchen to December 1983. "Yeah, I think that would work out. What did you have in mind?"

Sam and Jeanne Mayo, pastors of a church in Nebraska had invited Tom to come help them with the upcoming Christmas musical, "Mary and Joseph: A Love Story." After finishing up with the phone call, Tom began to think about what he might need for the upcoming trip to Bellevue, Nebraska. Vicki would pack his clothes for him so all he needed to think about was teaching notes, overheads, and maybe some sheet music. It would take several weeks to get everything in place. Tom didn't relish the thought of being away from his family, especially with Vicki being pregnant, but it would help pay the bills. It could also be a time to get away to seek God's will for direction in his life now.

"Steve," asked Pastor Sam Mayo, "can you pick up Tom Elie when he flies in this week?"

"Sure, Pastor," answered Steve, twenty-something, with light features, slim, and average height.

Later that week on the way to the airport, Steve thought about Tom Elie and wondered what the well-known music minister from

Minneapolis would be like. The contemporary church services at JP were a model for other churches to follow. And the musical productions that came out of JP under his direction were raved about nation-wide. Steve checked his watch. He didn't want to, but he was getting nervous. Sometimes well-known people in the ministry intimidated him. They seemed otherworldly; a step closer to God than regular people. Other times they had so much on their minds before their time of ministry, that they hardly noticed the underlings around them. Steve tried to brush that last thought off, excusing the need for focus on the task ahead. Before getting out of the car and walking to the terminal, Steve checked out his brown hair in the rear view mirror and then his teeth for any leftovers from lunch.

At the baggage claim carousel, he noticed a tall lanky-framed man waiting for his luggage, his dark brown hair parted to one side.

Tom glanced around and caught Steve's look of curiosity, "Are you Steve Wajda?"

"Yes, I am. Are you Reverend Tom Elie?"

Tom extended his hand and smiled at the young man before him, "That's me, but please, call me Tom."

They shook hands and Steve asked him if he had a good flight and how the weather was in Minneapolis. Tom answered casually as if he was talking to one of his neighbors. Once the luggage came, Steve loaded it into the trunk and off they drove to the church. Steve had used up all the small questions he could think of and was trying to think of a good ministry question, when Tom broke the silence.

"So, Steve, what do you do when you're not picking up strangers at the airport?"

"Oh, I work the night shift from 3-11 p.m. and volunteer at the church during the day."

Tom wanted to learn more about this young man. He seemed

so alive, so fresh with passion. He asked Steve how long he had been helping Sam and Jeanne Mayo, and what he was interested in doing at the church.

Steve was mildly and happily shocked at Tom's interest in his life. "Actually, Mr. Elie, I mean Tom, I'm certain God is calling me into the ministry."

"Really?" Tom slid his elbow over the back of the car seat and leaned toward Steve, his eyes fastened on the young man. "Have you attended any Bible schools?" he asked.

"Well, no, but I've been looking into a few."

"I know a good one in the Twin Cites area, North Central Bible College. I'm acquainted with a few of the staff and they are great people."

The next day, after Tom met with Sam and Jeanne Mayo, he needed a ride to a local radio station to do an interview. Tom saw Steve and gave him a grin, "Hey, Steve, how's my chauffer today?"

"Great, thanks, Tom. How about you?"

As they drove to the station, Tom asked Steve about his spiritual background growing up. "So you gave your life to Christ just a few years ago and you're already having thoughts about going into the ministry. What area of ministry do you feel the most passionate about?"

Steve answered in an animated fashion and Tom listened, invigorated by being around someone with enough energy to take on the world. He decided he really liked Steve and hoped God would bless him with an anointed ministry. In fact, he would remember to take some time to pray with Steve before he left Nebraska.

"Steve, I'd like you to meet my wife when she gets here." Tom was excited, his Vicki was making a special trip to Nebraska to see him. He had always worked a lot of hours at JP, but they had never been separated like this before. He was so lonely for her.

Steve watched Tom from a distance during his time in Nebraska, except for traveling in the car with him. He couldn't help but be drawn to this man. Tom's seminar on praise and worship, his ability to play the piano, lead worship, and direct the Christmas musical, only sealed what Steve had heard about Tom: he was gifted musically. Steve realized that Tom reminded him of someone he had never met formally. It was David the Psalmist, from the Old Testament, who was a gifted musician in praise and worship with a heart that God had said was "after His own heart."

Back home in Minnesota, a new birth of a spiritual community was about to take place in Plymouth. For the last six months, Tom and Vicki had prayed about starting a new church and the time had finally come for their first official service. The crisp winter air blew into the living room adorned with Christmas decorations, as people arrived for the first service. "Merry Christmas, welcome!" Tom greeted the guests as they came in.

Troy and Ryan helped people with their coats and hats. Everyone wanting to be part of the new church had been eager to make Christmas Sunday, 1983, their first official church service together. It was a bittersweet morning as people tried to put the past behind them and walk in forgiveness. Twenty-five souls squeezed into their living room hungry for companionship and spiritual fellowship. Tom opened in prayer, "Lord, we thank you for this Christmas morning of new beginnings. We thank you for the gift of Jesus. Thank you for the gift of each other here this morning." Tom played the piano and soon Christmas carols filled the Elie home.

The small group began to grow and soon it became necessary to look for a building, but they had no budget. Together they prayed, "Lord, you know our needs and you know our budget. We also know we can trust you to provide us a place to meet."

An answer came. The president of North Central Bible

College, Don Argue, spoke with Tom and said they would allow the new fledgling church to use their music room for six to eight weeks. "Sorry, Tom, that's all we can do for you; we do not want a campus church. Our philosophy is to have our students involved in area churches."

"Welcome to Praise Assembly!" Tom greeted the group of fifty or so gathered in the music room for Sunday worship, including his parents, Ruth and Al, and his sister, Beth. After a few announcements, Tom asked everyone to join him in prayer and then he walked over to the piano and started playing the opening song. "Let's give our hearts in worship to the King of Kings and the Lord of Lords this morning."

Tom began worshiping God with all his heart. Soon the presence of the Lord could be felt in the room as people forgot about all their earthly desires and worries. They entered the throne room of God, seeking the One who reached out to them with grace in one hand and mercy in the other.

Before the new church had started, Tom had been thinking about what happened at JP and had sought out an overhead governmental structure that could come in and help provide oversight. He never wanted to go through that nightmare again. He knew that in emergencies, denominational leaders could come in and take over before the church broke up completely. God had given him grace to forgive and to move on. But sometimes it still felt as though there were many loose ends. He knew of so many people struggling to move on, who were still stunned by the whole situation. Mistrust of leadership could be such a wounding thing. Still, so many lives had been changed and the eternal work of God would live on. Tom pictured a time when they could all get together again and thank God for all the good that had happened, instead focusing on the way it ended. For now, though, he had to press on and do what God was calling him to do for this season of his life. How that was going to look, he wasn't sure. All he knew was that the passion to see people come into a relationship with the Lord was as strong as ever.

Chapter Twenty Four

Del and the Bat Cave

Tom looked through the mail. His eye caught something from the Assemblies of God with a name he didn't recognize, Delroy Grages. It was a request to visit his church in Dassel, Minnesota, to do a praise and worship seminar. He scanned the letter, learning that Delroy along with his wife, Wendy, had begun a Christian Teen Center, which had turned into a small young church. Tom's heart was stirred. Here was an embryo of new life reaching out into the community with the message of Good News. After introducing himself to Delroy on the phone, Tom was eager to talk with Vicki about it. The spark in Tom's eyes touched Vicki's heart. He was always so positive, always looking to the future. She felt a contagious ray of hope slip into her heart.

During the drive to Dassel, Tom thought back to his conversation with Vicki shortly after they had left JP. "Vicki, I've been praying, and I think I will pursue being licensed with the Assemblies of God. I'm ready for the guidance a denomination can bring. Maybe at last I can be free to travel like I've always pictured."

Vicki had reached out for Tom's hand and with a smile had reassured him, "God will bless you for first honoring their request to not start another church for six months and also for stepping out in faith to test the waters. I guess we need to move on. Sometimes it feels like such freedom to be done with JP, but some days it feels like I'm walking in a dark cave. It's all so confusing. I feel some of the same feelings I had when my father died. I know I'm not supposed to doubt God, but I'm struggling. How did this happen?"

Tom had given Vicki's hand a squeeze, "Better days are ahead, Vicki. I just feel like we've learned so much through ministering at JP that we could encourage others to step out and become active in a worship ministry. I've been thinking about all these small churches that don't have praise and worship teams. I know there is probably talent sitting in every one of those smaller churches just waiting to be discovered. I think if I walk alongside the pastor by doing a seminar it could be the jump-start that he's looking for."

With a hopeful heart, Tom pulled into the parking lot next to Christian Teen Center in Dassel. Previously a restaurant and bar, it had been converted into a place for teens to hang out, with a soda and ice cream bar, and hamburgers. Teen services were held Saturday nights. As Tom walked through the door, he noticed a bulky-built young man in his mid-thirties walking toward him with a grin that Tom would always think of as Del's trademark smile. "Hello, you must be Tom Elie!" his massive hand gripped Tom's like a long-lost friend. His eyes sparkled as he continued, "I'm Delroy Grages, but just call me Del. So you found the place okay?"

"Yes, I did. You gave good directions and what a nice drive it turned out to be. The fall colors really hit their peak this year." Tom sensed Del's sincerity immediately and it didn't take long for the awkwardness of a first-time introduction to fade into friendship. There was something about Del that made him a friend instantly. He didn't seem to size you up, he just accepted you.

"Just let me know what else you need, Tom, and I'll do what I can,"

Del said, showing Tom around the Teen Center. After Tom had set up for the weekend seminar, Del and Tom fell into conversation about getting licensed with the Assemblies of God and its denominational doctrines and philosophies. By coincidence, they were both applying for ordination with the AG. "Say, by the way, Del, are you going to the pastors' and wives' seminar in January?"

Tom noticed Del's eyes drop for a moment. "Well, I've looked at the information. It sounds real good. I know my wife, Wendy, wants to go, but I not sure what we're going to do."

When Tom returned home from Dassel, he told Vicki all about it. "Vicki, they are the neatest people. The offering was small from their church this past weekend, and I am sure they don't have enough financially for the upcoming pastors' and wives' retreat in January, but I felt in my heart that God wants them to go. How would you feel if we sponsored Del and Wendy to go?"

Vicki thought for a moment about how tight their finances were since Tom left JP. With out a steady paycheck they were living week by week, but suddenly she felt a peace about helping this couple out. "Sure, Tom, why not?"

Wendy opened up the small envelope with the return address from Tom Elie. Inside there was a check and a small note in Tom's handwriting:

I feel led by the Lord that you're supposed to go to that seminar. I know sometimes it's hard financially when you are first starting out, and I just wanted to help because God has been so faithful to me.

Wendy sat down and began to cry, "Thank you, Lord!"

She removed her glasses and whispered through tears, "Bless Tom and his family for their generosity. I know they are between ministry jobs and probably don't have two nickels to rub together themselves, and yet they have freely given. Thank you, Lord, for an example of your love toward us. May you bless them in their future ministry, whatever it may be and wherever it may take them."

As her tall frame straightened up, she pushed back her short warm chestnut hair from her brown eyes, replaced her gold wire frames, and went about her day with joy.

During the time Tom was setting up praise and worship seminars at other churches, there was also the possibility of a different facility for Praise Assembly. Tom's enthusiasm was contagious for everyone: "I think we might have a place to rent that we can afford. It's pretty cheap. It's a black Pentecostal church in Minneapolis located near the Metrodome, across the street from Bethlehem Baptist Church. They run their services in the evening, so we could rent it for Sunday mornings for a while until we can buy our own building. I think it could be a good steppingstone."

After parking their cars, Vicki and a few others stood in front of the church building. The sign read "Holy Ghost Temple." Her face showed her disappointment, "This is it?" Her heart sank. It was so different than the ornate State Theater building that JP had been in, but it was available for the price they could afford.

"At least we can have a Christmas musical this year," he told her, hoping to sound upbeat.

Vicki took Tom's hand in hers trying to be positive, "That will be nice, honey. I love Christmas musicals," she reassured him.

Now that she was over the shock of the condition of the building, she would support Tom as best she could. She knew it wasn't easy for him either, but now he would be able to be involved in another music project and that would keep him focused on something. He would be happy organizing people and music. She sighed. Tom was able to look into the future with such hope.

When Tom dropped off the papers for the rental agreement and a first month's rent, he noticed it was a bit drafty in the church and had that Minnesota winter feel to it. "Is there a problem with the heat?"

"Oh, that's that old furnace going out again. We're getting a new one."

"Will it be getting fixed soon?"

"Oh, definitely," the man reassured Tom.

During that summer, Steve Wajda moved from Nebraska to Minneapolis as a registered student of North Central Bible College and was thrilled to begin serving at Tom's new church. Perhaps, he thought to himself, he could intern there some day before he left for cross-cultural work overseas. When Tom began playing the piano and leading worship, Steve could feel tears coming to his eyes. He was so grateful to worship God with this group of believers, to be at the college, and to be around Tom. The more he got to know Tom the more he liked what he saw. He was a spiritual giant, to be sure, but he was so ordinary, so humble. Tom was the same whether driving around in the car or in front of a group of people. He was just Tom: a guy who loved God and sincerely wanted to serve God with all his heart. Steve knew he shouldn't put Tom on a pedestal like this, but he needed someone to model his life after. No one in his family had aspired to be in the ministry. He didn't have a clue how to go about it. He needed a mentor, so why not Tom?

The summer passed and when the fall came the old furnace had been taken out. However, the new one hadn't been put in yet, so people kept their coats on. As they sang, little puffs of air could be seen coming out in sync with the worship songs. Hands were rubbing together, while cold-pink-noses were scattered in rows like a strawberry patch. The next week a few people brought blankets with them. Tom made an announcement, "I know these are humble beginnings for us, but hang in there. If the furnace isn't hooked up by next week, we can use a couple of those propane heaters from the rental shop."

By the next week they had rented two propane heaters to take the chill off the cavernous sanctuary, positioning them so nothing would catch fire when the orange flames shot out with a giant SWOOSH. The heat was appreciated, but the sound was something like being at an airport. When Tom began preaching, he realized that he would have to time his sentences around the swooshing sound of the flame-throwing heaters.

On the way home, one of the boys remarked, "That place is like a meat locker!"

Later that day Tom asked God, "What are you doing?"

It's not brick and mortar; it's my presence.

Tom reflected on what the Lord had said to him. It wouldn't be the building that drew people to Jesus; it would be the Lord's presence. God would build the church by his Spirit, not by human power and might. All Tom had to do was be who God made him to be: an evangelist who stood between God and the congregation. God would build this church with new believers and disenfranchised believers who wanted their hope renewed in a living God, instead of an institution. This would not be a church built from people shopping and swapping churches, it would be what some in the ministry called a "church plant,"—one that would usually see more new people come into faith than older established churches.

The Holy Ghost Temple was located near North Central Bible College and attracted a lot of students. So, in they came for a Sunday morning service, young people in their early twenties, dressed in the fashions of the mid-1980s. Steve Wajda was among them and he settled in the balcony section with a group of students who were enthralled to be a part of Tom Elie's church. He had met Tom last Christmas in Nebraska and now he was here for Tom's first musical with the new church. Steve glanced up to the deteriorating ceiling and wondered if they would need buckets when it rained. The church smelled as old as it looked and he noticed the rickety risers weren't any better. The students helped swell the attendance that morning to over 200 adults and children.

In came the new choir of fifteen "Praise Singers," which had several students from North Central Bible College. They stepped onto the risers, which creaked with every step, and waited for Tom's signal to begin. Tom finished greeting the congregation gathered in the rented sanctuary of The Holy Ghost Temple. It was his first Christmas musical since JP and he had enjoyed doing something that was familiar to him. The students looked eager, full of promise for the future. White shirts with red and black ties or bows, coordinated with black skirts and pants, made them look unified. The surroundings were humble, but Tom thought back to the manger in the stable. It was going to be a holy moment, a fond memory to look back upon one day. God was in this place.

The musical started and Tom was standing in front of the audience directing the choir. Everyone was singing with all their hearts. All the harmonies were blending. The tone and emotions built with the musical crescendo stirring hearts and souls. There was even a chorus of audible responses from the audience. Tom's lips broke into a confident smile as he thought to himself: *"Oh, they must be enjoying this."*

As the college students in the balcony watched Tom directing the choir, movement in their peripheral vision had caught their attention. It didn't take long to figure out what it was though, because it started swooping down over the audience. Every time the small black form took a dive, the audience responded. Only then did Tom notice the distracted Praise Singers. The sounds of the audience were getting louder. It sounded odd—waves of "ooohs and ahhhs" filled the cavernous room. Tom's curiosity couldn't be restrained. He had to have one little peak to see what was going on. He turned his head just in time to see a bat flying directly over the audience. His expression went from a look of shock to horror. As the little winged creature swooped back and forth dive-bombing people, cries of fear were elicited from some of the crowd, while much to the delight of others. People were ducking and covering their heads. Where were the ushers? Tom had the same feeling he used to have at JP when the church was new and ushers were still barefoot and in basic training. He turned back toward the choir, trying to regain some sort of order.

Defeat began invading his thoughts. *Oh God, where have you brought me?*

From doing sixteen performances of "Scrooge" at a Broadway level of professionalism before thousands of people…to this!

He sank lower in despair.

Doubt crept into his mind for the kill. *Have I missed you? What is going on?*

He looked at the choir before him. Their faces were like mirrors of his despondent thoughts, yet they were trying their best to finish the song. Soon the bat hovered over the choir and began dive-bombing the vocalists. The girls were visibly frightened and had to fight the desire to flee off the risers. A stampede would probably cause an accident and, after all, Tom Elie *was* their director. If he wasn't quitting; neither would they.

One student in the balcony whispered to another, "Can you believe it, Steve? This is the same Tom Elie of Jesus People Church."

The student leaned over again to Steve, "Well, so much for the pedestal."

It was an awkward moment for everyone: Tom, the choir, the musicians, the audience and the Bible college students. Steve's hands twitched. He had that helpless feeling of wanting to help Tom, but how? He felt like the musical was a lame horse, and he just wanted to shoot it, and put it out of its misery for Tom's sake, but all he could do was watch and endure. Finally, someone grabbed a broom and started an offensive attack on the winged kamikaze and vanquished their foe. But it wasn't the last they had seen of bats. This one had relatives and soon they would also be paying a visit to the Holy Ghost Temple.

Nevertheless, for Tom it was onward and upward, and he kept looking toward the future God had for Praise Assembly. The congregation kept growing and God kept sending key people to help. One of them, Audrey Johnson, began attending Praise Assembly at Holy Ghost Temple in 1985. Her short stature was offset by her sparkplug personality. Her brown-skinned hand shook Steve's white hand and they began a conversation. "So, Audrey, when did you enroll at North Central?"

"I started at North Central College this year. I've been church hoppin' for a while trying to make up my mind. I've come a few times now, because I see a heart of evangelism in the pastor."

"I came to North Central last year. I've also been with this church since then, and yes, Pastor Tom is very evangelistic. We're going to start going down to the Drake Apartments building on Saturdays and minister to the homeless with food, clothing, and the Gospel. If you're interested, you could meet us at the church office. It's one block from the Lutheran church across from Elliot Park off of 11th and 8th."

"I'll be there!" Audrey was decisive and friendly with a generous heart. From then on she was a friend of Steve's for life, a sister in the Lord, and they labored together at Praise for several years.

Chapter Twenty Five

The Bottom Line of Serving

Since the inception of Praise in 1984, Tom and Vicki, and other leaders, had set a goal for every member to be involved in something inside and outside the church. Consequently, they were very intentional about how they would accomplish this goal. Their main outreach was called Mission of Love, an outreach to the homeless people of Elliot Park in Minneapolis. It grew from a weekly Saturday outreach in the park to the homeless shelters in Minneapolis. When the announcement was made regarding the new ministry to the homeless, the reaction was overwhelmingly positive; that is, until one Sunday the homeless started coming to church and sitting in the pews next to the freshly groomed suburbanites. It took a while for some suburbanites to adjust to the street people who seemed so different. The thawing process continued and the warmth of God's flame of love flickered in most of the hearts of congregants for these new type of sheep entering the flock. Tom kept encouraging people to participate and the momentum of ministry kept growing. The people of Praise began to drive a bus full of clothes to a shelter for the homeless and invited the people to come outside and "shop" for free. The following morning, the bus would come back and pick up those who were interested in attending service. On the way home, the church bus would stop at a fast food restaurant and pick up a bag lunch for everyone. Eventually, they had three busses being used for the homeless ministry and for children's church. Volunteers sorted clothes, brought food, and shared what God had done for them with the people at the men's and women's shelters, which had been the Drake Hotel.

Meanwhile at home, Vicki tried to balance all the responsibilities of four children and keeping a home, besides helping Tom pioneer a new church. Creative meal planning and bargain hunting were her specialties. Once in a while something special would occur that enhanced the Elie budget that normally would not be possible on a minister's salary. One day while browsing for coupons and sales, Vicki happened to see an ad in the paper about a modeling contest for boys and girls between the ages of three to five for Carter's children's wear. The child who won would get a free trip for three family members to Universal Studios, including a complementary week's stay in a resort. They had never had a family vacation where they flew somewhere with the kids. Vicki felt in her heart that if she entered Jon into the contest that he would win. So she bought the required Carter's outfit, choosing a light blue vest and shorts set with a white shirt and new white shoes. Then she got Jon ready for the photo shoot.

Tom and Vicki were going out on a date night, but before they left, Vicki was trying to take pictures of Jon, who was going through separation anxiety with the thought of mommy going out for the evening. He would cry and then Vicki would tell him to smile and he would. Then, as soon as she took the picture, he was back to crying. This went on for six pictures. After they got the pictures developed, Vicki picked out the best one and mailed it off. She just felt in her heart that they were going to win. Three weeks later they got the phone call that Jon was one of the winners! The company paid for Tom, Vicki, and Jon's airfare and all the other expenses. Darren was only one year old, so they arranged for someone to care for him while they were gone. Now they only had to purchase Troy and Ryan's tickets.

The weather in California was beautiful and the resort was wonderful—no cooking or cleaning for Vicki for a whole week. The first day of the modeling contest Vicki got Jon dressed in a Carter outfit provided by the company, "Oh, doesn't he look adorable, Tom?"

"Yeah, he sure does. Do you think he takes after me?"

Vicki ignored Tom. "Okay, Jon, let's go down and have your picture taken."

Jon stuck his bottom lip out, "No, Mommy, no!"

"But, honey, that's why we came all this way, so you could wear these nice clothes and have your picture taken."

The lip protruded farther, "No, Mommy, no."

Jon fussed for a few more minutes before he acquiesced to his mother's request.

Tom and Ryan flew home a day before Vicki, Troy, and Jon. On the way to the airport, Jon got sick and threw up all over the bus. Then he threw up on the plane. Still, the trip was a blessing, and Vicki tucked away a little mustard seed of faith in her heart, learning that God provided even for special times of family bonding that were so desperately needed with Tom's working hours.

Now it was back to regular family life and it didn't take long to start with a bang.

"I wish I was older!" Ryan pouted, after being told he couldn't do something that Troy was allowed to do. His parents both laughed, "Ryan, you're seven going on thirty."

Vicki kept praying for her boys that they would learn obedience to their parents, as well as to the Lord. On another occasion, Ryan ran out of the house with a loud "NO!" and tore down the road on his bike. His seven-year-old feet pedaled his new bike as fast as his legs would go. He tried navigating a corner at the end of his street and "skidded out." He limped home with gravel embedded in his knee that left a permanent scar.

"Ryan, it's okay to obey your Mom," Vicki said, as she cleaned off his knee. "I'm telling you this to explain to you that parents tell you things to protect you, not to take away your fun. Now, just because you obey us doesn't mean you will never have anything bad happen to you. But it's still the best bet in town. Does this make any sense to you, honey?"

Ryan nodded his tear-soaked face, "Thanks for not being mad, Mom."

"Oh, don't be silly, Ryan. I'm not going to yell at you for falling down and getting hurt, even if I did tell you not to wear shorts." Vicki hugged Ryan, tussling his hair with her hand, "You know, Ryan, this reminds me of how sometimes I don't want to listen and obey God, even though it's for my own good. Then after I mess up, I feel ashamed and afraid he'll be mad at me and not want me as his child anymore. But he's not like that. His love is so strong and pure. He's always close by, waiting for me to turn around and find his arms. I guess that's one of things I love about God."

Ryan listened to his Mom and wondered how she knew so much about God.

Family life kept things moving in Vicki's life and each day brought new changes, one of which was a humorous delight. Tom held Darren up after changing his diaper, "There you go, big guy, you're all cleaned up and ready for another 10,000 miles."

Darren smiled back and wiggled his free chubby legs in the air as if to say thank you to his daddy. Then Tom carried Darren over to Vicki for a moment so he could wash his hands thoroughly. Vicki snuggled her fourth-born son and then held him at arm's length, "You are getting so big, so fast."

Tom was out in the kitchen remembering how he hadn't really changed any of Troy's diapers, thinking that was Vicki's responsibility, and not his. However, over the years he had a change of heart and began helping a little more with each new arrival. By the time Darren came along, he was getting past the smell and was able to change a diaper as well as changing tires in a pit crew at the car races. With all that Vicki had to do around the house, and four children to care for, there was no way he could just sit back and not help. After drying off his clean hands, he sat down by her, his wonderful bride and friend. He reached out his arms to his son, "Okay, big guy, come back to Daddy." Tom smiled at Darren's filled-out baby face. "You know what, Vicki? I preach about being a servant and you live it."

"Tom, what do you mean? You help plenty of people and serve people all the time."

"But I didn't serve you. When Troy was first born, I couldn't bring myself to change his diapers and left it all up to you. And because you were more mature than me, you didn't put up a stink." Tom caught himself, "No pun intended, ha! Hey, that reminds me of a good marriage joke we could use in a class sometime."

"Well, try it out on me first. And by the way, I'll always be more mature than you, because I will always be older than you, if only by a few months."

Tom proceeded, "Okay, here goes: One day the wife told her husband, 'You ought to be sharing in these stinky diapers!' She tried to hand the baby off to him for a change. The husband refused, and said, 'No, I'll do the next one.' The wife stomped off but waited until the next stinky diaper and again brought the baby to him. This time the husband said, 'No, I meant the next baby!'"

Vicki smiled, "So how many babies did it take for the husband to come around?"

Tom caught her tease and went along with it, "Oh, only four or so."

Darren bounced up and down on his daddy's knee, totally impressed with the conversation.

Chapter Twenty Six

The Pearl of Great Price

Everyone needs a Pearl in their life. It was 1985 and Pearl Sanders was looking for a church. "Someone recommended I come here. So I came," was the straight-forward no-nonsense answer. Pearl's serious face was framed by gray hair and sensible glasses. She was an older woman with a thin, strong frame. Her complexion matched her name—white, but not pasty white. Not overly tall. A hard worker and honest.

Vicki had just introduced herself, "Well, I'm glad you could come today, Pearl. What part of town did you come from?" Vicki noticed she seemed like someone who had had a tough life, not by her own choice, but one who had survived the hardships that life had thrown along the way.

"Right downtown."

"We'll give you a ride home," Vicki offered after finding out Pearl had taken the bus. Just then Tom came around the corner. "Oh, Tom, this is Pearl Sanders. We're going to drop her off on our way home today."

"Hi, Pearl. It's nice to meet you." Tom acted like they dropped somebody off every week after church. "I'll get the car and swing around to the front door."

On the way to Pearl's apartment, Vicki began making light conversation. "So how did you like the service this morning?"

"Well, it was fine except I only noticed three other older people besides myself. And the one woman didn't seem to have any gray hair at all."

Vicki laughed, "You must have seen Tom's parents. His mom still looks very young."

"This is my place right here. You can just stop at the curb and thank you for the ride. It was nice meeting both of you."

Tom gave Pearl a warm reply, and Vicki added, "We hope to see you again, Pearl." Vicki's smile was genuine. Although they had mentioned how wonderful it would be to have more people her age at the church to help balance out the energy of youth with wisdom of age, there was no pressure to come again. Pearl wasn't sure what to think. She knew Tom was way past eighteen; why, he had four children, but he looked like he was eighteen! As far as she was concerned, a young church meant one thing: a lot of work. She had been around churches and pastors for years. She had volunteered and served on various boards and it was always the same with young pastors. Instead of providing spiritual oversight, they always seemed to need guidance themselves. Or if they were older, they were sometimes like the pastor she visited the previous week: bitter and worn out preaching sermons on the verge of anger. "No," Pearl Sanders thought to herself, "I'm all done with all that helping stuff."

Two weeks later, Pearl found herself going up the steps of the temporary building of Tom's church again. It was an old building in need of many repairs, she thought. It matched her mood. Tom sang his heart out in worship. He wasn't trying to get others into the spirit. He was just doing what he did at home—worshipping his Lord. Pearl thought his demeanor was so humble it was refreshing.

And the preaching wasn't bad, either.

Afterward all the young adults flocked around Pearl. They were so friendly that Pearl was overcome by the sense of family they had with one another—a family that wanted to include her. All of her nine children were grown up and she lived alone. It wasn't like her family didn't stay in touch with her or look in on her, but still, they were busy carving out lives of their own. Would she come again, they asked? Pearl left with a smile. But for some reason, on her third visit to the church, she left in a huff. It wasn't anything anybody did or said wrong it was just that, well, that nagging thought that this bunch needed some kind of help. But what kind of help? She couldn't put her finger on it until she walked out the door onto the front steps. Suddenly she was stopped in her tracks.

You are not only coming back, you are going to pray for this young man for the rest of your life.

And the Lord didn't say it gently like he normally did.

Pearl's face clouded up in anger as she headed down the steps. Instead of taking the bus, she began to walk in the direction of her apartment. She had followed the Lord a long time before she had learned to discern his voice. Ever since she had asked him to fill her with the Holy Ghost, their relationship had grown deeper. She wasn't given to arguing with the Lord being he was the ruler of the universe and all, but, boy, she had about had it with him this time. If someone had watched Pearl stomp along with her lips moving, they would have thought she was in need of psychiatric help. The next thing she knew she was standing in front of her apartment building, her pearl white cheeks flushed pink from the walk and her thoughts. She hadn't even remembered crossing street corners or watching for lights and traffic! Finally, Pearl gave in, "Oh, all right, Lord. You win. If you want me to pray for this man and his family for the rest of my life, I'll do it. I suppose that means I have to join the church too, doesn't it?"

Pearl didn't hear an answer, but she knew the answer just the same.

The next Sunday before the service, Pearl walked right up to Tom, who was in a side room used for prayer before the service. "The Lord told me that I'm supposed to pray for you."

Tom heard the voice of an older woman, opened up his eyes, and smiled, "That's nice, Pearl." Tom noticed Pearl didn't seem all that pleased by his response, but he didn't know what else to say. She turned and walked to a pew in the back. She didn't seem to smile the rest of the service.

The next Sunday Pearl came again. After the service Tom's father, Al, approached her, "Pearl, why don't you start greeting? You would be great at greeting."

Pearl nodded and managed a yes. She really didn't think she would be good at it, but Al was so kind in the way he had asked her, and she knew she had to do something around that church besides praying for Tom for the rest of her life. On the way home Pearl repented of those last thoughts. She would ask the Lord for a good attitude and be a greeter. Tom would eventually figure out that when she had said she would pray for him, it was more than a sentimental "God bless Tom." It would be intercession, not wrestling with flesh and blood, but unseen forces of darkness with assignments: Assassins of the dark kingdom that delighted in destroying pastors and hindering their efforts to advance the Kingdom of Light.

"Pearl," Al said as he walked by, "smile." He said it so gently.

Pearl tried her best but it wasn't her usual countenance. Sometimes she would be thinking so hard about something that she didn't realize she had a scowl on her face. It would take her a few years before it became natural for her to smile. Meanwhile, the thing Pearl had to figure out about prayer was how to go about it. The ten minutes a day she was spending in prayer wasn't going to cut it anymore, but how to change that was unclear to her. "Lord, I need to learn more about prayer."

Pearl began to talk to people about prayer. What were other people doing? Some people referred to it as their "prayer life." At ten minutes a day Pearl didn't think she had much of a prayer life, it was more like a prayer gulp and then submerge for the day. The next Sunday that would begin to change. Tom announced a new series on prayer: "I feel the Lord has laid on my heart that as a church community we should focus on prayer for the next several weeks. I know a lot of you come from various denominations or have no faith background at all. I want to learn more too, so we'll all be learning together. In the original Greek, the Bible calls the Holy Spirit the 'Paraclete.' Paraclete means someone who comes alongside to teach and guide. This morning let's ask the Holy Spirit to be our 'Paraclete' and guide us in learning about prayer."

Pearl left church that Sunday smiling. And she didn't need a reminder from Al, either.

As a greeter, Pearl began to get to know everyone and started to become the "Grandma" of the church. Without meaning to, she also heard a lot of comments people made while coming in and out of the church.

"He didn't say anything that I didn't already know," one person said to another as they passed by Pearl.

Pearl heard someone else say, "I want to forget everything I ever learned from the Catholic Church!"

At this point, Pearl couldn't help herself. "You can't do that!" she exclaimed. "It's still the Word of God. It's not right to discredit the past, you have to honor what the Lord showed you at the Catholic Church." The person's face went from critical to shock, and then to humility.

Another Sunday, when Pearl was greeting people at the door, she heard another group complaining that the music was too loud and that there weren't enough hymns. The next group was complaining about too many hymns and the music being too soft. Pearl was sure she had a frown on her face because Al was making his way toward her again. She brightened up her countenance as best she could, and he merely passed her by with, "Good morning, Pearl."

During the sermon Tom had challenged everyone to pray around the clock. "Sometimes we need to rethink about when to pray. I used to think that prayer meant once a day in the morning and then you're set for the day. In the New Testament we read, 'to pray without ceasing,' so now I try to pray throughout whole the day. Now this might seem like it's over the top, but try this for the next few days and see what happens. Look at your watch and every hour on the hour ask the Holy Spirit who and what to pray for."

So Pearl began to pray every hour on the hour at her job cleaning houses. Her job also gave her plenty of time to think about other things, such as reviewing her life. She had done the best she could raising the children while being married to a man with health problems. Now she was living alone in an apartment. Her life hadn't turned out the way she had dreamed it could be. Would she wrap herself in bitter disappointment or turn to a life of prayer for her family and for Tom and his family?

At home in her apartment, Pearl opened up her prayer journal and wrote at the top of the page—1985. Next she wrote a scripture reference for 1 Samuel 13:14: "a man after God's own heart" and then James 4:10 and the word "humility."

Through the years Pearl, prayed about things that could influence Tom's ministry. Pearl watched Tom grow and saw God's hand on him. She was heard to say, "Tom is very much his own man. I'm an old lady now and I think I'm a pretty good judge of character by now. Just sweet-talkin' doesn't do it. And Tom is not that kind of person."

Then she added, "He doesn't preach to certain individuals, and he's always gracious if people make negative comments about his preaching. He just preaches the Gospel and lets it fall where it will."

Pearl's life had changed. Prayer had changed her. Only she was experiencing a weight inside of her that she couldn't explain. "What is this, Lord?" After church, people made small talk but Pearl just greeted and smiled. A man in his mid-thirties who looked on Pearl as an extra mother, offered her a ride home from church. "But you live in St. Paul," protested Pearl.

"I need to go downtown Minneapolis on the way home for something, so it's no bother, really." He was a tall slender man—a family man, kind and gentle.

Pearl gave in, "Okay, Brian. I'll be ready in a minute."

Brian smiled triumphantly; Pearl wasn't the easiest person to help. On the way to Pearl's apartment, Brian asked her a question, "Well, Pearl, how's it going with you these days?"

Pearl let out a sigh. "Ever since Pastor Tom began the prayer series, I have been getting these—what do people call them—prayer burdens? I start praying for Tom and his family and I get these huge prayer burdens lifting, then returning, and then I get these 'words.' Only they seem like they're more for the church, not for me. I pray about all of this and it just keeps getting stronger."

Brian was a man of prayer and had been involved with the church for a long time. "Pearl, give me some idea of what those burdens are."

Pearl told him knowing their conversation would go no further than the car. He listened thoughtfully to all she said, "What you're getting is a 'confirmation word' for Pastor Tom. You need to tell him what you just told me. I'll take you back and then just tell him the word you're getting for him. There's no need to discuss it with him. The burden will be left there with Tom."

Tom was surprised to see Pearl come back into the church. "Hi, Pearl, I thought you had left already."

"I did leave with Brian Djerf, but he explained to me on the way to my apartment that I have been getting a prayer burden for you that is really a 'word' I need to give to you. So Brian drove me back and is waiting for me. He said I ought to tell you."

"Well, what is it?" Tom was both surprised and amused. There was only one Pearl. People often promised to pray, but she had taken it seriously. Here was a steadfast woman.

Pearl shared the insight from the Lord, which concerned a current situation at church.

"Thank you, Pearl. What you've just told me is something I've been thinking about and asking the Lord to confirm in several ways, just to make sure I don't make a mistake like I have in the past. I am learning about hearing from the Lord, too. It's a continual process being guided by the Holy Spirit."

That day, a new friendship began between the older woman and the young pastor. And Brian had been right. The burden had been lifted right off Pearl's shoulders, until the next one came. But now she knew what to do with them. In three cases that year, the Lord helped guide Tom about decisions he was making regarding the church and his ministry by using Pearl. Often she would be the first to give him a word before he received other confirmations from other sources. "And don't forget to wait for at least two more confirmations from the Lord, just to make sure."

"Okay, Pearl, I'll remember."

Chapter Twenty Seven

Northeast

It wasn't long before they were adding another service at Praise Assembly with attendance running 250-300 people every Sunday. They had started with fifty people back at North Central Bible College. New people were getting saved on a regular basis and a new community of Christian fellowship had formed. It was time to start looking for a building to buy instead of paying $1,000 a month in rent. After nearly three years at the Holy Ghost Temple, a.k.a. the Bat Cave because of its wildlife residents and the cold, cave-like conditions in the winter, the church moved to northeast Minneapolis. The growing congregation kept the name Praise Assembly of God, but a lot of people were calling it Northeast, because of its location, and the name just stuck. People's energy levels were high as they went in and began remodeling, making the necessary upgrades.

Finally, the name of the church was put in signage and bulletins with the new address were printed. In addition to preaching, Tom led worship from the piano with a worship team of about fourteen different soloists and gifted musicians. In the years that followed, Praise Assembly was known for its music, evangelism, and outreach into the community.

It was the same problem every week. A fruitful church is a blessing, and having children is a blessing encouraged by scripture, but the nursery schedule of volunteers wasn't as blessed. In fact, it was very difficult to get volunteers.

"All these kids! What are we going to do?" The head of the nursery department let out a sigh. "Even if they do volunteer, they fail to show up when they are scheduled! It's a nightmare every Sunday."

Tom assured her that he would again announce the need for more help in the nursery and headed for the pulpit.

After worship Tom looked over his congregation. They were such a great group of people. Besides a full nursery, they also had a lot of young couples. The crowd of white faces interspersed with Nigerians, Latinos, inner city people, and suburbanites were fun, outgoing people. One of the highest compliments visitors gave was how friendly the people were. And the icing on the cake was a lot of people were getting saved; almost every service someone gave their life to Jesus and made him their own.

"Before I start my sermon this morning, I just want to let you all know about a need in the nursery. I know I make this announcement almost every time I'm in this pulpit, but that's just the way it is with a healthy growing church."

Vicki listened to Tom, while looking over the new bulletin with the new address: Praise Assembly of God, 1424 Monroe Street NE, Minneapolis, Minnesota. Her eyes glistened as she looked around the beautiful building with stained glass windows and a real pipe organ. Her thoughts drifted back to her childhood days, sitting in church with her parents and listening to the organ music of the Lutheran church. She was glad to start a church again. She knew the family life of a spouse in ministry was a challenge to keep it all balanced, but it was still better than having a husband on the road all the time. The boys needed their father around on a daily basis. Even with four boys and a home to keep, Vicki still found time to sing with the praise and worship team and help Tom facilitate small groups, including marriage classes with young couples.

Tom had been the only paid staff member until Luisa was added in 1985 as the all-around church secretary. A hard worker, she was efficient and organized. A year later Dave was added as an associate pastor. He was relational and connected well with people. His large build with warm dark hair, made him seem like a cross between a linebacker and a teddy bear. Additional staff was added as the church continued to grow. Two years after buying the Northeast building, the volunteer treasurer, Rod, joined the Praise Assembly staff in 1989. A man of average height, with a beard flecked with gray, he oversaw the many small groups meeting in homes. He was a godly man, who loved people genuinely from his heart. He had left a lucrative career with Sperry Vicker Corporation after a few years of helping Praise from its embryonic stage to the present. Much of his five years with Praise was also spent on building projects. His petite wife, Connie, was a giant in prayer, always attending the early morning prayer times before services. Rod and Connie were loved for their smiling outgoing personalities and their intense commitment to the Lord and Praise Assembly.

Soon the services were swelling to 500 people and Praise was known as one of the fastest-growing churches in Minnesota. Eventually, Jeff was hired to oversee the children's ministry. Steve Wajda, who had come up from Nebraska, was asked to be in charge of the singles' ministry called Singles & Praise. It was part of his internship portfolio and he would preach occasionally on Sunday evenings. Since the church's beginning, God had done so much and the people of Praise were truly humbled to think they had been a part of building God's kingdom through the power of the Holy Spirit.

Tom was especially excited to see a lot of people getting saved and he wanted to keep it that way. "We need to be intentional about reaching the inner city." Tom's enthusiasm was contagious. "This summer we are thinking about entering the Northeast Parade, which is the second largest parade in Minnesota besides the Aquatennial. We'll walk down Central Avenue for about a mile, beginning at Broadway and proceed north. The streets will be lined with about 10,000 people, so we can offer them a positive message and invite those who do not have a church home to visit Praise Assembly."

People got on board and created an entry that was a block long, full of live music, ornate banners flowing in the hot July air, and a large cross mounted on the back of a pickup truck. They also had kids rolling on their bikes or being pushed in strollers, while others were handing out literature. The banners and music created a festive joyful celebration of the Good News of the cross. They even won best entry! They were encouraged and continued participating in the parade for several more years.

After the summer parade, Tom was on to fresh ways of presenting the message of the Gospel. "Next month we'll be having a drama company come down from Canada to do a new drama called *Heaven's Gate and Hell's flames*. Think about one of your friends or family members who you've been praying for, and ask the Lord who you should invite."

The response to the drama was so overwhelming that people began to talk about doing their own version. So Tom and a group sat down and wrote *Eternity: Hope or Horror?* The storyline was along the same theme of two people who suddenly die in an accident and find themselves thrust into eternity with two choices before them. They are allowed to view both options: heaven that is filled with hope or hell filled with endless days of horror. But what would their destiny be?

Ministry and outreach continued to grow and Tom found himself announcing some good news, "We are blessed with an awesome children's ministry outreach under the direction of Jeff. It has grown so quickly, we are going to rent the Logan Park Community Center just for kids on Sunday mornings. It's only a block away from the church. The adults will be in the service while the grade school children will be down the block at the community center. We own three busses, but we'll need to rent some more. Consider contacting Jeff about any area in which you can help, and don't forget to pray for him and his volunteer staff. God is doing amazing things with the children in our community."

People got involved, and at its peak they had 400 kids at the Logan Park Community Center Sunday mornings. Tom knew he may never own a large piece of real estate or build up his portfolio of assets, but he would take pleasure in building God's kingdom.

Meanwhile, Steve kept plugging along with his classes at North Central Bible College, which included his internship at Praise Assembly, working closely with Tom and the Associate Pastor, Dave. As Steve researched and practiced his sermon diligently, he thought back to the last time he preached. It had seemed a little off-kilter, so he was more determined to have a polished sermon. After the praise and worship time, he launched into his sermon with passion, his concentration fixed, and everything seemingly under control. The power of God was there for sure—he could feel it. After about half way into the heart of the sermon, he heard gasps and laughter that did not seem like appropriate responses to his message. He kept right on preaching, though, while noticing some flurry of activity off to one side.

Oh, no, not a bat in this building too! Well, it's not going to get the best of me.

Steve seemed to heat up his preaching another ten degrees. Meanwhile, two ushers had each grabbed a broom and managed to scare the bat up to the balcony. Once up there, they started taking deathly swings at the flittering creature. Unfortunately, one of the ushers over-swung and hit the other one, who almost flipped over the balcony railing.

"Are you blind?" echoed through the sanctuary.

The usher tried to apologize, but the fruits of the Holy Spirit, such as peace, forgiveness, and patience, had dried up in the injured usher, and there was no calming him down. He took aim at his co-usher.

Steve preached even louder and harder. *God, have mercy, I'm following in Tom's footsteps of preaching to bats!* Luckily, the injured usher missed the other usher's head and accidentally connected with the bat, and after that things settled down.

The next day Tom called Steve to see how the previous night had gone. As Steve relayed the story, Tom tried to sound sympathetic, but this was just too humorous.

"Welcome to the ministry, Steve! It seems God initiates all preachers these days with bats at their services!"

Despite his wounded pride, Steve joined in and had a good laugh, too.

Tom continued, "If there's one thing I've learned about serving God in the ministry, it is this: count these times as a blessing when you can laugh them off, because every once in a while a real trial comes along that isn't funny at all."

Tom hung up the phone laughing; he couldn't wait to tell Vicki. Through tears of laughter, Vicki managed, "Poor Steve! I do feel sorry for him."

"You know what, Vicki? Ever since I laid eyes on Steve I've liked him. He's becoming more than someone to mentor."

Vicki looked thoughtfully at Tom, "You trust him enough to be a friend, don't you?"

"Yeah, I guess that's a good way to put it."

In the midst of all of this, Tom was about to repeat family history. With Praise going full steam ahead, Tom's mind was constantly in gear trying to decide what to preach, who was doing what for worship, sound, outreach ministries, and building maintenance. About to leave his home in Plymouth to go on an errand, Tom decided to bring Darren so they could have a little father and son time together. After helping three-year-old Darren into the car, Tom started the engine of the car, and then realized he had forgotten something.

"Now don't you touch anything," Tom said firmly to Darren, before shutting the door of the car. He left the engine running with the car parked at the end of their rather long driveway, ran inside, and upstairs to retrieve his forgotten item. What could happen? They had taught all their boys to listen and obey, especially in matters such as safety.

Vicki glanced out the window facing the driveway, "Where's Darren?"

"In the car," Tom replied.

"Where's the car?"

"In the driveway."

"No, its not," Vicki said.

Tom's long legs darted down the stairs three at a time, not able to imagine what she was talking about. He came out the front door and saw a completely empty driveway. Looking all around the front street, his mind began churning with irrational thoughts, wondering if his three-year-old son could actually drive the car down their street.

Where was the car? And where was his youngest son, Darren?

His adrenalin kicked into high gear as his head turned around in all directions at once. His thoughts raced with concern for his son and knowing Vicki would be hysterical if anything had happened to…he proceeded over to the left side of the house. There was a steep hill behind their house. Tom felt faint and his heart sank at what he saw.

There was the car alongside the next-door neighbor's house. The engine was still running. The front left tire had somehow lodged into the basement window well on the side of the neighbor's house and had prevented the car from going any further. Tom threw open the door with trembling hands and put the car in park. He cut the engine. He gently carried Darren back to the house. The errand would have to wait.

After humbly returning his son to his mother, he knocked on the neighbor's door. Embarrassed beyond words, he asked them if they could help push the car out of their window well. The neighbors took it all in stride, being on good terms with Tom and Vicki, thinking this was normal protocol for the Elies!

After thanking his neighbors and the Lord, Tom looked at the path the car had taken to get to the neighbor's basement window well. The car should have gone straight through or around the garage, which would have put it on a hill heading to other homes. But there was no possible way the car could have turned left at a 90-degree angle and arrived in its final position. The car would have had to run over a group of one-inch maple saplings. Yet none of the saplings were damaged. Relief flooded Tom's heart as he counted his blessings: no injuries to Darren, no damage to the car or his neighbor's house! Tom went back into the house and asked Darren what had happened, "Were you scared, son?"

"No, Daddy," he said in his three-year-old voice with innocent eyes, "I saw a big angel looking in the window. The angel talked to me and said, 'Don't worry; everything will be just fine.'" Tom's guilt for endangering his child was severe. "How could I have been so thoughtless, Vicki?"

"Everyone's okay, honey. God was there," Vicki reassured.

When Tom's parents, Al and Ruth, heard what had happened, they were shocked and a memory flashed into their minds. Years ago, Al had left young Tom in the green sedan 1954 Oldsmobile while he went back into the house to get Ruth and newborn Tedd. They had been visiting Ruth's parents in the farm country of Alexandria. Al recalled, "I came out of the house and there's the Olds in a ditch after narrowly missing a tree with little Tom inside."

Ruth wryly commented, "Like father, like son."

How the car managed to swerve to the neighbors and catch on the window well, was a question Tom and his family would always attribute to God's angelic assignment to intervene in the situation. Even as an adult, Darren would be able to vividly remember his angelic visitation in Plymouth, except for one detail: how he got the car into gear!

Back at church Tom stood in front of the attendees for the evangelism class and asked everyone to turn in their Bibles to Acts 1:8. He began to read the verse, "But you will receive power when the Holy Spirit comes on you; and you will be my witnesses…." (NIV) He paused, looked up from the text and began to explain, "The word 'witness' comes from the same Greek word from which we get our word 'martyr.' So it would not be an inaccurate rendition to say 'you will receive power from the Holy Spirit and after that you will become martyrs.' God has called us all to be dead to self and alive to Christ. Did you know that eleven of the twelve disciples became martyrs for their faith in Christ? First they were eyewitnesses of Jesus. Then they were commissioned by Jesus go into all the world with the Gospel, but not until they were filled with the Holy Spirit. That's why they were able to do so much for the kingdom, because they didn't care what people thought or said. God's power enabled them to be bold, to be a witness…to be a martyr." Tom let the words sink in for a moment. "Another verse to look at is Galatians 2:20: 'I have been crucified with Christ…I no longer live….' (NIV) Paul is trying to teach the Galatians to embrace brokenness. You see it's only in brokenness that God makes a humble heart ready to be filled with his power, to love, to witness, to be a martyr. And yet we cannot seek after brokenness as a way to earn our salvation—or a way to seem more spiritual than others. Paul's first letter to the Corinthians also reminds us that God is looking for the weak things in this world to put to shame the mighty. He's looking for the foolish things in this world to confound the wise."

People were sitting at tables with their Bibles open following along as Tom was reading the scripture passage; some were taking notes.

Tom continued, "So no one can stand up and say, 'Look at me. How good I am.' As I embrace brokenness, I come to grips with my failure, my humanity, my own flesh. It brings me to a place of brokenness where I depend on God and pray, 'Lord, I need your touch if this is going to be successful today.' I can be only one-hundredth of my potential in my own strength. But through Christ and by dying to self, my potential is fully realized."

Tom paused, desiring to bring balance to all he had just said. "Don't misunderstand me. I'm not talking about guilt motivating you to witness. Only the Holy Spirit can empower you with boldness to share your faith. One of the key ways for me to keep that boldness is through prayer. Asking the Holy Spirit regularly for compassion and boldness, so we are not ashamed of the Gospel of Jesus Christ, is going to help all of us be his witnesses with joy."

Tom not only taught evangelism, he lived it. After settling into the Northeast building, Tom decided to go around the neighborhood and introduce himself to people and invite them to a morning service. He was only one block from the church when he found himself standing in front of a dilapidated porch hanging onto a tired-looking house. Tom prayed as he knocked on the door. It opened a crack and a woman cautiously looked Tom over. A man came to the door. From Tom's experience at Jesus People Church, he knew this medium-height man, with a full build, looking slightly annoyed at the moment, was what people called a "druggy."

Tom reached out to shake the man's hand, "Hi, I'm Tom Elie, and I was just inviting people from the neighborhood to come to church this Sunday morning." There was something about this man that filled Tom with compassion, but he couldn't quite figure it out, so he just kept praying, giving this family over to the Lord.

The wife and kids came to church a couple of times and then the man came. His name was James and Tom knew he wouldn't want to tangle with James in a dark parking lot at night. He was gruff, yet tender, when Tom talked to him about God. James came to church one day and surrendered his life to Christ. Tom was elated, until he learned that after only a few months the new believer had gone back to drugs. Something fierce rose up in Tom and he started going to visit James every Sunday morning. Tom would get to church early and then quick run over to the house and knock on the windows, "Come on! Come on!"

Finally, after many Sundays of knocking and asking, James surrendered his life again, went into Minnesota Teen Challenge, and graduated from their recovery program a changed man. Tom went to the graduation program and they hugged each other with joy. James' warm dark face sparkled. He was neat and trim and hardly resembled the same person he was the day Tom first knocked on his door. "Thank you, Pastor Tom. I don't know what to say except you've got yourself some determination from the Lord and that's why I'm here today." After that, the transformed disciple of Christ became a pastor in south Minneapolis.

However, there were times when being a witness for Jesus wasn't as easy in practice as it was in theory. Being an optimist, Tom usually didn't hang on to a lot of the negatives and failures when witnessing to people. He knew in his heart what God had called him to do and that was to give people a chance to respond to the best news in the history of mankind. If someone responded negatively to him, he would just let it go and know that he was obedient to what God had called him to do. But one time stuck in his mind as a reminder not to hesitate when prompted by the Holy Spirit to share his faith.

Tom was at the end of a family vacation in Florida staying at a Ramada Inn. While going down to the lobby in the elevator to check out, Tom felt the Lord directing him. *I want you to talk to the man at the checkout desk.* A million excuses began to flood Tom's mind: "I'm sure he will be busy, it's checkout time, everybody will be mobbing the desk, I don't know what to say—I don't even know this guy!"

The doors opened to a massive lobby, a huge front desk, and one lone desk clerk, with not another soul in sight. Tom walked up to the desk convinced he had heard the Lord right on this one. Tom started chatting about the weather and then sports. He could feel the opportunity slipping away from him, but he was powerless to stop it. Fear gripped his heart and mind. Why couldn't he make the transition to a spiritual topic? Soon people's voices could be heard approaching the lobby. The clerk began to notice the other customers approaching the desk, made the polite wishes for a good day, and turned his attention away from Tom.

Out in the parking lot, Tom threw his luggage in the back seat and slowly backed out his 1976 Ford Grenada. Through the front doors of the hotel he could see the man at the front desk of the lobby. Tears began to roll down Tom's face and a cry of anguish escaped. "Lord, I'm sorry. I failed you. Please send someone else who won't fail this man. You put him on my heart. I know you did. Please don't ever let me forget this experience!" Tom knew that instead of being filled with compassion for this man and his spiritual needs he had been more concerned about himself and the kind of impression he was making on the gentleman. It would be a day he would often reflect on and learn from.

Other days came with fresh opportunities for Tom to be a witness for Christ. Tom had met George at a gas station and sensed God telling him to witness to the elderly black man. After striking up a conversation, Tom learned that George was what people in the church called a backslidden Christian. Somehow George had lost his way and his life was a mess. But he came back to God and church, and never missed a service.

"Morning, Pastor, that sure was a good sermon this morning."

Tom beamed. George was one of those people Tom felt comfortable being with. His life wasn't totally all put together, but he loved the Lord Jesus and had come a long way over a hard long road. "Thank you, George. How's the ushering going?"

"Oh, pretty good, but sometimes I get to playin' with the children so much I forget I'm on duty."

Tom laughed. He knew George was getting to be one of the favorite adults with the kids. "Say, George, don't forget to come over for turkey next week. You'll have to check with Vicki about the time, okay?"

"Okay, Pastor, I'll be looking forward to that. There's nothin' like a good home-cooked meal."

Chapter Twenty Eight

The Intern

Tom got home from the hospital and sat down for dinner after greeting Vicki with a hug and quick peck on her upturned face. First he told her about Steve, the intern that had just come aboard from the college. Vicki listened as she helped the children with dinner—there was always an intern coming and going at Praise. She tried to get to know each one, but it was hard keeping track of them. "You met him when I did the Christmas musical in Nebraska before starting Praise." Then Tom began telling her about Steve's car accident, "They took x-rays; he broke both of his legs."

"No, really?"

Tom nodded while pouring milk for one of the boys.

"That poor guy, I feel so sorry for him," said Vicki, full of mercy as usual.

"You know, Vicki, I was thinking, this single young man is away from home at college with no one around to help him. I mean, how can he recuperate with two broken legs? He's supposed to sit up even when he sleeps. So, I was thinking, that maybe he could come and stay with us for awhile, if it's all right with you?"

Vicki's mouth dropped open, her eyes widened with fear, "What?!

I don't even know him! Who is this person you're inviting to my house to live with us? Good grief! I only briefly met him in Nebraska…and I've seen him at church only a few times. That's it!"

By now Tom was used to Vicki's expressive ways. He tried to hide his smile as best he could and waited a few minutes for her to think it over. He knew her mercy side would win over her fear of having a stranger in their home with four young children.

She let out a huff and conceded, "He can stay in the basement in the recliner!"

"Thanks, honey, you'll like him once you get to know him. He's really a nice guy."

Vicki started clearing the table, banging a few pots around in the kitchen while getting the dishes ready for washing, "I'm sure he is, Tom."

While Steve lived with the Elie family for six weeks in their basement, he spent the majority of his time in the recliner. Vicki had asked Ryan if he could assist her by bringing Steve his food and helping him to the bathroom. Ryan was eager to help this stranger with two casts, sprawled out on the recliner, and soon they were friends. Sometimes Ryan would sit next to Steve and they would watch TV together.

Then one day Vicki came down with the ironing board and began setting it up in a corner. "I thought maybe you could use a little company."

She went back up and got the laundry basket and the iron. Every other day she would bring down some more laundry and visit with Steve. They soon began discussing everything under the sun and everyone in the Elie household had the best-ironed wardrobe on the block.

On the day Steve was able to go back to his apartment, he

thanked Vicki for all her hospitality. They embraced and Vicki teared up, "You're welcome, Steve. I feel like I finally got the little brother I never had growing up."

Now it was Steve's turn to choke up, "You're the best, Sis. I'll never forget what you've done for me. You all are my family away from home." Steve tussled Ryan's sandy brown hair framing those huge soft eyes that melted his heart every time he looked into them.

"Hey, buddy, once I get all the way recuperated you are going to get the basketball match of your life."

One of the things Vicki and Steve had discussed during ironing sessions was someone special that Steve was finding himself attracted to. Not long after Steve moved back to his own place, he invited her to church.

"I want you to meet Vicki."

They walked over to where Vicki was visiting with someone and waited for their conversation to be over. "Vicki," Steve touched her lightly on her elbow, "I'd like you to meet Kim. Kim this is Vicki."

Vicki's eyes got as big as her smile, "So this is the mystery woman I've heard about; Kim, it's so nice to meet you." Vicki shook her hand and clasped her other hand over both their hands.

"It's nice to meet Steve's angel of mercy who took him in off the streets," Kim's face beamed with that look of instant bonding with a new friend. Her blue eyes complemented her brown hair and striking features. They made a handsome couple, Vicki thought.

"Well, let's not be strangers. How about if the four of us get together for dinner or something?" Vicki asked.

"Yes, that would be great!" Kim replied, immediately feeling free to be herself around Vicki.

Soon Kim was attending Praise Assembly on a regular basis. Vicki leaned over toward Tom and whispered, "Don't you think they make the nicest couple?"

Tom agreed. "So you think this stray I dragged home from the hospital is okay after all?"

"Tom!" Vicki gave him a little poke with her elbow. Her eyes sparkled as she looked up at him, "Yes, I do! And I like his girlfriend too!" Then she gave him another little love nudge to emphasize her last point.

Over a period of several months, Vicki and Kim's deep love for the Lord and their humorous ways of looking at life, drew them together as kindred spirits. They began going out occasionally together as couples and Vicki had them over for dinner several times.

Tom kept thinking about Del Grages, the pastor who had been running a teen center with his wife Wendy, whom Tom had first met right after leaving JP, and decided to give him a call. "Hey, Del, what do you think about going to Mexico with me?"

Through the denominational grapevine, Del had heard Tom was taking an outreach team on a bus trip to Mexico. "I don't know, Tom," he replied, hesitantly, "I've never gone on a missions trip before."

"Well, there's always the first time. It would be a blessing to have you, Del."

"I don't know where the money would come from, but I guess I could pray about it with Wendy."

"Ryan is going, so maybe you should think about asking your daughter to come, too."

Del laughed, his hearty bear laugh, "Tom, you are always dreaming big with God. Now that means double the money."

"He's a big God, Del. If you're supposed to go, God will provide. I feel in my heart that God has something for you in this trip."

A few months later, Wendy walked up to the lay-a-way counter and asked for the $100 she had put down on a winter coat. She had really liked the coat and her current one was getting downright shabby looking, but she couldn't stand the thought of her daughter not going to Mexico while mom strolled around in a new coat. With that additional $100, the funds were in place for Del and eleven-year-old Jessica, who was excited to go along and hang out with her pal, Ryan. Gradually, as the two families began to spend more time together, they became like cousins in their friendship.

The day came and Wendy saw them off in the church parking lot with the other families. Other team members greeted Del and Jessica as they boarded the bus. Someone with an outstretched hand and warm smile caught his eye, "Hey, Del, glad to have you aboard!"

"Thanks," Del grabbed his hand and squeezed it with a hardy shake. Introductions were made and Del felt the anticipation of things to come.

Finally, Tom boarded the bus, stooping slightly as he made his way down the aisle. He looked for Ryan and saw that he and Jessica were already bouncing up and down in their shared bus seat with matching grins. What a pair, Tom thought as he slid in next to Del. The diesel engine had been patiently humming, waiting, and now it roared into gear, ready to head for the border, ready for an adventure with God.

Mexico opened up Del's eyes to the rest of the world and he became permanently hooked on missions. On the journey back, the man who had first introduced himself to Del, came up to him and placed some folded-up bills in his hand. "Here, God told me I should give you this."

The man turned and sat back down in his seat. Del slowly opened up the carefully folded money. There was exactly $100 in his hands. Del smiled with a grateful heart to God and thought about how nice Wendy would look in her new winter coat.

After that first trip to Mexico, Del ended up going on more than thirty trips to Mexico. Looking back, Del and Wendy always believed that God used Tom to plant that first seed of cross-cultural missions in Del's heart.

During the holidays, Northeast would put on large musical productions. Jon played Joseph a couple of years and Ryan sang a solo for one of them, but nothing topped what they did for Mother's Day one year. It was spring and Mother's Day was fast approaching. Tom was secretly arranging a special musical number for the all the mothers at church, but this year he also wanted something special for Vicki. He began discussing his plan with all four of his boys.

The youngest, Darren, would be the hardest to convince to not tell. "Now this is a secret, Darren. We want to surprise Mommy with this song on Mother's Day. Do you know what I mean by secret and surprise?"

Darren nodded his five-year-old head.

"He'll tell. He always does. He's a squealer," Jon offered with his arms crossed over his chest.

"No, I won't!" protested Darren.

"Well, I think Darren will be able to keep this a secret, won't you?" Tom encouraged him.

"Yes, I can, Jon!"

Tom didn't like his boys to argue but perhaps this once it would serve the greater purpose, and Darren would keep quiet if it meant showing Jon he could keep a secret.

On Mother's Day Tom got up to introduce the special music for the offering that day. "To celebrate and honor all the sacrifices of the mothers in our midst, we have a special treat today that I hope all of you will enjoy. Okay, boys, come on up."

Tom watched Vicki out of the corner of his eye as he got all four boys arranged in a group on the stage. Vicki's mouth dropped open and a look of utter shock was on her face. Tom whispered to the boys, "I don't think Mom knew a thing, good job on keeping this a secret."

The boys were all smiles and stood a little straighter and taller, waiting for Tom to start the music. They sang the chorus together and then each one of them had a little solo. By the time they finished, Vicki had tears streaming down her face. There were her four boys: Troy was now fourteen, Ryan was eleven going on thirty, Jon was eight, and little Darren, with his baby face, was able to keep a secret. What a satisfying feeling it was to have a family. All the work and the heartaches just seemed to vanish in the moment. It was one of the most touching things Tom had ever done for her.

Chapter Twenty Nine

Great Scott!

For five years Praise Assembly was an organic part of the neighborhood. Many of the local neighbors became regular attendees and the church population grew. One of the associate pastors, Rod, had left nine months ago to pastor a different church. This left a hole in the pastoral staff at Praise, but they had worked through the transition. Tom still had Dave, an associate pastor, working alongside him.

"Tom, can we meet in your office?" Dave asked.

Tom was used to meeting with Dave on all sorts of matters, "Sure, Dave." After they were settled in, Tom asked, "What's up, Dave?"

"I had a prophetic word over me recently and God is leading me on."

"What do you mean by 'leading me on?'"

"I want to start a church of my own."

Tom was silent for moment as he thought of losing Dave as his associate pastor. "I don't know what to say, Dave. Are you sure about this?"

Dave nodded, "It's a word from the Lord, Tom. It's time for a church plant. The two services are full. People are ready for this. I can feel it."

Tom felt his chest tighten up, "I don't want you to leave, Dave. We make a great team. Can't something be worked out?" Tom realized the answer would be no as soon as he asked it. "If you're going to leave, Dave, then you have to help me find a replacement. That's all I'm asking of you. I want you to help me find someone to take your place."

Dave replied with eagerness, "Oh, Steve would be the perfect person, because he'll stay. He's a loyal person, and he's been at the church long enough to know the ropes. You won't have to bring in a new person and take months to orient someone new to the ways of Praise and the people."

After his conversation with Dave, Tom decided not to waste any time and approached Steve about taking the position of associate pastor. "Steve, can you come into my office for a minute?"

After hearing Tom's proposal Steve looked at Tom with a look of unbelief, "What? You want me to take Dave's place? But I'm going overseas as soon as I graduate, you know that, Tom."

"Steve, please take some time and pray about this."

"But I'm not called to be a pastor. I'm called to live in a different culture."

"Steve, please, could you just take some time to seek the Lord about this?" Steve walked out of Tom's office stunned.

Later Dave asked Steve to meet with him. "Steve," he said, "I know you want to come with me on this church plant and I really want you to come, but I think you should stay."

Steve had been praying about the situation after meeting with Tom, but it was still a shock to have Dave ask him point blank to stay with Praise.

"Stay?" Steve thought about all of his friends going with Dave to do the church plant.

The next day Steve and Tom met in Tom's office again. The

atmosphere was charged with emotions rising to the surface, "Tom, this is a lot to think about." Then Steve acquiesced, "But I have had some Holy Spirit encounters that have prepared me for this moment. I will seriously consider this in prayer and let you know when I sense a confirmation from the Lord."

"Thanks, Steve, I appreciate it."

Tom thought about the saying, "If the parade is going to happen anyway, you might as well join in and help lead it," and decided to help Dave launch his church, even though Tom didn't have a "word" from God on it. Dave was Tom's friend and that's what friends do. Northeast raised $1000 a month to help Dave and the church for the first year. Tom tried to part as friends, "God Bless you, Dave. I wish you all the best."

Others weren't so forgiving of Dave, but Tom wouldn't play into their comments. To ward off negative talk, Tom would simply say, "Dave's a neat guy. I wish him well."

In private, though, Tom wrestled with forgiveness, "Lord, I choose forgiveness, but I still wonder who gave Dave this prophetic "word" to launch out? And why didn't I hear it too?" Tom sighed. "People will let me down; that is life. But you, Lord, are faithful, just, and good. I choose to trust in you even in this situation, though I do not understand it."

At home Tom tried to practice forgiveness as well. Ryan was mad, "Come on, Dad, why won't you let this guy have it? Look what he's done to the church. Why didn't you put this guy in his place?"

"Look Ryan, I know it's hard to see all this happen, but it's out of my control and being angry and bitter about it isn't going to help anyone. It will only make matters worse. Try praying for him, Ryan."

Later on Ryan approached his mother, but Vicki wasn't about to criticize Dave either. "Honey, we need to pray for Dave and his new church that God will bless them."

Sparks flew in Ryan's youthful green eyes, "I can't believe it! Now we are down to one service because we've lost so many people and that's your answer—pray for God to bless him?"

"Honey, this isn't some Sylvester Stallone movie. This is real life as a Christian. Forgiveness is just as powerful a force to be reckoned with as revenge."

Ryan wasn't so sure he liked his mom's answer, but deep down he knew she was right.

"Ryan, before you stomp off, I want to tell you one more thing." Ryan lifted his stubborn chin and his eyes met his mom's. She was tearing up. As usual, her heart of compassion came through her eyes like windows into her heart. Ryan began to soften a little, "Okay, Mom, I'm listening."

"Sometimes God is more intent on watching our reaction than he is on the other person." At the time it seemed like only motherly advice, but in time Ryan would see its wisdom as preparation for a life in ministry for himself.

Tom kept busy trying to do what a pastor does: work on upcoming events, prepare for praise and worship, work on future sermons, help solve maintenance problems with the building, and make phone calls to people who were sick or in a crisis situation.

Tom walked to the pulpit and looked over his congregation. Would the challenges of life ever get easier to handle? It had taken a while for Praise to build back up after Dave had left. They were still at one service, but it was full of new faces and that energized Tom. Hope was always around the corner filtering its rays out into the darkness.

"This morning I would like to read from the Psalms 121:1: 'I lift my eyes up to the hills—where does my help come from? My help comes from the Lord, the maker of heaven and earth.'" (NIV) Tom's hazel eyes looked up from the text. His tall frame filled with a breath and he straightened his shoulders, "Let me ask you a question this morning. Is this just a statement of passivity? Perhaps it's just a crutch, as some people call it, when we say our help comes from the Lord, instead of doing what our culture teaches about reaching down deep into our inner strength."

Out of the corner of his eye Tom noticed Vicki, his Vicki—what a girl he had married. Then there was his mom and dad, still coming to Praise, still helping. And in another pew sat his little sister Beth, her husband Kevin, and their children. They were supportive, too. His other siblings, Tedd and Barbara, though out of sight in another state, were not out of mind. Whenever they had contact with him he knew they were in his corner. Even his four boys, though they didn't understand it all, were willing to lend a hand wherever needed around the church. And what about Pearl? She and others like her had promised to pray for him and had been faithful to do so. Yes, he had a lot to be thankful for. Surely better days were ahead.

Steve had reluctantly told Dave he would stay, but it hadn't totally been resolved within himself until he had wrestled through it with God.

"Okay, you win. I'll stay," Steve flopped into one of the chairs opposite Tom's desk in his office. Tom pushed away from his upcoming sermon and rested his hands behind his neck. His easy-going smile flashed across his face, "So what happened?"

"Well, I prayed like you asked me to, and then one day God spoke to me at chapel: *Steve, I want you to give up your cross-cultural call and stay in this city.*"

"Don't look so happy about it, Steve."

"Yeah, I'll try. Sometimes this obedience stuff with God gets a little tough to swallow."

Tom looked at Steve with a new appreciation, "You're right, Steve, sometimes obedience is the harder pill to swallow; but speaking from experience, you'll be glad you did. Serving God involves risks and laying down our own agendas for his. It doesn't mean you'll never get overseas, Steve."

Tom and the members of his board were discussing the financial situation and what to cut. Because of the large number of people who left to help with the church plant, the budget quickly became rather tight. It was getting late, and before they wrapped things up, Tom asked Steve for a report on missions. By now Steve had graduated from North Central and had been asked to be the Missions Director. "It's unfortunate, but with the missionary budget coming from bi-annual pledges, some of these pledges have gone with the people who left. I think I'm going to have to write a few of those letters no missionary likes to receive, 'Sorry, we have to reduce your monthly support.'"

Nobody in the room was happy. Brian Djerf and Don Newman, who served as deacons, were going over the numbers. Tom thought for a moment, "Let's cut ministry projects instead of cutting our missionaries' salaries. Some of these missionaries have been with Praise since they were new believers. While some of these non-profit organizations are worthy causes, it will not mean a family leaving their work to come back to the states." They put their heads together and trimmed off the budget somewhere else.

A few weeks went by and it was time for another board meeting. As Tom moved from one item to another, Steve checked his watch. Luisa, the ever-faithful church secretary, was at her post taking notes. By morning she would have the notes all neatly typed up. Flanking her were the deacons, Brian and Don. The meeting was lasting so long that finally one of the guys suggested ordering pizza to help keep the meeting alive.

"It's the pizza guy," Steve said, "I'll get the door for him."

In the room came the Pizza Guy with the savory pizzas. Everyone brightened up and said hello. Tom introduced himself, "Hey, thanks for making the delivery. Are things busy for you tonight?"

"No, not too busy." He had a friendly personality that was obvious for all to see. He was an average-looking guy with a mustache and black-rimmed glasses framed with dark brown curly hair.

Steve looked at his watch again and tried not to let Pizza Guy see the subtle eye contact with the other board members and faithful Luisa. Steve couldn't believe it! He was with Tom a lot and sometimes Steve would privately groan: *Tom, would you take a break?*

Then another board member took interest in Pizza Guy. Steve knew the business meeting could go until one o'clock in the morning and now Tom and the others were taking their sweet time with Pizza Guy!

In the weeks following, Pizza Guy showed up at church a couple of times. Then he made a delivery. After the door opened Tom recognized the young man, "Hi there! We meet again!" Tom asked the young man his impression of church and found out that the young man lived down the street a few blocks. Another invite to church was made. This time Pizza Guy came to a Wednesday night service.

Tom decided to pay the family a visit. The young couple felt safe in Tom's company and opened up. "Our lives are in a mess right now. I felt something about you and your church that first night I delivered pizza. And then I felt the same warmth and friendliness when I came to a service."

Tom invited them to come on Sunday. He never knew what God would do, but he knew God was at work again.

The following Sunday, Pizza Guy came with his family. After Tom was done preaching, they walked up to the front to pray with tears streaming down both of their faces. Steve watched with his mouth open while Tom prayed with the young couple.

Through the years Steve watched the couple, Craig and Nancee Scott, grow in their faith, serve with Audrey Johnson in the children's ministry, have more kids, home school their kids, and finally prepare for service in missions. Before they left for Australia, Nancee said, "Praise Assembly was the place where Craig and I got our foundation for everything we've done with our life. We will always thank God for bringing us here and for Pastor Tom inviting Craig to church that night he delivered pizza."

Chapter Thirty

Black Sunday

"What do you really think of Tom Elie?"

It was Sunday morning; another worship service was wrapping up at Praise Assembly and someone was fishing for gossip.

Steve discerned the motive and decided to cover his friend's back. "Well, I've had a bird's eye view. When you attend someone's church you have one view. When you intern with them another view, work with them another view, and when you live with them you have yet another view." Steve paused, the listener was waiting. "And my view is: here is a man who is generous and consistent in a lot of ways, most of all, in prayer. From his life of prayer flows his entire ministry. I've been around Tom in a lot of different situations and what you see is what you get—consistency around the clock."

"I see." The listener wasn't finding any good pickings for the grapevine from Steve and excused himself.

Pearl came up to Steve, "Looks like you were interviewed, too. There's something dark brewing around here, Steve. I felt it before today. I'm going to have to double my intercession for Tom this week."

Steve was not aware of the internal conflicts, but over a year ago one of the associate pastors had left for a position at another church. His leaving raised some questions. About nine months later another associate pastor left. It was called a church plant, but some felt it was a split after he had a personal prophecy given to him privately.

Steve would later recall: "I observed Tom handle these crises and the ones to follow with integrity; not perfection, but with integrity. Dave had left to go do his church plant with about fifty people and the financial support of $1000 per month, for about a year, from the Praise budget. It was controversial, to say the least."

Everyone had an opinion about everyone and every situation. After the church plant, there were issues with the children's pastor and at a meeting with the board they begged him to stay. The board members offered him whatever he wanted: time off and paid counseling to work through his authority issue with Tom. But when it came right down to it, his mind was made up.

Then Black Sunday came. It was the end of the Sunday morning worship service at Praise Assembly. After the children's pastor announced his resignation, several people spontaneously stood in succession, blurting out negative opinions about the whole situation and about Tom's leadership.

Steve looked over at Tom's face, which had a look of sheer pain, while Brian, one of the deacons, stepped to the front and asked everyone to please calm down. "I understand this is difficult, but let's not be hasty in our judgments. It was his decision to resign, not the board's decision. This is not the time, nor the place to air your grievances."

People reluctantly sat down, others had a look of shock on their faces. Brian continued, "Tonight there will be a meeting to air any grievances you might have. All are welcome; however, I would like to advise those of you who support Pastor Tom to consider staying home. There is no need to hear some of the negative things that will come up during this kind of meeting. Some of it will be misinformation. Do yourself a favor and stay home. We know that many of you love and support Pastor Tom, and if you want to help him out, please consider staying home."

After driving six blocks, Tom walked into his home on Madison Street for lunch. Delicious aromas greeted his stomach like a long lost friend. After praying for the meal, the family began talking about lighter subjects, when suddenly, Troy burst out with a question he had been thinking about all morning, "You don't worry about your reputation much do you, Dad?" He was a teenager now and felt the injustice of the situation.

Tom laughed, "What reputation? I've got enough other things to worry about; that's one of the things I've learned to leave in the Lord's hands. The proverb about 'whatever is done in secret will one day be shouted from the rooftop for all to hear' rings true for me. Time has a way of leveling things out. And even if the truth doesn't come out in this lifetime, when I get to heaven I won't even care. It's not my job to protect my reputation, but to try to honor God and love my family to the best of my ability."

After the meal Troy started in again, "Dad, how can you stand there and listen to people say the kind of stuff they said this morning during church? You should bring the truth to light!"

"Time will tell all, Troy. I just need to be faithful to the Lord and let him deal with it. He'll take care of it."

Troy couldn't stand it anymore, "Dad, how come you're always letting people push you around like that? You've earned the right to set people straight. It's okay to defend yourself."

Tom put his hand on his son's shoulder. Troy was getting taller, his hair had darkened, but he still had those piercing hazel eyes. "I'm sorry, Troy, you shouldn't have to trouble yourself with these things. In the ministry there will always be people who disagree; we are only humans, imperfect humans. We all say and do things that hurt each other."

Troy shook away from his dad. He didn't like what he was hearing. He ran to his room, slammed the door, and flung himself on his bed. As his thoughts whirled around in his head, he had a flashback of all the trouble at JP. Then an idea popped into his head and his eyes narrowed as he worked up a plan in his mind.

Trying to be discreet, Troy overheard the details concerning the meeting that night. He could tell by the hushed tones and serious faces that it wasn't a normal dull church meeting about finances and what color the new carpet should be. He made a mental note of the time and began thinking about his plans for the night. It would take him ten minutes if he walked to the church, or five minutes if he ran.

Troy looked at the kitchen clock and then checked around the house to see where his mom was. She was in the living room talking to Kim, Steve's girlfriend. They were going to stay at the house during the meeting. He would have to hurry if he was going to see anything worth seeing. The night was chilly so he pulled up the collar of his jacket. When he got to the church he checked a side door. He hadn't thought of what to do if he couldn't sneak in through a back entrance. Luckily the door was unlocked so he wouldn't have to use the main entrance. He crept along a corridor, finding a dark corner near the balcony, and positioned himself in a way that he could both hear and see who was speaking. All those TV shows about cops had finally paid off.

The evening meeting lasted three hours. It would forever be remembered as the infamous Black Sunday. Tom sat on the platform where he normally did every Sunday, listening to people's comments. Steve, who was now an associate pastor; Brian, the youth pastor; and Don, a board member were there in support of Tom. What they didn't know was that someone else was there in support of Tom who had slipped in unnoticed through an obscure back entrance.

As Troy sat in his stakeout spot, he began thinking about everything. He saw Grandpa Elie come in and take an inconspicuous place to sit. More people filed in, some of them had left the church in the past year when the other pastors had left. Nobody seemed to have their Sunday morning church faces on. This must be serious business all right.

Troy was worried about his mom. She had such an open heart to everyone. She took people at face value and tried to give them the benefit of the doubt. She was so sensitive, so tenderhearted, he was afraid she might get crushed under the weight of all the malicious accusations. He knew his dad often shielded her from the outrageous things people would say to him, using the name of the Lord as some kind of loophole.

The meeting started and his thoughts continued. He might be only a fifteen-year-old kid, but he had been around church people plenty and had made a few observations. Especially good at giving harsh advice and correction were those people who considered themselves to have a prophet's personality, as though this gave them a license to be more caustic if linked with truth. In the name of having the motivational gift of being a prophet, abrasiveness was honored more than the law of mercy.

Troy flinched at some of the comments that were made. These angry people must be direct descendants of the Pharisees in the New Testament who were always giving Jesus a hard time about breaking the rules. Troy just wanted to run out and scream at everyone in defense of his dad. How could these people who had been his dad's friends say such things? He had never heard Christians talk like this before. Man, why would anyone want to be in the ministry and put up with this kind of nonsense? Troy held on until the very last second of the meeting and then slipped out the door and ran back home as fast as he could.

After the meeting was over, Brian said to Tom, "You know what, Tom? Even though this has been hard, at least now we know the truth about why everyone left." All Tom could do was look at Brian, who continued, "People leave and never tell why. They leave in such a huff, which is why churches split. People carry offenses and are unwilling to give forgiveness to those who they feel offended them—whether it was one of their friends, or a favorite pastor."

Steve had overheard, "It's the people closest to you, those you love the most, that can hurt you the most."

Tom sighed, "It seems a lesson we all continue to learn our whole life through, but there are always a few who cover your back. And I thank the Lord for you guys." Tom added, "Brokenness is a hard path to walk, but if we let the Lord have his way there can be good spiritual fruit from it."

Brian looked over at his pastor with mercy and compassion, "I'm sorry, Pastor."

"For what?"

"That you had all that mud thrown at you tonight."

"Brian, please forgive them. It's really Satan who is trying to get us to fight with one another instead of uniting against him." Tom paused for a moment, "I made mistakes along the way too. It wasn't like I was the perfect one and they were all wrong."

"Point taken, Tom," Steve said, "but it was like a mob mentality tonight. It wasn't exactly a dialogue of thoughtful conversation back and forth around a table."

"Steve, just let it go. It's over now. Let's pray that God will guard our hearts and let peace be in our thoughts so hurt won't turn into bitterness."

After praying with Brian and Steve, Tom walked over to the side prayer room. It had been a very grueling and sometimes caustic meeting. Tom found his thoughts rattling off as if he were writing in a journal:

We called for the meeting because we wanted to err on the side of communication. The meeting was only for people who felt they needed more answers for our leadership decisions. I felt that people should be able to at least ask questions, even if we couldn't always give a public response that satisfied them. I knew I couldn't please everyone, nor could I divulge all information to all people. Sometimes a family keeps its own squabbling and inner turmoil to itself. I also know I wasn't a perfect leader. It's just that we were doing the very best that we knew how at that time. I was discovering that leadership is risky business. And not for the faint-hearted.

Suddenly out of nowhere, his dad was there beside him. Their eyes briefly met. Tom couldn't talk. *I have to let my emotions out. I can't internalize everything one more second!* Tom clung to his dad tightly and cried like a baby. Deep and long sobs seemed to help clear his buildup of damaged emotions. He had never experienced anything like this before. It was one of the most painful moments in ministry for Tom. But now there seemed to be a release for him, his earthly father was now taking the place of his Heavenly Father, holding him tightly, and not saying a word.

On the drive home Tom felt exhausted, like a soldier heading for a refuge after a battle. Vicki and the kids would be there waiting for him. And what a comforting thought that was.

Many months later, one of the former associate pastors came to Tom and Vicki and tearfully apologized for the manner in which he had conducted himself that evening. Tom would always respect the man's humility, and be able to say, "If offenses hurt much, sincere apologies heal even more."

Chapter Thirty One

Working it Out

Vicki was at home cleaning in the living room, "I know, God, that we are called to the ministry for your name's sake, not our own. Please help me to walk in forgiveness." Vicki prayed the same prayer she had prayed an hour ago. It had been a hard day. She knew Tom tried to shield her from negative reports, but she wasn't blind to all that went on at the church. She saw and heard things he didn't.

"Lord, your love and forgiveness is greater than my hurt and their hurts. Help us all."

She continued to dust and vacuum. It felt good to be doing something physical.

"Lord, create in me a clean heart and help me to get this house cleaned in time for company."

Vicki worked her way into her bedroom and seeing the bed, she slid to her knees and bowed her head. Ryan had gone to the kitchen for some milk and overheard his mom praying. She had been asking God for strength to forgive all who were speaking against them. When he passed her room again, she was asking God to reaffirm the call on their lives to be in the ministry. Ryan felt like he was eavesdropping on a private conversation, so he tried to pass by quickly and silently. Mom was working it out with God again. She had some kind of hotline connection to heaven, or something like it, by the way she prayed.

It was Monday night, which meant family night at the Elie household. A favorite meal was made and a competitive board game followed around the table. Monday night also meant family devotions. When they had finished, Tom and Vicki called a family meeting to discuss recent events at church.

Ryan, who had heard all about the meeting on Black Sunday, was the first to voice his opinion, "They turned on you, Dad! After all you invested in their lives; after all you did to meet them on their bridge!"

"I know this is hard for you, but the Lord will take care of it. I've been through this type of situation before and I've learned that the best way to handle this is to let God deal with them and me in his own way and in his own timing."

Ryan sighed, but Tom continued, "You'll see. Down the road everyone, including me, will be able to look back and learn from this and see his or her own mistakes. Truth can sometimes take awhile to float to the top, but eventually it does. And God is constantly teaching me the painful lessons of leadership, too."

"And if it doesn't?"

"Well, that is part of trusting God until he takes you home."

"Oh, brother. This isn't at all like the cop shows on TV where they get their man at the end and throw him in jail."

"Ministry is one of the greatest privileges of my life. I want you to know that being a pastor has been a good thing." Tom looked over his four boys, "Let's pray for those who have spoken out against me. Not to call down fire of punishment from heaven, but the fire of the Holy Ghost that brings forgiveness and healing."

The boys mumbled something that resembled yes and bowed

their heads. Why did their dad have to be so…so nice like this?

"Lord, it's only through forgiveness that we can walk through such struggles as this. Please help those people who are hurting to be healed. Please bring humility and restoration to all of us. Bless their minds and homes with peace. I lay down my own reputation and agenda at the foot of the cross where you shed your blood for me. In Jesus' name, Amen."

Vicki had tears in her eyes. All the boys looked at her, "I'll be okay, boys," she said, wiping her eyes, "the Lord looks after me every day."

As the boys started getting ready for bed, Ryan could hear his parents talking and couldn't help but perk up his ears for a moment. His dad was saying, "Along with the joys of ministry come great sorrows, but I still think the good always outweighs the bad. The good times eventually outshine the negative ones."

Later on that night, as Vicki lay in bed next to Tom, she thanked God for a man who would show such a powerful example of living out his spirituality in the home as well as in the pulpit. She patted his arm, "You're a good example to the boys, Tom. Thank you."

Tom was exhausted and barely heard her, but he knew Vicki was near his side in more ways than one and he slipped off into a night of peaceful rest.

Vicki was going to make sure her boys had the little extras in life that she had gone without growing up in a single-parent home following her dad's death. She began cleaning a few houses to begin with, but when Troy and Ryan began attending Fourth Baptist Academy, she added a few more. This way the sports fees were covered and also another extra in life: the family vacations. Tom and Vicki had been chatting in the living room and were overheard by a few of the boys. Soon there was an in-depth investigation going on.

"Where are we going on vacation?"

"When are we going?"

"Who's coming with?"

Sometimes Aunt Beth and Uncle Kevin would join them on vacations. They were younger and a lot of fun and could do all kinds of neat stuff, like throw you in the lake, or play tennis and ping-pong with Uncle Kevin. Juggling vacations with the intense schedule of ministry was a challenge, but without that family time it was hard to think about saving the world. Tom and Vicki knew people in the ministry who rarely vacationed or spent little time together as a couple, and so they were determined to make time for family trips. It was their only real escape from the demands of Tom's job. If a Call to the ministry was a sacred and noble calling—so was being a family.

Later that night during dinner, the telephone rang. It was for Tom. Someone in the church needed to talk to him. "It'll only take a moment," he promised, "I'll be right back."

After the kids finished eating they helped clear off the dishes. "What do you want me to do with Dad's plate?" one of them asked.

Vicki was transferring leftovers into plastic containers, "Oh, just leave it on the stove, he can finish when he gets off the phone." Ryan threw the forks and knives into the soapy water. The clattering against the sink was so loud Vicki shot him a look, "Ryan, what are you doing? You're not throwing a bunch of rocks into the lake. It's our tableware!"

Ryan didn't say anything back to his mom, but exchanged knowing looks with Troy. They both hated it when their dad took phone calls while they were eating supper. It made them feel less important. Why couldn't he take a half hour from work to eat with his family? That's when they all got to share about their day or banter back and forth with varied opinions until someone would say something funny and get them all laughing.

"Time for family devotions,'" Vicki called out around the house rounding up the boys. Tom found the booklet that had Bible lessons for families, his Bible, and settled down in one of chairs in the living room. Groans could be heard around the house as boys reluctantly stopped the pleasures they were pursuing after a family Monday night dinner to heed their mother's call. One of them had been outside tossing the football.

After the kids left, Tom complained to Vicki, "They act like we are torturing them."

"Oh, Tom," Vicki chided him, "deep down they like it. Someday they'll appreciate it. Can't you remember being a boy and just wanting to play outside?"

"Every chance I got I was out there." He thought back to practicing the piano. One of the boys called through the front door, "Come on, Dad, I'll throw you a pass!"

Tom jumped up and grabbed his jacket and headed for the door. His kids had to share him with a lot of people, but not tonight.

Later that night they settled in to watch a little TV before going to bed.

"Here's the popcorn!" Vicki brought in a couple of big bowls of warm salted popcorn for everyone to devour.

Troy glanced over at his dad for a moment before he introduced his idea, "Dad, there's this new movie I want to see. Everyone says it's really neat."

"What's it rated?"

"Well, that's what I wanted to talk to you about. It's rated PG-13, but I don't know why. Everyone that has seen it says it really should be a PG rating."

Tom looked at Troy, "You know the standards we have around here. We don't go to PG-13 movies."

"But, Dad!"

"Sorry, Troy, maybe you can find a different movie to go see with your friends."

"Yeah, sure, Dad, I heard there's a new release of *Benji the Dog Saves the World*."

"Troy, watch that mouth of yours."

Troy glanced away with a pout, but didn't say anything further. Ryan began looking down at his lips while rolling his eyes back and forth. His chin was sticking into his chest. Vicki caught sight of his antics, "What on earth are you doing, Ryan?"

"I'm watching my mouth. Look, it's moving."

Everyone laughed. Ryan had broken the tension again with his comical humor.

In the morning as the kids got ready for school, they filed in and out of the bathroom. They could see their dad sitting off in the corner reading his Bible. Usually Mom had to help them get ready and then she would pull out her Bible and read it in her bed or wait until late at night before going to sleep. Tom and Vicki never harped on the kids to read their Bible every day or pray, they just modeled it by doing it themselves.

One day at the Northeast house, Troy was arguing with Vicki about some plans he was making with his friends. They were standing in the hallway between the kitchen and bedrooms, when suddenly Troy's anger got the best of him. He just wanted to slam his fist into something. Vicki's eyes widened in horror as Troy sent his fist through the sheetrock with a bang. All the rest of the kids stopped what they were doing. The quiet in the house was like the stillness in the eye of a hurricane. And then the storm began again as Vicki ran down the hallway to her bedroom in tears.

Immediately Troy felt terrible, "I'm sorry, Mom. Really I don't know what came over me. I just got so mad I didn't know what to do." He stood at the bedroom door, "Mom, I'm sorry."

Vicki answered between sobs, “Troy, I’ll talk to you later. I just need a few minutes to myself.”

Troy turned away from the door to find three faces staring at him like he was a monster from some creepy horror movie. As he passed by, one of his brothers quietly said, “Boy, is Troy gonna get it when Dad gets home.”

Grandpa and Grandma Elie were over for another family dinner after church. Everyone was passing food and talking up a storm, except for one teenager. Troy’s medium-length hair reached just below his ears and touched the back of his collar. He sat at the dinner table looking down at his food. Grandpa glanced at him, “So, what’s new with you these days, Troy?”

Troy barely looked his direction, although he knew Grandpa was genuinely interested, “Nothing much, I guess.”

Grandma probed a little. “Well, there must be something new. Anything new at school?”

Troy got annoyed. “No, but I’m thinking about getting my ear pierced.”

Ruth considered how his hair would look with a pierced ear, swallowed her own opinion on the matter, and managed a quiet “Oh….”

Tom, on the other hand, felt very free to express his opinion, “You do that, young man, and I will rip it right out of your ear the first time I see it!” Tom regretted his words as soon as they left his mouth.

Grandma and Grandpa exchanged glances and decided to help clear off the table. Later they went to Troy’s door and knocked.

“Who is it?’ demanded Troy.

“Just Grandma and Grandpa, Troy. We’re leaving now and we would like to say good-bye.”

“Come on in.” Permission was granted and they walked in.

Troy got off his bed and tilted his head to one side. There he stood, a tall stubborn sixteen-year-old trying to figure out life.

Grandpa embraced him, "You're a wonderful young man, Troy, and we love you."

Troy softened and hugged Grandma with true affection when it was her turn. "Troy, we're always here for you. God bless you, dear."

"I know and thanks." Troy meant it. They always had a listening ear and didn't boss a person around like his mom and dad. Sometimes they seemed like his only allies in the battle, except for Aunt Beth and Uncle Kevin.

As Al and Ruth were going out the front door they gave some free advice to Tom and Vicki, "Don't worry, he'll come around. Just give him some time to figure things out."

Tom watched his parents walk out to the car. His dad must have said something funny to his mom that she didn't think was appropriate. All Tom heard was, "Oh, Al!"

Tom couldn't see it, but he knew that there was a twinkle in his dad's eyes as he backed the comfortable Buick down the driveway and headed for home. Tom sighed. His parents had seemed so confident when they were raising a family. Tom didn't remember all these struggles. What was he doing wrong? Vicki noticed the concern written on his face, "What is it, honey?"

Tom slipped his arm around her, "It's hard raising kids. Harder than I imagined it would be."

Chapter Thirty Two

Mission of Love

"Who do you think we should make gift baskets for this year?" Vicki asked her family gathered around the table for dinner.

"Pass the potatoes and I'll give a suggestion," someone called out.

"And what about Thanksgiving dinner. Is there anyone you know of who doesn't have a place to go this year?"

Everyone started talking about different people at church who might be left alone at home if they didn't have an invitation.

"Dad, why are some people poor and some people rich?"

"That's a good question; one I've asked myself at times. All I know is there always have been both rich and poor, and always will be. So the question I ask myself is this: What is my response to the needs of the poor? One thing I've learned is that rich people can still be poor in many other ways besides money, while poor people can be very rich in the things money can't buy."

Vicki added, "Your dad and I want to share the blessings we have with others, not because we have to, but because we want to. You should always give out of generosity, not out of guilt."

Vicki finished her little inspirational talk and the family began partaking of the meal she had prepared. Tom and Vicki believed in teaching their four boys proper table manners. However, while they were eating, their conversation got so intense that somehow they started pointing at what they wanted on the table instead of interrupting the conversation. During the meal Vicki began pointing to the salt. No one noticed her, so she tried again with an extra wave of her arm. No response—not even a glance in her direction. Four boys and a husband, and she couldn't get them to pass the salt. So this time she waved her arm so vigorously she let out an enigmatic sound of "M-m-m-m!" until she swallowed, and then erupted with, "the salt!"

Everyone turned to her in silence and then burst into laughter, including Vicki, "Well, I was trying to point to the salt and nobody was listening!"

One of the boys made a comment about their mom "yelling" with her arm and they teased her about it from then on.

"Ryan, can you get the mail for me?"

"Sure, Mom," Ryan checked the mailbox. In it were the usual bills and advertisements. Then he noticed one square envelope that wasn't either one. He knew it wasn't close to his birthday. Who had a birthday coming up? The return address wasn't from anyone he knew. He bounded up the front steps and into the kitchen, "Here you go, Mom."

"Thanks, honey."

"Oh, look at this!" Vicki opened up the card. Ryan's curiosity got the best of him and he peered over his mom's shoulder as she sat down at the table to read the card. Her eyes started to moisten up.

"What is it, Mom?"

"It's a thank-you note from a couple at church that your dad and I used to spend time counseling with after they gave their lives to the Lord. Now they are done with their training to become missionaries and are ready to go wherever the agency places them."

Vicki looked out toward a distant place of memories, "I remember when they first came. They were so hurting—so lost, and their whole world was falling apart. They were with Praise for several years and then felt the call to the mission field. It's so nice to hear from them." She let out a sigh of contentment, "This makes my day, in fact, my whole week. I'm sure your dad will enjoy reading this, too."

She set the note in a place where Tom would be sure to see it later. These were the little gems God gave her to keep her going. It wasn't like she was looking for accolades; it was encouragement for the road. The journey of being in the ministry needed these little oasis stops. Vicki looked up to find Ryan studying her, "Ryan, I know being a family in the ministry is hard sometimes, but there's a lot of good that goes along with it, too. You kids don't often see that. In fact, even Dad and I don't often see it; still we press on because the Lord sees it."

Ryan measured her words and stored them for another day.

It was early morning and bus drivers, clothing organizers, and cookie bakers were assembled together, ready for another Saturday of ministry to the homeless. Mission of Love, as it was called, had begun five years ago and would continue through the years to be a vital part of the outreach ministry at Praise. One morning before they left for the shelter Tom prayed, "Lord, we just want to do our best. You called us to do this, regardless of how many people get with it and escape from the homeless lifestyle. We recognize that for some it's a transient mobile lifestyle. It's not up to us to understand their ways, only to share your love with them. Bless them all as they come and go. In Jesus' name we pray, Amen."

"Amen," responded the gathered group as one; then they went to the homeless shelters bringing homemade cookies, a hug, and the words of life to the people the world would call the least, but whom

God had said to serve.

On Sunday the church bus went out in search of the homeless who wanted to attend Praise. Because Tom had the heart of an evangelist, he preached the Gospel with repentance, so many of these people would come forward Sunday during the morning service and pray to commit themselves to Christ. After the service Steve would lead them to another room where he would discuss with them what they had just done, pray with them, and then connect them with people at the church to do follow-up. Often there would be several wanting to be baptized, so Tom and Steve would take turns doing the baptisms, which were done once a month on a Wednesday night. People had to be serious about their commitment and come back to Praise more than twice, and also go through the pre-baptism class taught by Steve. One of the seven homeless people in Steve's current pre-baptism class was T.L., who had hair down to the back of his belt, along with several creative tattoos. His life of drugs had really messed things up for him, but today marked a new day: T.L. sincerely wanted to be baptized. Steve had been with him in a couple of classes and had seen him come to church consistently for a couple of weeks.

"Okay, T.L., I'll baptize you this Wednesday night. Just get on the bus when it comes and come to this same room before the service and I'll explain how we do the baptism."

Wednesday night came and sure enough so did T.L. with several other homeless people who wanted to be baptized. Sitting on the platform watching Steve officiate the baptisms, Tom rejoiced to see the believers give a public expression of what God was doing in their lives. Baptisms were so powerful to watch, as people went down into the water and came up retelling the death and resurrection of Christ. T.L. was the last one in the group to be baptized. Steve breathed a sigh of relief, "Almost done, no mishaps with the aging tank, and no microphones in the water. Thank you, Lord."

T.L. walked out through the door onto the platform, his eyes on the baptismal tank. The previous people had walked right up to the front of it and waited for Steve to give them the signal to climb down into the tank. The tank was just big enough for one person to lie down and the pastor to stand in the tank. Steve waited in the water at one end of the tank as T.L. came to the threshold of the doorway and came to a stop. Steve smiled at him and nodded for him to come to the edge of the tank as the others had done, when all of a sudden T.L. had a strange look in his eyes, Then taking a flying leap, and pulling in his knees to his chest, he did a cannonball into the tank!

It took all of three seconds to happen, but for Tom, Steve, and the congregation, time was suspended. Audrey came up the stairs at the back of the church just in time to see T.L. make the leap. Her mouth dropped open with a whisper, "He's crazy…."

Tom panicked, looking at Steve with an expression that asked: *Why did you let him do this?*

Steve shot back his own look: *Like it's my fault!*

As T.L. took the leap, Tom and Steve could hear a deep sucking sound emit from the congregation. With one breath held, they watched him fly through the air with the greatest of ease and splash into the baptismal tank. Water flew everywhere.

T.L hit his head on the top rung of the ladder with a thud. Steve thought he was going be knocked unconscious and prepared himself for a rescue operation. Instead, T.L. popped up out of the water like a dolphin and shook his long hair like a dog getting out of a lake. Steve got a second splashing. Nothing like this had been written in the textbooks at Bible college.

The congregation exhaled, waiting to see what would happen next. Unfazed by it all, T.L. smiled and shook Steve's hand and said, "Thank you, Pastor!" thinking he was going to leave the tank.

"No, T.L., no. We need to baptize you correctly." So Steve did everything he had done with the others, "Have you made Jesus Christ your Lord and Savior, T.L?"

A joyful 'yes' was said loud enough for all to hear.

"All right then, before God and these witnesses I baptize you, T.L., in the name of the Father and of the Son, Jesus Christ, and the Holy Spirit." Down went T.L. under the water and up he came a baptized member of the Body of Christ.

Audrey's mouth finally closed as she stood in the back. It would be a night to remember for the rest of her life.

It took a while for things to calm down around Praise, but eventually it did and church life continued. A lot of quirky people would still come to Praise because no matter who they were, Pastor Tom and Vicki accepted them. Some of the "church people" would look and wonder, "What are they doing here?"

But the quirky ones knew they were accepted at Praise and would say, "Pastor Tom is my pastor." They didn't have a home, but they had a pastor. And it was because Tom and Vicki loved anybody.

Meanwhile, on another front, the service was about to start and Vicki didn't see Kim anywhere. She usually was here by now and would at least give her a wave across the sanctuary. Vicki looked for Steve. After the service Vicki made a bee line to him and coaxed him off to the side of the room, "Steve, why isn't Kim here this morning? Is she sick?"

"No," Steve didn't make eye contact.

"What's wrong, Steve?"

"Oh…I don't know, Vicki. I guess Kim and I just need to rethink our relationship again."

Vicki grabbed both his arms. "Steve!" Instantly the floodgates of her eyes burst with tears, "You cannot break up with Kim again.

My boys can't take this and I can't take this. We as a family can't take this!"

Steve didn't know what to do. His eyes began to moisten. He felt awkward crying in church about this. "I don't know what to tell you, Vicki."

"Well, is this what you really want, Steve?" Vicki's voice was rising in pitch.

"Not exactly."

"Go to her and straighten this out. And then call to set up a counseling appointment with Tom and me. Sometimes it helps to have another set of ears and eyes to see a situation better."

Steve and Kim meekly came into Tom's office and sat down with Tom and Vicki. The door was shut and heads were bowed in prayer for a few minutes before the counseling session began. Kim's eye's filled with amazement as Tom and Vicki listened to their concerns and then offered practical examples from their own married life of how they had learned to work through different issues in their relationship.

"Wow, thank you so much," Kim said, as they finished up. "You didn't give us canned answers from the marriage handbook."

"Yeah, thanks," Steve said as he looked at his friends with new admiration.

Kim spoke again, "I really enjoyed observing how you complement each other by seeing things differently. It helps me see that Steve's and my differences can also complement each other rather than cause conflict, if we will work to let those differences fit together."

Tom and Vicki left the church office in a warm glow. Sometimes ministry with couples ended sadly after many hours of investing heart and soul. Eventually, Tom and Vicki's calendar had a wedding date written down for Steve and Kim in June of 1990.

Later on that evening Tom settled into his favorite reading chair to check out the sports page and whatever else might catch his attention. As he scanned through the newspaper he realized he couldn't concentrate. He kept thinking about Troy, and the fact that lately they had clashed a lot. Troy was his first child and Tom wanted to do the best job he could do as a parent. Unfortunately, sometimes that meant being too firm and rigid, which added fuel to Troy's anger. How was a parent supposed to navigate through all of this? Tom kept asking the Lord for help. Gradually, as time went on, Tom mellowed and learned to choose his battles. He started praying, "Lord, is this battle worth it? Do I want to bleed on this hill? I ask for wisdom as a parent. Music and preaching seems to come so easily for me. It's so logical. But parenting is so hard. Please help me to see Troy the way you do and respond to him in a better way."

Chapter Thirty Three

New Hope

Troy began attending Edison High School and one day he got in a fight outside the bus. He defended himself saying it wasn't his fault, but Tom thought he better nip this kind of thing in the bud, so he grounded him. Even Troy's grades were slipping. Maybe it was time to look for a new neighborhood with a different school for Troy. After searching, Tom and Vicki found a home with enough bedrooms for their family in a northwestern suburb called New Hope. The name seemed to fit the situation. Before the Elies moved into their new house, Troy was transferred to Armstrong High School and lived with Tom's sister, Beth, and her husband, Kevin, for six months and seemed to settle down a bit. The living arrangement gave Troy and his parents some needed space, relieving the pressure on both parties, and in the end, Troy's bond with his aunt and uncle deepened—they became more like siblings.

Ryan peered into the mirror at his twelve-year-old face while brushing his teeth. They had just moved into their new house in New Hope and already he was splattering the mirror with white toothpaste flecks. Jon came in looking for his toothbrush. He was nine; he could find his own toothbrush. Shortly after, Darren ambled in with pillow hair, "I need to brush my teeth, too."

Ryan dug out his toothbrush and wet the brush.

Darren grabbed the tube of toothpaste, "No! Let me do it!" At six he certainly didn't need help!

Troy had moved back home by this time, but he was still sleeping.

It was a nice neighborhood full of families and kids. In the summer it was all sports for the boys, especially around the basketball hoop. Football was also played a lot, and some baseball. Sometimes even the adults would join in. Tom played a lot of football with the boys. If they weren't playing football they were watching it. Monday night football with a fire in the fireplace was a great Elie family tradition!

Every Monday night Vicki would make somebody's favorite meal. "What should I make for dinner tonight?"

"Tomato soup casserole!" yelled one of the boys.

"Yeah, Mom; make tomato soup casserole, please!"

"All right, I will. What should we do tonight, play a game or do some chores?"

"A game!"

The boys began discussing which game to play while Vicki got out the tomato soup and other ingredients needed for the casserole. After Tom prayed, everyone dug in and started eating. They talked about the events of the day and significant things that happened over the weekend. Pretty soon they were laughing over something someone had said and Ryan would elaborate with his own improvised version. Someone started calling him the King of Comedy after he had finished one of his antics and it stuck.

Whenever they had talks around the dinner table, future plans would come up in the conversation about what the kids wanted to be when they grew up.

Tom never put any pressure on his kids to feel that being in the ministry was the best choice. "Serving God well in whatever you do brings honor to him, and what could be better than that?"

When Ryan was about seven years old, he knew God was calling him into the ministry. The Elie home was a musical home. All the boys learned to play an instrument or sing in school choirs. Ryan had begun his musical career at age three by helping his dad with many musicals at Jesus People, always wanting to be by his dad's side.

"Ryan, you're three going on thirty!" his parents had exclaimed not for the last time.

A few years later he began singing in any kids' musical he could. Eventually, while in his teens, he began traveling with different evangelists singing with them. "I want to be an evangelist. That's my heart and that's what I want to do."

Tom relived some of his youthful passions about cars when Troy got his driving license, and eventually father and son went out car shopping. The first car a guy bought was so important. The speed and power of a roaring engine was exciting to a young man coming of age. The owner handed Tom the keys, "This is the biggest engine they made that year."

It was truly a connecting moment for Tom and Troy as they test-drove the car—a used blue 1986 Ford Mustang. They both could understand the universal language of cars and engines. Tom couldn't help feeling he was sixteen again driving his 1962 Nova. He had always wanted a bigger engine, but hadn't been able to afford it. Tom's normally budget-conscious thinking went out the window as they cruised around town feeling the power of the 5.0 Mustang.

"Wow, Dad, this car is so cool! Can we get it?"

When they arrived back at the house Tom had a plan formulating in his mind, but all he said was, "Let's think about it, Troy."

Troy knew his dad was a frugal man so he readily went along even though his heart was pining for the car. Later, Tom went back to the owner and requested to borrow the car just for the day. Smiling on the way home, Tom snuck the car into the garage and closed the door, slipping into the house with the secret pounding in his heart. As nonchalantly as possible, Tom called for Troy. As the sixteen-year-old came into the kitchen, Tom said, "Troy, I've got something to show you."

Troy didn't seem to know what his dad meant and followed him through the service door to the garage. As soon as Troy's eyes landed on the blue Mustang, he yelled, "DAD!"

Tom didn't know if it was good parenting to try to live vicariously through Troy in order to fulfill his own dream of owning a fast car, but at the moment he didn't care. He just wanted to lavish his love on Troy. Tom set up a payment plan with Troy for the Mustang. Eventually Ryan bought the car from Troy and it was kept in the Elie family for many happy years.

It was Friday night, their date night, and Tom and Vicki were already in bed for the night, tired from an especially busy week. Relaxing and enjoying the unusual quietness of their home, they lay in bed in their pajamas and slippers reading. The sound of newspaper crinkled as Tom turned the pages of the sports section looking for golf updates. Vicki reported on anything she found interesting, including the weather.

They heard the sound of a door opening. "One of the kids must be home," Vicki mumbled to herself, and turned another page of the newspaper. Men's voices began to drift up to their ears. Vicki put her newspaper down, her eyes widening to the size of large pancakes.

"Anybody up there?" the deep-sounding shout came. "It's the police!"

Tom jumped! He sat up in the bed, for once his eyes were as big or bigger than Vicki's, and managed to get out, "Yes!"

Vicki let out a screeching whisper, "Oh my, oh my, tell 'em you're the owner!"

Tom decided this was good advice, "I'm the owner!"

Again the authoritative voice spoke in simple commands, "Get down here. Show your hands."

Tom leaped out of his bed and fumbled to get his bathrobe on. He didn't notice Vicki draping hers on and following him like a shadow.

"I'm the owner!" Tom shouted again, as he turned out of the bedroom and began slowly walking down the hallway. It was a short hallway with a slight bend to it so you couldn't see directly downstairs, which was nice if you wanted to sneak to the bathroom unnoticed in your underwear. Only now it seemed like a long dark tunnel in the Frankenstein horror movies.

Tom kept repeating his new found mantra, "I'm the owner. I'm the owner." Vicki crept along behind him.

Once again the command boomed, "Let me see your hands!"

Tom came to the angle with his arms stretched forward as far they could be stretched in front of him. His breathing was accelerated. He could feel the drum-drum heartbeats inside his chest with each step he took. Vicki peered around Tom as best she could while maintaining a protective position behind his back using Tom as a shield. She didn't want to be shot, but she didn't want to miss anything, either.

Tom gave out one last "I'm the owner!" as he stuck his hands around the angle of the hallway. It was all hands for a moment, then the long arms appeared, and finally a tall Norwegian frame followed.

The next thing Tom knew he was at the top of the stairs staring at a gun pointed up toward him from the bottom of the stairs. One officer was back a few paces as a cover for the first one. A flashback of the 1970's Starsky and Hutch TV show snapped in and out of his mind. The two uniformed police officers with their guns drawn took one look at the bath-robed owners, who looked like cats about to be thrown into a lake, and burst out in laughter.

Tom and Vicki let out a unison cry: "What is wrong?" Tom noticed Vicki was behind him for the first time.

One officer finally managed, "So you're 'the owner,' I take it."

Tom didn't make the connection he was being teased, and nodded seriously, "Yes, officer. I'm the owner."

The other one motioned toward the front window, "See your son outside there?"

Tom and Vicki turned toward the window. It was dark outside. "Where?" they asked in unison.

One of the officers offered, "He's out there behind the squad car, sir. Crouched down by the mailbox." The other officer signaled to Troy to come up to the house. Tom's legs began to turn to jelly as his adrenalin rush began to subside.

Troy's seventeen-year-old frame came through the door. His sandy brown hair set well with his hazel eyes, and his chin was becoming more defined and rugged-looking. However, his expression was still very much a young teen, "Oh, hi, Dad! Is that you? What are you doing home?"

"I live here Troy. I'm the owner."

"I didn't think the car was home and saw the service door from the garage to the kitchen was slightly a jar so I ran to the neighbors and asked the Andersons to call the cops while I kept an eye on the house."

Tom couldn't believe his ears, "Well, you walked right by the car. It could have almost bit you!"

Troy continued his story, "I got out of my car and saw the door open and said to myself, 'My folks are on their date night and the door's open. Someone must be in the house!'"

Vicki offered her assessment, "Troy, you've been watching too many of those cop shows!"

The police officers enjoyed watching the family interaction for a few moments and then headed toward the squad car with a smile. Tom apologized for the inconvenience and thanked them for their service, nonetheless. He wasn't in the habit of standing in his front yard in his bathrobe and quickly headed back into the house for the night. It would always be a date night to remember.

Chapter Thirty Four

Turning the Corner

It was another typical Sunday at Praise Assembly in northeast Minneapolis. People filed out shaking hands with their pastor and making small talk. The comments were as varied as the people.

"You don't have the warm and fuzzy pastoral personality that a lot of people are looking for. But I'm sure you care about people in your own way."

"Is my reserved Norwegian heritage showing too much?" Tom tried to lighten the comment. It had stung a little, but he knew who he was and who he wasn't. He loved people just as much as any other pastor and worked on expressing that the best he could, but he wasn't born in a Latin American family where people were naturally more "touchy-feely," as they say. "Some people just seem to exude warmth from the core of their being. I think my Scandinavian background cools some of that down."

Tom shook another hand, "Thank you, Pastor, for being there for me. I appreciate how much you care about my family and me. I can just see it in your face when I talk with you."

"Why, thank you."

And another hand, "You know, Pastor, I don't mean to complain, but the drums seemed a little loud lately. In fact, the whole worship team seems a little loud lately. Is it just me or what?"

"I don't know. I'll check into it, though, and at the next staff meeting I'll bring it up."

And another, "Oh, Pastor, I just loved the praise and worship this morning. It was just the thing to get my mind off my troubles. The louder the better, I say."

On the way home Tom smiled as he replayed all the comments people offered him after church that morning. No doubt Vicki had heard a few, too. They would have to compare lists. "Lord, bless them all, every one, and thank you for placing them in my care. I pray that however they were touched by you today, whatever you wanted to impart to them by your Holy Spirit, would remain in their lives and produce fruit. Amen."

And speaking of fruit, I'm starving, Tom thought to himself as he drove the last few miles home for lunch. His stomach growled back at him as if in reply to Tom's thoughts.

Another week passed and it was a bright sun-filled Saturday and the morning chores were finished. Vicki left to run some errands and Tom decided to toss the football with the boys before evening dinner. After a while he went back into the house to go over his sermon, making a few final changes. He heard someone come into the house and run up to the bathroom. "Is everything okay?" he asked.

"I'm fine, Dad. I just cut myself on the basketball hoop trying to slam dunk one." It was Jon. He was almost thirteen and his voice hadn't started cracking and croaking yet like Ryan's and Troy's had.

Tom went up the stairs to the bathroom just to make sure everything was all right. "What did you do, Jon? Are you okay?" He opened the door and found Jon had gotten out the box of Band-Aids and was rinsing off his finger.

Jon looked up at him, "Dad! Are you okay?" Tom leaned against the wall in the hallway. His face was pale.

"Let me help you get to your room." The twelve-year-old coaxed his dad to the edge of the bed.

Tom bent his head over, "I'm fine, really, Jon."

"Just wait here until I'm done getting the Band-Aid on, okay, Dad?"

"Oh, all right, but don't forget to put some hydrogen peroxide on your cut first."

"I will, Dad." Jon cleaned up everything making sure there wasn't any trace of blood left in the bathroom or any tissue paper with blood left on it lying around. Then he yelled out as he bounded down the steps, "I'm going back out to play, Dad!"

Jon told the other boys what happened; after that they did their own doctoring when mom was gone. If they heard their dad coming near the bathroom they would quickly shut the door tight and yell out a warning, "Don't come in, I'm bleeding."

A few weeks later at the Elie home they were sitting around the table eating dinner; Grandpa Elie had prayed his usual prayer of thanking God for Calvary and all the many blessings they enjoyed. As the food was being passed, Grandma noticed Jon had a couple of Band-Aids on his finger. "And what happened to you?" Once the story was told Grandma was amazed, "You mean to tell me you cleaned yourself up and put those Band-Aids on all by yourself?"

"Sure did; Mom was gone and Dad, well, you know how he gets around blood."

"You know, I have a little story about your father," Grandma declared. The boys always enjoyed hearing stories from Grandma and Grandpa. "When your father was a little boy he used to go out to the sandbox and play in the sand. After a little while he would toddle back into the house and ask to have his hands washed, so I obliged him and helped him wash his hands. Well, after about three trips into the house, I thought I can't be washing his hands all day long, so I got a wet washcloth and told him to bring it with him out to the sandbox. And do you know that wet washcloth did the trick!" Grandma's eyes lit up, "As long as he wiped the sand off his hands every once in awhile, he could play in the sandbox."

"Is that true, Dad?" Jon asked.

Tom laughed. "Yes, I'm afraid so. I've never liked getting dirt or grime under my fingernails."

"But you enjoy cars and all that stuff so much. What's the deal, Dad?" Troy asked.

"I don't know. I don't really work on the engines all that much because of the grease. If I do, I usually wear gloves. You see, the part I like about the cars is wheeling and dealing with them, finding a good car at a low price that needs a little bit of work to make it worth a little more and then selling it."

Darren chimed in his two cents, "It's a good thing you didn't become a missionary to Africa."

"Yes, it's probably good I wasn't Stanley or Livingstone. And that's a lesson in life that you just have to be yourself, the way God made you to be. There are some things God gives you the grace to overcome, and some things you just have to accept about yourself, and be content with that."

"I would be content with not having the grace to do dishes," Ryan, the King of Comedy, informed everyone amidst laughter at his remark.

Steve was staring out his office window watching the spring rain give way to the sun. He wasn't relishing the thought of going into Tom's office to tell him that the time to fulfill his Call to go to overseas had come. He looked at the calendar. Was 1992 really the year he would finally follow God's calling to the mission field? There had been so many detours. Of course, he had learned a lot and God obviously was in it all. He was genuinely glad both Kim and he had been there with Tom and Vicki at Praise as they weathered the storm of several pastors leaving in such a short span of time.

He began thinking about all the preparation he faced: getting passports, visas, and required immunizations. Added to this was the enormous task of raising sufficient funds for his family while they served overseas. There it was again, that feeling of chafing at the bit, desiring freedom to run in abandonment toward the Call of God that was in his heart even before he was a student at North Central.

Tom looked down at his desk. It was messy, full of papers and books, and other odds and ends. Neat and orderly in every other way, it was his one outlet for organized chaos. He liked to think of it as brainstorming in the physical realm. Steve sat down in a chair across from Tom and they made small talk for a few minutes. Then Steve got to the point. Tom had the look of "*here we go again*" covering his face. It changed to a hint of fear, "How about when God tells me, then you can resign."

It wasn't a demand, just a simple plea, to give God time to confirm to Tom that it truly was time for Steve and Kim—his and Vicki's closest friends in ministry, to go on their grand adventure with God that they had talked about and dreamed of for years.

"Tom, we've walked through a lot together and remained friends. Let's part that way on good terms. You can't hold onto me." Steve tried to soften the situation for Tom. He knew he would feel the same way if he had been in Tom's shoes. "You have to let me go fulfill my Call just as you have to fulfill your Call."

Tom left the church to go home for dinner. The fresh April air greeted him warmly, but it didn't do much to change the way he was feeling. Wait till Vicki hears this, he thought to himself.

"What? Why now? We need them so much, and not just for the sake of staffing Praise. They are our friends…more than friends,"

Vicki said, visibly upset. She couldn't believe their dearest friends in the ministry were leaving them to go across the world.

"Let's pray, Vicki. Let's go to the Lord." They closed their eyes and opened their hearts to the Third Strand in their marital cord: the Lord Jesus Christ. It had been the three of them since the day they were married in 1973.

The bright summer sunshine poured through the stained glass windows of the sanctuary, causing dust particles to illuminate in the air like tiny snowflakes. After a time of praise and worship, Tom strode up to the pulpit and faced his congregation. He was so proud of Kim and Steve and wanted the best for them. It was the tear of separation that was killing him. "Good morning, everyone! Before I begin my sermon, I would like to ask Steve and Kim to come forward so we can pray for them before they leave."

He glanced at Vicki; as usual tears were streaming down her face. Tom thought back over nine years ago to the first time he had met Steve in Nebraska. After that, Steve had come to Minnesota and had interned at Praise until accepting a paid position as missions director, and then associate pastor. Through bats, Black Sunday, long board meetings, and a cannonball baptism, they had forged quite a bond.

After praying for Steve and Kim, Tom asked Jeff Kennedy, and his wife, Becky, to come forward. "The leadership board and I sought the Lord for Steve's replacement and we feel Jeff is a worthy candidate. Let's pray that God will bless him and his family as he steps into this new position of service in the ministry." Tom thought to himself with contentment: *Now this is how it feels when things are healthy in a church and God is simply moving the pieces around on the board. Right motivations, without carrying offenses, brings unity and, as the Palmist put it, "commands a blessing."*

Another gathering of family and friends at Al and Ruth's home was underway as Vicki and Betty embraced each other warmly, then found a quiet corner to sit and visit. The Petersons had watched Tom toss Vicki over the side of the boat like a sack of potatoes while vacationing with Al and Ruth, and had been humored by the event ever since. Betty's warm brown eyes glistened with joy as they talked, "So, Vicki, I hear from Ruth how busy you are these days with four boys, a husband, a home to care for, serving at church, and cleaning homes."

"Well, it gets a little crazy sometimes."

"How many years has it been since you and Tom started Praise Assembly?"

"Oh let's see, I think it's been about ten years now."

"Vicki, you are such a good helpmate for Tom. You are in the very mix of things at church and help with everything. And you don't create barriers or walls between yourself and the church people as other pastors' wives sometimes do in order to survive. There are no formal classes on how to be the pastor's wife, but you've done marvelously at it."

Vicki's eyes filled to the brim with tears, "Why, thank you, it's so kind of you to say such things."

"And another thing I've noticed is how hospitable you are. Your house is always open to so many people for dinners and meetings. It's not a common thing."

Vicki didn't know what to say. She felt so humbled by Betty's comments and so cared for by Betty's interest in her life.

Betty continued, "And it's so good to hear the good news about how Troy has come around and is going to a nearby Bible college. Following God is a lot to figure out sometimes. It's a free gift of salvation, but it takes some wrestling of the soul."

After the dinner Betty and Pete said their good-byes to everyone. As Pete started the car, Betty glanced up at Al and Ruth's home.

"I'm worried about Vicki," Betty said. "She is working too hard in the church and doing so many things."

"But she likes to do all that stuff. It makes her happy."

"I know she does, but there is a balance to everything. Sometimes overdoing it can cause problems. I think sometimes she feels so responsible that it gets the best of her. She's only one person."

Pete took Betty's hand in his, "You're right, Betty. Let's remember to pray for Vicki." After that Pete and Betty began to pray for Vicki on a regular basis. It became their way of supporting her and sharing some of the load she bore as a pastor's wife.

Churches are fluid—like rivers—people coming and people going. While Steve and Kim had begun preparing for their life overseas, Del and Wendy Grages had moved back to the Twin Cities after several years of ministry in Duluth, a harbor town of Lake Superior. They were worn out and had joined Praise Assembly for a season, which gave Tom and Del a chance to get reacquainted again. Del hadn't seen much of Tom since the day they were both ordained Assembly of God pastors in the same service several years ago. Two years had passed since Del and Wendy felt the renewed call to go back into the ministry, and knew their time of resting at Northeast was coming to an end. Wendy glanced around the building, looking at the people milling about after the service exchanging conversation. She said to Del, "I treasure the time we spent with Tom and Vicki at this church. It helped us grow in the ministry."

They were eager to begin a new life in Monticello, a country-type suburb, but they couldn't help but reflect on all they had learned from Tom and Vicki while at Northeast. "You know, Del, it wasn't so much the actual instruction from the pulpit or classrooms, it was the way they did church. It was more like a community."

Del was quick to add, "It wasn't an outpost of God's kingdom hunkering down until the return of Christ, either. They got out of their four walls and loved those outside the church."

Del had also watched Tom open his pulpit to guest speakers from other denominations, which helped the congregation to have a broader picture of the kingdom of God. In the future, their relationship with Tom and Vicki would continue in a way none of them could ever imagine. For now, however, it was a season of parting their ways, until God's plans and purposes would bring them together again.

Part Four

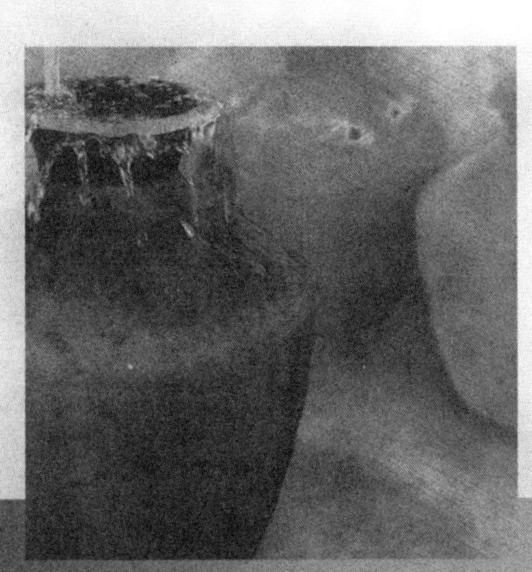

The Oasis Years

Chapter Thirty Five

The Long and Winding Road of Faith

India 1995

Lakshamakka's face held age. Her skin had succumbed to the heat of the sun and many years of toiling in her small village of Sirivaram, with dirt roads and long walks to the low-caste well. Her feet had well-worn calluses, yet her body was strong and full of life. Her hope of the church building had not been realized so she kept nursing her seed of faith, watering it with prayer. Her fulfilled dream of her son, Yesaiah, becoming a believer and then a trained pastor, gave her joy, but it was mingled with the sorrow of her departed husband. Matthaiah was with the Lord waiting for her amongst a cloud of witnesses. One day they would meet again. What a day that would be to see the glory of the Lord surrounded by all the heavenly beings and the saints in white robes. The longing for that day lingered as she walked to the low-caste well with her clay pot on her head.

She had two daughters and many grandchildren to help with the task of getting water, but the walk was a time to think and reflect. In her mind she could picture the church building. It had been a prayer of hers for many years as the monsoons and summer heat came and went.

Since her fourth child, Yesaiah, had been forming inside her, she had prayed. Since her husband's eldest brother, and eight other families had formed the first Christian community in their village...since Samuel had foretold on his deathbed that Yesaiah would be a pastor…since Yesaiah had become a pastor before he had reached the age of twenty...since her husband had died, she had prayed. God had been faithful and she knew she could trust him with a church building. She would keep praying with a quiet confidence and wait for God's timing in this matter.

When Lakshamakka arrived back at her stone house with wooden beams, she began to pray. She pushed back a few stray strands of graying hair into the rest of her long salt-and-pepper hair. Gracefully she slipped the gold-trimmed end of the emerald green pallav over her head. Words in her Telegu language ebbed and flowed until the intensity blended into a peaceful hush. A stirring inside her told her something was about to happen. What it was, she wasn't sure. Her brown eyes sparkled with hope. The green saree swished its yards of fabric as she rose from her knees with a smile. It was time to boil water for the evening meal of rice and vegetables.

Chapter Thirty Six

Crystal

Tom and Vicki watched the new year come in; if they had been able to see ahead, they would have realized that this was more than a new year, but a new era in their lives. Changes had come, but more were coming. God would lead them one step at a time, but first they had to start the year 1995.

It had been twelve years since the first service of Praise Assembly at their former house in Plymouth. The fledgling congregation had grown and a building purchased in northeast Minneapolis gave the church more room to grow. For Tom and Vicki, the good times of life had eventually outweighed the bad times, and through it all, the Lord had been faithful. On the home front, Troy had graduated from Armstrong High School and had a few years of college under his belt. There was also the possibility of something exciting happening with Troy and a special someone he had met. Ryan, who was sixteen going on thirty, would graduate next year leaving Jon and Darren to keep things lively at home. In addition to all of this, Vicki treasured every visit with her mother, Ruth Marie Wolden. When her oldest sister, Linda, would come into town from Florida, they would all get together, including Vicki's other sister, Gretchen, who lived close by.

Life was keeping Vicki busy with cleaning houses, helping her mom, being a wife and mother, and also helping Tom with all the needs at Praise Assembly. It was a full life, an abundant life, and she enjoyed it.

At Praise Assembly many of the young couples with children had moved to the suburbs causing a reshaping of the Northeast church. Because of this, a group had looked into renting space at an elementary school in Brooklyn Park for a sister church. Things were pretty much in place when Tom got a phone call.

"Hello, this is the pastor from the Assemblies Church in Crystal."

Tom's memory went into gear, "Oh, yes, hi there. How are you doing?"

The other voice was friendly, yet a bit hesitant. "Well, Tom you're not going to believe this, but I was in the shower and I think God told me to call you about something."

Tom had to laugh, "All right, go ahead. I've heard of the burning bush, but not the talking shower."

"I know it sounds a bit crazy, but you know as well as I do that you can't put God in a box." With that the caller came straight to the point, "Are you still looking for a place to expand your church into an additional campus?"

"No, we've secured a place in Brooklyn Park at an Elementary School."

"How about my church here in Crystal?" he let the words sink in a moment before continuing. "Tom, my time here is done. I have thirty-six members left who don't want me to go, mostly because they don't like change. But the fact is, I'm resigning. They need a pastor who can help them walk out this transition and you need more space. Instead of starting from scratch with set-up and tear-down in the school every week, you could just move in here. It's pretty close to Brooklyn Park." The pastor finished his proposal with, "Could we meet and discuss it?"

Tom's mind was reeling, "Okay…let's meet. We can discuss it, and then I'll pray about presenting the idea to the board and the congregation."

"Tom, I just want you to know that the remaining people here at Crystal are good people. They will be loyal to you and help you, but they will need to be eased into any change that might occur. It could take a few months of patience and kindness on your part. But once they are on board, you will see what great people they are."

Tom met with the pastor and the Crystal congregation. Thirty-six people with various shades of gray hair were settled into the pews waiting to hear what their pastor had to say. Part of the "builders generation," they came from good stock and were, as the pastor had said, good people. But they were also afraid. Tom could see it in their faces.

Their pastor began the meeting with prayer, and then after formally introducing the Rev. Tom Elie, he told them as gently as possible, "I have known Tom for many years. He is very well respected in the Christian circles, as well as the community. He is not in any way, shape, or form, trying to take my job from me. I am resigning and I am recommending Tom to you as your pastor. Not only do I think he is the best pastor for you, but also his congregation was already looking to expand into another campus with a group of young families."

Their pastor paused and then gave them a hint of what the future could look like. "Wouldn't it be great to have nursery problems again? These young families could benefit from all the collective experience in this room."

A few smiled. They all loved their grandchildren dearly. One woman spoke up, "And we could probably benefit from them as well. It might be good for all of us." Then she added, "But, Pastor, we're going miss you. You've done a good job."

The ice had finally cracked. Before this time no one would say much. Tom had chatted with Pearl previously after church about the older congregation. "Pearl," he said, "you've got to pray for me. I can't get the people over at Crystal to open up and talk. How can I know what is going on with them if they don't talk? I don't want people thinking I came in and steamrolled them and they didn't have any say about anything. But they won't talk."

"Okay, Pastor," she smiled, determination written all over her creamy white face crowned with silver. She adjusted her glasses, "I'll rally the intercessors and we'll begin to pray this through."

Pearl was just saying good-bye to Tom when Vicki came around the corner. "Hi, Pearl, hi honey, ready to go home for lunch yet?"

On their way to the parking lot Tom asked Vicki, "Honey, can you make it to the next meeting with the Crystal people? I think they would enjoy meeting you. It might help them not be so afraid of me."

Vicki laughed, "Oh, Tom, they're not afraid of you are they? Scary old you?"

"I don't know what it is that makes them afraid of me, but they are."

"Oh, I think it's more of a loyalty issue. Somehow, if they are loyal to you, it makes them feel disloyal to their pastor."

Then Vicki added with a little tease, "Honey, remember how my mom felt threatened by you at first because of facing the change in her life? You won her heart and you will win these people's hearts as well. It will just take a little time, that's all. They'll begin to see the Tom that my mom saw and they won't be able to resist you."

Tom slipped his arm around Vicki, "Well, I won you over too and that wasn't easy, either."

Vicki smiled sweetly, "I didn't really give that much resistance."

Life was good. No matter what happened, his Vicki stood

with him. She really was his best friend and he thanked God often for her.

The two churches met together and then voted the merger. It was arranged that Tom would office at the Crystal church and an associate pastor of Praise would office at the Northeast location. Tom started preaching at the Crystal location the first Sunday after Easter. To keep the consistency of a two-campus-one-church-feeling, the same worship team, led by Vicki and Ryan, would begin the 9 a.m. service at Crystal and then head over to the Northeast location. Meanwhile, Tom would preach at Crystal. If he wanted to close with a song he could do it himself or simply have a pianist play while a vocalist led a hymn or chorus. Tom would then walk into the Northeast church in time to preach by 11:45 a.m. It was a well-oiled operation on Sunday morning, a different way to do church, but they didn't have too many models to look at for inspiration; so as usual Tom just ventured out and pioneered.

Family life kept moving along with the demands of ministry and Jon and Tom were butting heads again. The tension between them thickened as they discussed Jon's latest infraction. Finally, Jon exploded, "Well, maybe if you were around more you would know what's going on!"

Vicki's eyes widened, "Jon Elie! I can't believe it!"

"Well, it's true. I'm sick of how much time the church takes Dad away from us. I want a father who throws the football around the yard like the other dads in the neighborhood." Jon stomped off to his room.

Tom sat down in his chair stunned. "He's got something there, Vicki. He's not just being a smart aleck." Tom thought for a moment and then got up, "I'm going to talk this over with Jon."

Later Tom spent time in prayer with the Lord asking for balance in his life. He knew the call on his life to be in the ministry required sacrifices of everyone in his family, but there were limits.

"Lord, what good is it to save the whole world and in the process lose my kids? Help me to humble myself and really listen to what Jon is saying through his anger. Help me to be the kind of father he needs—all my kids need. Help me to draw the right kinds of boundaries in my life."

Tom was determined not to be the kind of father who comes home just to discipline the kids and sort out the conflicts of the day. He knew he had taken time in the past to play with his boys, but the demands of ministry had crowded in again on his family. He could change and he would change. From then on Tom made sure he played all the football he could with his boys, often including the neighborhood kids.

The New Hope house took a beating, but it held the greatest memories for the boys. While Troy's expertise had been holes in sheetrock at the Northeast house, Jon excelled at bathroom doors. Because of closeness in age, Jon and Darren could really go at it, especially when it came to getting ready to go out for the night. Jon was in his bedroom and had just donned a new outfit. His dad would probably say it was too flashy, but Jon thought it looked cool. He checked his watch. Only five minutes left to fix his hair and get out the door. At fourteen it took him longer to get ready than it used to. Just as Jon left his room, Darren slipped into the bathroom from the other direction.

Jon knew his friends would be waiting. "Darren, I gotta go!" Pound, pound, pound, went Jon's fist on the bathroom door. The hollow oak veneer door vibrated with each assault of the battering ram. "I'm supposed to meet my friends! How long are you going to be?"

Nothing except a terse, "Too bad!"

Jon began again. Pound, pound, pound! Crack!

The wood gave way and suddenly Jon's arm was through the door. Darren nearly jumped out of his skin and started the only defense that worked in these types of situations: "Help! Jon's gonna kill me! Help!"

Tom came flying around the corner and stopped dead in his tracks. There stood the door, cracked in two with Darren backed up against the tub area, his face white with fear. "Dad, save me!" he cried.

"What's going on here?" Just when Troy and Ryan had finally grown up and left their foolish ways, here was round two with Jon and Darren, "Okay, settle down now…" Tom gasped, "What did you do to this door?"

Jon faced his dad sheepishly, "He slipped in ahead of me on purpose and then he wouldn't let me in. He knew I was going out with my friends. He did it on purpose. He's always doing stuff like this, but you and Mom never catch him at it."

"Looks like we're making a trip to the hardware store, Jon. Right now. And you're paying."

"But what about my friends?"

"Maybe they want to come with us?"

Tom decided to wage a deal with Jon, his days of fighting and dying on the hill of every battle were over. Being rigid hadn't helped with Troy at all. In fact, if he was honest with himself, it only fueled the anger in Troy's stubbornness.

"Okay, I'll cut a deal with you, Jon. If I let you meet up with your friends tonight, then you have to be grounded extra time and pay for the door."

Jon agreed and was out the front door.

"I can't believe you're letting him go, Dad!" Darren sputtered.

Tom thought it was better than having those two in the house together tonight if he wanted any peace and quiet. "Don't worry, Darren, he'll pay up the rest of the week."

Tom started down the stairs thinking maybe he would survive being a parent after all.

Another year had come and gone for visits at the nursing home with Grandma Wolden. Vicki would stop in and visit her mom and compare notes with her older sisters about their mother's declining health. November 11, 1995, was a sad day for all the boys when they found out Grandma Wolden had passed away. Vicki hugged each one of them, reminding them how much Grandma had loved them and how much joy they had brought to her life.

Jon was miserable, "I only wish I would have had my driver's license before she died. I had promised her a ride in the car to Arby's." Before Grandma Wolden had moved into the nursing home, Jon had often stayed at her apartment when he was "sick" on school days. After Vicki would drop him off for the day while she cleaned houses, a "miracle" would occur. Then Jon would push Grandma Wolden in her wheelchair to Arby's for lunch. They had an understanding about such things.

"Oh, honey, I'm so sorry you didn't get a chance to do that with Grandma."

Ryan was thinking hard about all of this. "You know, I'm really sad, but now at least Grandma Wolden isn't suffering with her arthritis anymore. She's probably running all over heaven."

"That's right, Ryan. She's finally free."

Chapter Thirty Seven

Double Time

Since he was twelve years old, Tom had had a sense that God would use him to win masses of people to Christ. It was in some sense a quest. He had been the Minister of Music at Jesus People Church and now he was the senior pastor of Praise Assembly. He had watched many people give their lives to Christ at both churches. Both had satisfied the great "itch" inside of Tom to "win souls for Christ." Yet, looking back, his quest to be an evangelist had turned out different than he had pictured at twelve years of age. It was in 1996, though, when something happened that changed his life forever.

It was an invitation to go to Promise Keepers, a gathering for clergy and leadership in Atlanta. Held in the RCA Dome, known to the locals as the Georgia Dome, it would be considered by many to be an historical event because of the 40,000 pastors and leaders who attended. Some were coming because they were hurting; others were seeking a word from the Lord. Tom wasn't really looking for either, but men from Praise kept telling him, "You gotta go, Pastor. Promise Keepers has been such a blessing to me and my family!"

Another man would come up to Tom and grab his arm, "Pastor Tom, you've got go to this Promise Keeper's conference for pastors.

I just know it will be a blessing for you!"

At first he had resisted, but finally, as if pushed by the Holy Spirit, Tom found himself going to Atlanta. Before he had left for the airport, he had confided in Vicki, "I still don't know why I am going to this."

After checking into his hotel, Tom made his way to the stadium and into the interior of the Georgia Dome. Tom had never been to a Promise Keeper's conference before, so he didn't know what to expect, although he had been to many other conferences over the years, some of them as a featured speaker. He let out a sigh. Sometimes these events could be a real blessing and other times not so much.

Tom stood still for a moment overlooking the rows of seating wondering: *What do you want me here for, God? I'm listening.*

He made his way down toward the front and selected a seat. A warm and friendly gentleman behind him with a distinct Latin American accent introduced himself. He was a pastor from Ascuncion, Paraguay. They soon found themselves engaged in a lively conversation.

"So you came all the way up to Atlanta, Georgia?" Tom asked.

"Yes, sir, but before I was a pastor I was training for soccer in the Paraguay Olympics six hours a day. After I gave my life to Christ, the Lord said to me, '*I want you to give the same intensity to prayer as you gave to training in the Olympics.*' After that we started a church in my living room with a broken accordion, a tattered tambourine, and ten people. One of those people was a missionary, Dick Hedman, and we did it together with God. Now I'm at this dome looking for structure ideas for a new sanctuary because we're at 6,000 people. This is not typically seen in Paraguay. God is at work in a mighty way."

Immediately Tom knew why he had come. It was a "God moment." A thought about this Paraguay pastor was imparted to Tom by the Sprit of God:

I want you to go home and double your prayer time to seek my face and not my hand.

In that moment Tom dedicated himself to double his prayer time with the Lord from one hour a day to two hours a day, as much as possible. It wouldn't be a time of seeking God for needs or direction, but rather relationship, fellowship, and worship. Psalm 37:4 became a hallmark over the next seven years as Tom purposed to delight himself in the Lord. "Delight yourself in the Lord and he will give you the desires of your heart." (NIV) Another scripture that became significant to Tom was Proverbs 16:9: "In his heart a man plans his course, but the Lord determines his steps." (NIV)

Tom began his new season of increased prayer when he came back from Atlanta. At church he would spend time in the sanctuary delighting in his Abba Father. At home he would sit at the piano enjoying God's presence praying and worshipping. Sometimes Tom would be walking and talking with God or simply sitting knowing he was able to climb into his Heavenly Father's lap and enjoy God's unconditional love.

A month later Tom received two unexpected phone calls in one week. First, an invitation to go to India from a man he had briefly met at the Assemblies of God District Council. The thick Indian-British accent implored Tom, "Come to India and do a crusade; there the harvest field is ripe and ready."

After the call, Tom raced back to the sanctuary and danced as David had with unabashed joy before the Lord. Praises fell from his lips like a waterfall: "God, you did this! I get to preach at a crusade in India! I just know, God, this is your voice, this is your plan." Tom continued to offer up thanks in his heart to the Lord. What a privilege it was to serve the living God.

Tom couldn't wait to get home to tell Vicki all about it.

"Oh, Tom, that's so wonderful!" She knew how much this meant to Tom. Some guys dreamed of dollar signs, big homes, or big toys, but Tom dreamed of "soul signs" as Vicki liked to call it. "You can see all those souls in the villages waiting to hear the Gospel, can't you, Tom?"

Tom looked into Vicki's eyes, "Yeah, Vicki, I can see them."

However, they both knew what this meant. On the surface it can seem so adventurous to go to the mysterious land of India—especially if you're a rugged kind of guy who can easily rough it in uncomfortable conditions. Tom was all guy, but with clean fingernails. Raised in the suburbs with a fastidious housekeeper for a mother, Tom was a self-proclaimed city slicker.

"Tom, you know you like to be clean," Vicki began to smirk just a little at the corners of her mouth.

"I know, I DO like to be clean," he confessed freely. He caught the twinkle in her eyes. It seemed like no matter how many years they were married, Vicki could still make him feel like a schoolboy. And he loved it.

A few days later Tom was astonished to receive another call. This one was from the African pastor who had suddenly shown up on the front steps of the church one Sunday at the Crystal location. A deep voice, good for preaching, boomed out, "Good morning!"

After introductions, the African pastor declared, "You need to come to Africa and do crusades!" Again the invitation was extended, "Come to the harvest fields of Africa."

Tom couldn't wait to tell Vicki about the second call. After finishing his duties for the day he left the church office with a glow of happiness, looking forward to dinner and discussing travel plans. Shortly after bursting in the door he found Vicki. "I can hardly believe it, Vicki! Two calls in one week for two different parts of the world. I hardly get asked to speak in St. Paul let alone around the world!"

Vicki was getting the meal arranged on the table before calling the troops for dinner, "Oh, Tom, you do too get asked to speak. Give yourself a little more credit than that."

"But not opportunities like this. You know it's usually church people I'm speaking to—people who have heard the Gospel their whole lives. Most of the people coming to the crusades in India and Africa have never heard the name of Jesus Christ, let alone a clear presentation of the Gospel. When I think of the possibility of giving these people the opportunity to respond to faith in God through Jesus Christ...I hardly know how to put it into words."

Vicki could sense the moment, "You've always had this desire to see people find Jesus, and not just a few here or there, but hundreds and thousands. God put that desire in you for a reason. And now he's making a way for you to do that. I think the Lord is waiting, Tom. He's waiting for those people to come into his kingdom."

Tom began to pray about the upcoming trips. He knew he wanted a traveling partner. Someone had to stay home with the boys, so Vicki wouldn't be going with him. Who had some experience with other cultures and could communicate God's love in a way that was more than just speaking words? It had to be someone who was kindred spirit to his own openness to divine healing. Tom had been doing praise and healing services for a while and had even attended a John Wimber healing conference. He knew God wasn't a vending machine where you put in some formulaic prayer and out comes a healing. Healing was one of the mysteries of the Spirit of God and Tom accepted that. But one thing he knew to be true was this: in countries where people are more open to spirituality there seemed to be more freedom for the Holy Spirit to heal. It was kind of weird in a way, that a land with all of these millions of false gods would be such a place where God's spirit was the least inhibited. Maybe the greatest oppressive demonic spirits were intellectualism and secularism found in countries like America, where believing in God and his power to heal were seen as old-fashioned and relegated to religious fanatics.

Chapter Thirty Eight

India 1996

It was summer and that meant it was time for the Assemblies of God family camp at Lake Geneva. Tom and Vicki reconnected with Del and Wendy Grages at the church camp and decided to go out for dinner at a family-owned restaurant. The Grages and their two children, Josh and Jessica, had attended Praise, also called Northeast, for two years and "sat" as they described it, meaning they rested and were ministered to. It was a good time for their family and Jessica had gone on a Mexico trip with Ryan. Del and Wendy had since moved to an outlying suburb, Monticello, and had become involved in the church there. During this time Del was still going to Mexico and God opened doors for him to go to Cuba as well. Now Del was getting ready for his third trip to Cuba, but was having difficulty in obtaining his visa.

He had explained the situation to everyone at the table. "I don't understand it."

Tom said, "Del, God has opened the door for me to go to India. Although I've never gone, I believe this is part of God's plan to use me to preach at crusades. Is there any chance you would want to go with me?"

Wendy's and Del's eyes met for a brief moment, "Well, actually, I think I am interested, Tom. I've already raised all the necessary funds for going to Cuba. Wendy and I have been praying and asking God to make a way."

Del began to laugh his trademark chuckle, a good belly laugh, as people would say. "I guess I thought it was the enemy stopping me from going, but now I know better. It was the Lord!"

Over the years the Elies and Grages had become friends, not only as couples, but also as families. Wendy always enjoyed pulling out a picture of Jessica and Ryan going on their first trip together to Mexico. In turn, Jessica and Ryan would hoot and holler when they saw the pictures of their young gangly frames and toothless smiles ready for adventure. These two had a close friendship that would help them ride out the storms of life together. For Ryan it was like having the sister he never had, and for Jessica, an extra brother to chum around with.

After the family camp, Tom began earnestly praying about his upcoming trips. One evening at the dinner table he said to Vicki, "I think God is calling me to go to India long term."

Vicki looked up from her dinner plate and eyed Tom. "You mean as in 'Divine Call' to India? Honey, are you sure? You don't even like curry. Going on this upcoming trip is one thing, but an ongoing Call to India?"

Tom laughed, "I suppose it sounds crazy to you. I've never been there, it's thousands of miles away, twelve hours time difference, I don't know the language or customs, and here's this six-foot-three Norwegian trying to find some food to eat."

They laughed and then Tom leaned over the table, his piercing green hazel eyes locking with Vicki's. His visionary can-do-attitude carried through into everything, including going India: "We can do this. The harvest is so great over there. I can sense it in my spirit.

There are thousands of people ready to give their lives to Jesus Christ if someone will just take the time to explain it to them."

Vicki looked at the man she had been married to for over twenty years. By now she knew when the Call of God was on him to do something new. "Honey, sometimes I feel like I'm behind wild horses trying to keep everything together—trying to keep everything reined in with all your visions of things to do for the Lord." Vicki leaned back in her chair and sighed. "But I guess that's what visionaries are all about. If it's what God wants us to do, then we can do it."

She crossed her arms while her eyes sparked with a bit of a gleam, "It's never been boring being married to you, Tom Elie, I'll tell you that much!"

The day had finally come. Tom's tall lean frame boarded the plane followed by Del's bulkier frame. They both were pulling a carry-on suitcase. Vicki had packed some snacks in Tom's carry-on just in case the curry thing didn't work out. Tom felt regret of separation from his family for three weeks mingled with the excitement of going on a three-week evangelistic trip to India and Africa. Would this trip help him clarify in his mind if India was truly his future for ministry?

After landing in India, they journeyed to a town in southern India named Tenkasi, situated in the Tamil Nadu district. Nothing in all of Tom's previous travels to other countries had prepared him for India. Sights, smells, and sounds pulled at his senses. Cars, trucks, and families perched on motorcycles, swarmed down the road like an ant colony. Three-wheeled motorized rickshaws added to the cacophony of a fluid stream of traffic noise. Lanes in the road were merely suggestions. Animals and people lived in a sort of harmony as people and cows shared the same roads and sidewalks. The brightness of fabrics and homes contrasted with the dusty streets.

Living in the same town was the Assemblies of God Superintendent, Y. Jeyaraj. After introductions, the superintendent offered in his Indian-British accent, "Anything I can do for you, Reverend Elie, anything at all, please do not hesitate to ask me."

Tom and Del stayed with Y. Jeyaraj's son, who had been in the States for college. They ate their meals there as well, which to Tom's amazement agreed with his taste buds. Rice and flat bread were served at every meal, together with yogurt and different colored sauces with bits of chicken, or a boiled egg. There were also fresh, juicy, yellow mangos and deep-orange-fleshed papayas with soft black seeds.

Tom and Del had two different crusades there, after which the pastor of the second crusade told Tom, "You need to meet Pastor D. Mohan. He is the pastor of the largest Assemblies of God church in India, which has 12,000 people."

They continued their journey until they met up with Pastor D. Mohan. His warm brown face full of joy greeted them. "How is your first time to India?"

They talked about what God was doing in India, the many people turning to Jesus Christ, and the miracles that were taking place.

Tom's excitement bubbled out, "Seeing all those people pray and ask Jesus to become their Lord and Savior is worth the trip. But this trip is also significant to me because of the many miracles we're seeing, especially after the frustration of not seeing many in the States. I saw God open blind eyes and deaf ears! The Indians helping with the crusade try to validate each healing as best they can."

At the end of their conversation, D. Mohan gave him an invitation: "We would be pleased to have you come again, Brother Tom. Let's partner together for an evangelistic festival."

Tom thought to himself: *Who am I to have God's favor like this? It's almost too much to take in!*

Their next destination was Africa. In a suburb just outside of Nairobi, Kenya, they had a big open dusty lot where ten churches came together and had a crusade. At the end of the week Del got sick so they headed for their place of lodging at the United Nations Research Center.

Del had lost his appetite, but not his sense of humor, "At least it's a nice place to be sick in."

"Isn't it wild going from India to Africa in a few short weeks?"

"Yeah, they're both so different and yet similar." Del rested for a moment and then opened his eyes, "Are you coming back to either place?"

"How could I stay away?" Tom answered.

During Tom's first trip to India, Pearl opened up her prayer journal and wrote Psalm 139:5 "You hem me in—behind and before; you have laid your hand upon me." (NIV)

While praying, Pearl began to get a picture of a wide pathway through India. Tom was inside the pathway and alongside Tom was a large beautiful angel. There was not a mountain, not a hill, not brush, not anything on this pathway. The picture was about how the Lord would go before Tom and prepare the way. Pearl wrote down all that she had seen.

She also wrote down scripture references from the two books in the New Testament, First and Second Timothy. After that, Pearl paged through the New Testament to the letters Paul had written to his younger protégé, Timothy. Seven different verses, all from First and Second Timothy, the last one was from 2 Timothy 2:15 "Do your best to present yourself to God as one approved, a workman who does not need to be ashamed and who correctly handles the word of truth." (NIV)

They seemed to fit Tom very well. It was as if Paul would be mentoring Tom, much like he had done with Timothy. Only this time it would be Pearl praying and asking the Holy Spirit to do the mentoring using the text as a guide for prayer.

Tom's first trip to India confirmed in his heart what he had felt that day while praying at Praise Assembly in Crystal, Minnesota. He also thought back fifteen years to the meeting in the Perkins Restaurant with a friend, Mark Anderson, who had recently gone to India. Mark's stories and pictures of the crusades had impacted Tom immensely. All he kept thinking was, *"Oh, I need to do this! I need to do this!"*

It was a tiny seed planted fifteen years earlier. Now Mark was in Wyoming. Maybe someday Tom would have the opportunity to tell him what a difference that day had made in his life.

Vicki's high school graduation picture.

Tom's trip to Jamaica; Tom is on the far right.

A June wedding.

Kim Manning (Vicki's niece), Barb Elie, Gretchen Wolden Barsness, Linda Wolden Manning, Vicki, Tom, Tedd Elie, Steve Waage (Tom's cousin), Bob Christoph (JP singer), Don Manning, Beth Elie, Tia Barsness and Tona Barsness (Vicki's nieces), Donald Jon (ring bearer, Vicki's nephew), Steve Carlson, John Shand, George Ridge (JP singer), and Dick Barsness.

Tom playing piano at Lake Street location, Jesus People Church.

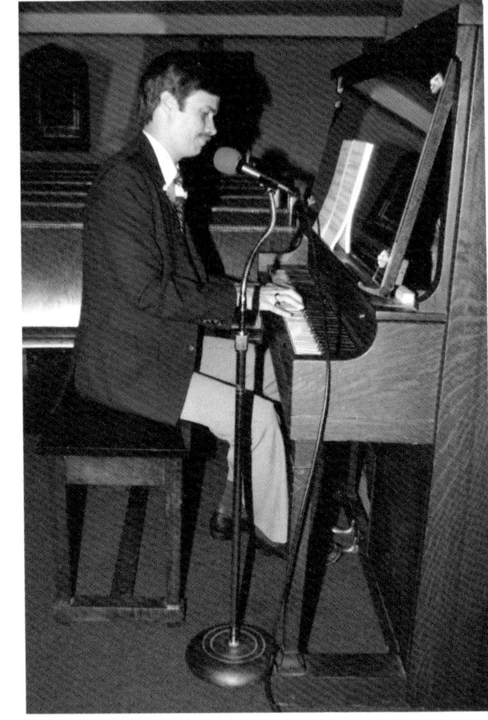

Vicki and Troy as townspeople in "Scrooge."

Tom and Vicki with Troy, Ryan, Jon, and Darren.

Tom sings on Mother's Day with his four boys at "Northeast."

Jon's contest photo.

Tom's Ordination (from left) Al, Ruth, Tom, Beth, Kevin, and Vicki with Troy and Ryan.

Pearl

The long awaited double anniversary trip with Tom, Vicki, Wendy, and Del in front of the Wailing Wall in Israel.

Steve (the intern) and Kim

The special 25th Wedding Anniversary party with Ryan, Darren, Jon, Tom, Vicki, Kristin, and Troy.

Festival crowd: a typical gathering of Indian people waiting to hear Tom preach the words of life.

Tom with little boy healed by Jesus Christ.

Tom excited to bring the words of life and water of life to the people of India. Pastor Thimothi Rao is left of Tom.

Festival Director in India, Pastor Thimothi Rao, and his wife, Johti, also preside over a Bible school.

One of the many wells Oasis World Ministries drilled because of sponsors partnering with the Indians.

Lakshamakka in between Wendy and Russ.

Sirivaram church dedication March 20, 2003.

"Del's church," to the right of Tom is
Rev. G. Peters (wearing a dark tie).

Chapter Thirty Nine

Oasis of Love

Pastor D. Mohan, who Tom had met on his first trip to India, had invited Tom back to have another evangelistic festival. The large church of 12,000 people had rented the beach for several nights and Indian worship music was attracting a large crowd. Tom preached a simple, straightforward message, pausing between sentences for the translator. The invitation to believe in the One True God was given and people came forward to pray. A new faith journey was before the Indians and Tom had been a part of it. Overcome with joy, Tom couldn't believe he was really a part of an outdoor crusade overlooking the Bay of Bengal in southeast India! He had asked Del to come again and they had both raised their own travel and festival expenses. The sound of the waves crashing upon the shores reminded Tom how great God is.

Because there was prayer for healing after the service, Tom and Del went down with the host pastor and interpreter into the crowd of Indian people. Tom glanced over at Del, who was having the time of his life. His large frame looked out of place next to the slender dark-skinned Indians, but Del's heart was right there with them.

After an Indian man requested prayer, Tom asked him in English,

"How can I pray for you?"

The interpreter translated Tom's question and the reply came back in Telegu, "I have a deaf ear."

Tom placed his hands on the man and prayed for healing of the deaf ear when all of a sudden he was interrupted by the Indian man speaking something in Telegu. Tom asked his interpreter, "What's going on?"

The interpreter told Tom with visible excitement, "He said, 'You don't have to pray for me, I was healed the moment you laid hands on me!'"

Once the interpreter had translated a little more, Tom found out the man's ear had instantly popped open. Tom was just as shocked and excited as the man he had prayed for, and they both rejoiced in the Lord. Wanting to make sure the gentleman had indeed been deaf, Tom decided to ask around and check with the locals. Those who knew him reported that, yes indeed, he had been deaf.

On the way back to their lodging that night, Tom had to laugh at himself. Because he truly believed the age of miracles had not passed, he had attended all the healing conferences he could in order to learn as much as possible about it. He had also prayed and asked God for miracles on this trip, together with all of those praying partners back home, yet he was still shocked when it happened!

Over the years, as Tom continued to travel to India, he would see even more miracles. Many people would be healed from blindness, mutes would speak, and deformities would be made whole by the power of God. As always, each miracle would be validated and testimonies would be screened, before the person would be brought up on the stage to testify of God's healing power in the name of Jesus.

On the way home from India, Tom leaned over his seat in the airplane and caught Del's attention, "You know, Del, we've had some good times doing beach festivals, but I've come to realize that there are evangelists coming two months before me and then two months after me. It seems like the larger cities are being penetrated with the Gospel. What about the areas that aren't being reached? They don't have people coming every two months. I bet some places have never had a festival like what we've seen here."

Del began to smile, "That's what I like about you, Tom. Like a pioneer, you always have to be moving forward to new things. So what exactly do you have in mind?"

Tom laid his head on the back of his seat. The drone of plane's engines filled the cabin, "I don't know yet for sure. But Rev. G. Peters, the superintendent I introduced you to, had some ideas of places in Andhra Pradesh with cities of maybe one hundred to two hundred thousand that never have hosted festivals. They aren't considered big enough. But I think that's where God wants me to go. People in the outlying areas need to hear, too. If we can encourage the few pastors that are in the area and help them, that's not all bad, is it?"

Del closed his eyes, but he was still smiling, "No, it's not bad at all."

Del was working at the Monticello Assemblies of God Church part-time and at a local garden nursery part-time. He had to raise his own money to go on every trip with Tom. Del and Wendy didn't have a lot financially, but Del just believed God would provide. Vicki always thought of Del as a man of faith. The Grages lived simply and went without, and yet they had what they needed for ministry trips. Del had a positive attitude and a hunger for God. Because he loved to teach the Word of God, he came along as one of the teachers for the daytime pastors' seminars.

After the second trip, Tom and Vicki decided to form their own non-profit 501(c)(3) corporation for their ministry. They began to see that down the road their ministry to India would need to be separated from church ministry. It would be a mess for all parties concerned if it wasn't handled properly with all the paperwork and legalities involved. A vision was forming in Tom's mind of a ministry that would not be exclusively one denomination, but would interface with many groups of people: some faith-based, some business, and the other categories Tom wasn't sure of yet. He would find out along the way. He knew from past experiences with God, that some of it was "trust and go." The details would work themselves out. They always had.

Tom continued his doubled time of prayer he had started after attending the Promise Keepers Pastors' Conference at the Georgia Dome. From time to time he would reflect on how the ministry should function. Tom wanted to work with the Indian pastors in each town as long as they had like vision in reaching out with the Gospel. Showing unity within the Christian community could be a powerful example of God's love. Another thing to figure out was the name. What would they call their non-profit organization? A song came back to Tom from the days of Jesus People Church called *Oasis of Love*. He had first heard it in the late 1970s when David Ingles, a nationally known Gospel singer/songwriter from Tulsa, Okalahoma, came to the church for a concert. Tom had always enjoyed the melody and lyrics written by David Ingles. He began reflecting how fitting the word *oasis* was because of the spiritual analogies with Jesus Christ—the Oasis of Love to so many people. In the Bible there was the woman at the well. She had come for physical water, but Jesus had offered her living water. One of the commands of Jesus before he left the earth was that believers in him should publicly show their faith through water baptism. In the book of Psalms, chapter one, it suggests that those who follow after God are like trees planted by water and their leaves do not wither, bearing fruit even in times of drought. An oasis was like that—providing relief in the midst of a dry and weary land. People were spiritual beings, dry and weary; thirsty for something that would give them life. A ministry of meeting Jesus, the Life Giver, through evangelistic crusades, or as they now were called "festivals," had been born.

After discussing everything with Vicki, she responded with, "I've always equated that song with the Lord being an Oasis to our hearts. We can do this!"

They began to look into the legal aspects of forming a non-profit organization. It seemed a daunting task until the Lord provided them with advisors who would volunteer their time and expertise helping Oasis World Ministries become a reality. It would take until the end of 1999 to get their official signed document declaring non-profit status. It would also be near the time of the dedication of the first church building and drilled well in November 1999 in Nalgonda, south central India. They had never thought of drilling fresh water wells when they chose the name of Oasis World Ministries in 1997, but that was all part of the adventure of following God. Their Heavenly Father knew what their future destiny would look like: an oasis giving life both spiritually and physically.

How all this was going to work with overseeing the two churches, Northeast and Crystal, was unclear to Tom and Vicki. But they knew from walking with God all these years that you never got the whole agenda, just one step at a time. And that's what they would do; take the next step. They started raising the funds necessary for expenses overseas and for operational needs stateside.

Chapter Fourty

Trust and Obey

The spring of 1998 came with changes and challenges for everyone in the Elie family. Troy had been the youth pastor at Crystal for a few years and had pioneered the youth group, Spirit Fire. Now he was moving to Iowa with his new wife, Kristin, and would work with a church in Sioux City.

It was time for the send-off dinner for Troy and Kristin, and the Elie clan had gathered for a meal at the New Hope home. Grandma and Grandpa were filled with joy when they saw Troy. "Congratulations, Troy! A college degree, a beautiful wife, and a successful run as youth pastor. We're so proud of you."

Troy hugged them both. They had always encouraged him in good times and the bad.

After sitting down for dinner, Tom deferred to his father, "Dad, would you like to say grace?"

Grandpa Al bowed his head to bless the meal. "Thank you, Lord, for the price you paid on Calvary for all our sins. May we never take for granted your shed blood. Thank you that we can go to you for forgiveness of sins." He continued thanking God for the food and every person there, concluding with, "Amen."

As they passed the food around the table, everyone was engrossed in conversation. Grandpa Al was enjoying the moment, "Ryan, it's so nice that you have taken over for Troy. I am sure it's a relief for him to know that the work he started with Spirit Fire will not die out now."

Grandma Ruth agreed heartily and gave Ryan a similar compliment.

"Thanks, you're both welcome to come whenever you want!" Ryan was beaming. He had finally gotten through his indecision about being youth pastor at Praise and the relief showed.

Grandma carefully replied, "Well, you young people really seem to like all that loud rock-n-roll music to praise God with, so we probably wouldn't be able to handle it. But you go ahead and serve God as you think best, Ryan. We'll be praying for you."

Ryan smiled. That was Grandma and Grandpa, always wanting to encourage him, even if they didn't go along with his methods of reaching out with the Gospel. To them the important part was that the youth would be touched by the love of God.

In June Tom flew down to Dallas to a conference for evangelists and it renewed his desire again for evangelism. Before leaving, Tom and Vicki had discussed his flight schedule, "I think I have it figured out. If I go down Wednesday and fly back Friday in the afternoon, I'll have time to wash up and change clothes for the open house."

"It starts at seven o'clock, so if you can get in some time in the mid afternoon that should work." Vicki threw in a teaser, "You don't want to be late for our 25th wedding anniversary party, do you?"

"No, I sure don't. Especially with the boys and Kristin planning it."

Vicki smiled at the thought of her boys taking the time and trouble to plan a special party for them. Of course, they were probably getting a little bit of help from a few female volunteers, but it was their initiative.

After the conference concluded, Tom drove to the Dallas airport with a cautious eye on the sky. Black voluminous clouds were forming. The wind was picking up and there was a smell of rain in the air as he exited his vehicle. Soon sheets of rain began to crash against the airport terminal. The clerk at the check-in counter apologized, "I'm sorry, Mr. Eel-lee, but the flight that was supposed to be coming into Dallas isn't able to land because of the storm."

"It's Elie." Tom didn't know why he even bothered with the correct pronunciation except that it was a force of habit. It was strange to be thought of as an eel-type creature from the sea.

The clerk apologized and mispronounced his name in a new improved version, "Sorry, Mr. Ell-lie, but we do have an alternative flight for you that leaves in an hour and a half."

"That would be fine. Thank you."

Tom searched the massive airport for a fast food restaurant. Settling into a spot, he set down his jacket and reading materials in order to pursue his lunch. After a few bites, Tom noticed a man sitting next to his table reading a book. An impression that he should share Christ with this stranger began to grow. After initiating some friendly conversation, Tom could sense that the gentleman was open to discussing spiritual matters. The man's reaction was positive and inquisitive. Tom thought to himself, this is a "God appointment."

Suddenly Tom noticed his watch. "I had better get to my gate." He thanked the man for their discussion, grabbed his Bible, and headed in the direction of his gate. When he got there the line was forming for boarding the plane. Tom began fishing around for his ticket. It wasn't tucked inside his Bible. It wasn't in his pants pocket. A despairing thought crept into this thoughts, "I must have left it back at my table."

But then he relaxed as he thought about how he must be in their computers with his luggage transferred over to the plane, and he did have his driver's license for identification.

"Where's your ticket?" the female agent asked.

"I think I misplaced it, but my name is in your computer."

"I have to have a ticket."

"Well, ma'am, I'm sure if you just look at the computer you will find my name. I just got transferred because of the rain storm."

"I have to have the ticket."

Tom's courteous, reassuring smile faded. He looked at his watch. He had twenty minutes to run back to the fast food place and get back to the gate. He had long legs, so he could do it if he sprinted a bit. He reached the restaurant in five minutes. Now where was his ticket? He asked the manager. Nothing had been turned in.

Now what was he going to do? Tom decided to head toward the main terminal that serviced American Airlines, but which one? It seemed miles away; nonetheless, with his long legs he got there in a few minutes. Through quick breaths he explained to the ticket agent that he had a huge problem on his hands, "I've just got to get home tonight!"

The agent was cool and calm; it happened every day on the hour. Some adult traveler was forever losing their ticket, "I'm sorry, sir, but you'll have to buy another ticket."

"No, that's not an option," then Tom considered his family, "How much?"

"Six hundred dollars, sir."

"No, that's not an option. Can I please talk to your manager?"

Tom could feel the panic swelling up inside of him. It matched the storm thrashing its elements against the windows. Disturbing scheduled flight plans and disrupting people's lives, the storm seemed to delight in all of this and take strength from it. Tom waited and prayed, "Oh, Lord, how did this happen?"

He thought of Vicki, all dressed up, smiling by his side. Vicki! He pulled out his cell phone. He finished explaining everything to Vicki when the female manager showed up at the counter. After clicking the keypad the manager began reading the screen, "The flight you lost your ticket for just taxied out."

Tom slumped his shoulders.

"But," the manager continued, "I see there is another flight leaving in thirty minutes."

Tom straightened up with hope, "There is?"

"Yes, but you will have to hustle because the gate is almost a mile away. I'll write you a note and you can get on that plane and get to your party."

"Oh, that would be wonderful. Thank you so much! If I don't make this party I will be dead meat—"

The manager interrupted him with a dry smile and a suggestion: "JUST GO!"

Tom ran for the gate. Suddenly over the intercom they began announcing a name, "Last call for Tom Eel-lee."

Tom turned the corner and saw the ticket agent, gave a slight wave, and panted, "I'm Tom."

"Where's your ticket?"

Tom bent over grasping the corner of the counter with his right hand. He cocked his head to one side to make eye contact, "I don't have a ticket. Here's the note." Tom felt like a kid in grade school as he began to go through the whole story again.

"Which terminal were you at? There are three of them and I need to call the manager and get verbal approval of this before I let you on the plane."

Tom couldn't believe it. He tried to not have a panic attack, "I have no idea which one I was at!"

The ticket agent called around but couldn't find the manager. Tom was ready to get down on his knees and start begging, "Sir...

listen… please," he gulped another breath of air, "I have a 25th wedding anniversary party to get to that my four sons planned. I have been trying all day to get on a plane. This is my third try. The party is at seven o'clock and I can't bear the thought of my poor wife standing there all by herself. Sir, my options are running out. I have to be on this plane."

The agent wavered, weighing out Tom's plight and company rules. Finally, he gave Tom the nod. "Go ahead. Get on the plane."

Tom gushed out a thank you and raced down the corridor to the plane. Over his shoulder he heard a faint, "…and Happy Anniversary!"

Vicki met Tom at the baggage claim and they looked for his suitcase, but it wasn't there. After waiting and waiting, Tom went to the customer service counter and explained the situation. He was getting good at it by now. The man behind the counter checked the computer screen and reported his findings, "Sir, it's not in our system."

"But it has to be. I checked in way before this flight on a previous flight."

The agent replied, "Oh, that's a horse of a different color," and began checking on the other flight. "Sir, your luggage hasn't arrived because the plane hasn't left Dallas yet. After the plane taxied out, it was delayed on the runway. In fact, it won't be here until," squinting, he checked the time, "9:50 p.m., it looks like."

Tom let the words sink in a minute. Through all that confusion the Lord had enabled him to get home. Tom could see it now. If he had gotten on that second flight he still would not be home. "Lord, you are amazing. Thank you!"

Something new was kindled inside of Tom about trusting the Lord. It wasn't that he hadn't in the past, but he knew his level of trust wasn't where it could be. This day and other previous situations had proved that. It was a day for Tom to look back on and share the story with humor like most people do. But he also came away with a sense of reinforced trust in the Lord's promise to order his steps. Almost like steel rebar placed down before concrete is poured in the form prepared for it. This was something Tom would need, something that would be tested in the future, and would hold firm.

Chapter Fourty One

The Big Fat Anniversary Trip

The episode of Tom's misplaced ticket for his 25th anniversary party had a sequel. This time, though, it involved Del and Wendy. In 1999 the two couples had planned a trip to Israel and India to celebrate their 25th and 30th wedding anniversaries—the Elies and Grages, respectively, which both happened to be on June 22nd. After Del and Wendy's son, Josh, had dropped them off at Tom and Vicki's house, they discovered that Del's briefcase was missing with all their travel documents in it—and the evening turned frantic. In the darkness of night, the black brief case had been left in the backseat of their son's car.

"What are we going to do?" Vicki lamented. "Here we have been planning this big anniversary trip for the four us to Israel and India for months and this happens!"

Tom calmly gathered the frazzled together and prayed. A few minutes later the phone rang. Ryan had been sent out on a mission to locate Del and Wendy's son and had been successful. The briefcase containing the tickets, passports, and visas, was on its way.

Wendy sank into the couch in a pool of exhaustion and happiness.

Tom let out a laugh, "Boy, this sure is an exciting way to start a trip of a lifetime, isn't it?"

Del joined in with a chuckle while Vicki rushed to the kitchen to finish up a few dishes. She wondered what else the trip would bring for Wendy and her. "Thank you, Lord, for your help. We will probably be keeping you busy for the rest of the trip."

As the plane flew to their next destination, Mumbai, formerly known as Bombay, India, Tom's head swirled with all the things the four of them had seen in Israel: the Wailing Wall, the River Jordan, and other historical sites recorded in the Bible. It had been Del's dream for years to go to Israel and Tom was happy he could share it with him. This would be their third trip to India together and he was excited that Vicki and Wendy were able to come along to see what the festivals were all about. After going through customs, they were greeted by an elderly gentleman. "Greetings, Brother Tom and Brother Del." His gracious manners, so typical of the Indian people, were evident even before he spoke. He wore large-rimmed plastic glasses, and his closely-cropped gray hair contrasted with his deep brown skin, but his smile and the twinkle in his eyes made him seem younger.

Tom began the introductions, "Hello, Brother G. Peters. As promised, I brought my wife, Vicki, and this is Del's wife, Wendy."

Then Tom turned to the two travel-worn women and introduced the Rev. G. Peters who bowed slightly, "It is a pleasure to meet your wives, Mrs. Tom Elie and Mrs. Del Grages. Welcome to India. I hope you will enjoy your time here." According to the protocol of politeness in his country, he made eye contact with Vicki and Wendy for only a moment.

Exotic sights, sounds, and smells, combined with the emotions of being in a world-famous city of ancient history, made their spirits rise. Immediately they were swamped with taxi offers and baggage handlers. A begging woman with a child on her hip and one clutching her skirt reached out for coins. Rev. G. Peters explained, "They are sure you are millionaires from America."

On the way to the hotel, the taxi jostled through the traffic. Tom and Del were used to the noise and congestion, but Vicki and Wendy were not.

"Oh, my, why are they honking the horns so much?" Vicki asked.

Tom explained, "It's their way of communicating to one another, saying, 'I am here, you may go ahead of me,' or 'I am passing on your left or right.'"

Vicki noticed something else. "There are six rows of drivers...but only three lanes are marked."

Wendy was looking everywhere, "Look! That lady is riding sidesaddle on that motor scooter with her family. How does she stay on?"

There was a sea of activity before them. A rainbow of colored textiles greeted their eyes as women passed by tucked inside auto rickshaws or driving motor scooters with scarves flowing behind them. In the modern city of Mumbai some women wore western clothes, but a great many wore the traditional Indian saree or two-piece punjabi.

The site of the evening festival was fifteen minutes away and every night they drove back to their hotel in the dark in the midst of 10 million people. One night as they rode home in separate taxis, one of the vehicles suddenly clunked over. The rear wheel had fallen off. Stopped in the middle of the nighttime traffic in Mumbai gave new meaning to the term "traffic hour."

One added element for this trip besides the nightly festivals was a women's seminar during the day. The Indian women enjoyed meeting Vicki and Wendy, observing their clothing and hair.

Wendy couldn't help blurting out, "I feel like I am on exhibition at the zoo."

Vicki laughed, "I suppose they don't see American women up

close very often and are just curious."

Vicki got up to speak to the Indian women. Whatever was on her soft heart was on her face: a desire to see people right with God, to see hurting people ministered to by God, and to see God's whole plan fulfilled on earth. Beyond her words there was something communicated of the heart that needed no translation. As Vicki and Wendy taught from the scriptures what the Lord had given them for this trip, the fans whirled above like a fleet of helicopter blades, dogs moved in and out of the building freely, and mothers nursed their babies. It was life lived out without the constrictions of the sanitized protocol of the West.

However, there were strict observances in protocol of honor, respect, and deference to those in leadership. Rank and class were observed and faithfully adhered to, although the Bible clearly teaches against class separation in Galatians 3:28 "There is neither Jew nor Greek, slave nor free, male nor female, for you are all one in Christ." (NIV) The adherence to honor and respect often clouded the line of separation between the two. Years of layers in the Hindu system of elevated classes and marginalized portions of societies, were often diluted by Christian teachings, but not completely erased. It weighed heavy on the hearts of some Christian leaders. The Brahmin caste had the most to give up. They needed humility and submission, to either lower themselves down to the level of lower-caste people or allow the lower castes a higher place. Which would it be?

As for the Dalits, they had been treated as lower-class, even by their Christian counterparts, for so long that they saw Christianity as another hierarchy of the "haves and have-nots" simply because of birth. Where was this new birth order that some spoke of where Dalits and Brahmin were grafted into the vine of Jesus? Surely Jesus was to be respected as a great teacher, but did Jesus really bring equality to those who follow him? Yes, there was freedom from reincarnation, but would there be a caste system in the paradise Christians talked about, for those who put their allegiance in this One True God above all the other millions? These were the questions of the Dalit people group.

During one of their few quiet moments together, Wendy and Vicki were alone relaxing at the hotel after another evening festival. As they chatted about India, and life in general, Wendy brought up one of her concerns about being in the ministry, "How do you do it, Vicki? How do you keep your vulnerability, that childlike faith after so many years in the ministry? It's such a temptation to become cynical."

Vicki's eyes softened as she considered her friend's question. "I think, Wendy, that the secret is simple forgiveness. It isn't always easy to get back up after you feel you have been taken advantage of. Sometimes it hurts to know that you gave and gave from the heart and someone just keeps taking and taking. But it seems to me they are so starved for love that they don't know any better. Once they can learn to love, they can overcome this."

"I see what you're saying, Vicki, but what about those people you trust and then they end up backstabbing you in the end. How do you deal with that?"

"Oh, it hurts, I'll admit it. I cry and then I pray. I just have to go to God with all that and let him figure it out, because if I try to…well, it's sort of like drowning. There really is power in forgiving from the heart, Wendy, or I wouldn't still be in the ministry. We are all just people. And people make mistakes—that's why we're called sinners. We are saints saved from sin, not perfect people."

The trip to India had cemented their friendship forever. Despite the hurdles of discomfort, it was a trip to remember and give God the glory for everything. They had taught together, laughed together, screamed together while traveling, and even cried together, at seeing people ministered to by the love of God. Would they ever travel to India together again? It would be hard to forget this land with its enigmatic culture. How does one explain such things to those who have never seen the expectant faces of new believers who have escaped the slavery of appeasing millions of gods?

Tom and Del dropped their wives off at the airport. As he said good-bye to his Vicki, Tom gave her a squeeze, "I'm so glad you came, Vicki. You did so well, everyone just loved you, I could tell."

Their eyes met with unspoken words, the pain of separation again, mixed with excitement from the trip. Vicki's heart felt gratitude brimming over as she reflected on the past week. "Tom, now I can see what a difference the prayers and resources from our partners in the States make. I knew it did, but to see it firsthand leaves no room for doubting that this is a good thing. I can't wait to tell all our supporters back home how much is impacted by their participation in Oasis World Ministries. I probably sound like a commercial, but it just blows my mind to see all of this firsthand. I know this is God's Call on our lives."

Chapter Fourty Two

Well Spotting, Vision Building

Tom and Del arrived in Palakol and met up with the festival team. It was on his third trip that Tom met Lee Ruud, who had a warm smile and a California tan. After making small talk, they began to discuss the Wells of Life. Lee explained, "We drill the well next to the newly-erected church building for the entire community to use, regardless of caste or creed."

Tom was intrigued. Could this be the next piece of the puzzle for Oasis World Ministries? "So, how does it all work?"

"Why don't you and Del come to Hyderabad and see for yourself? Could you meet me there at the end of the week?"

Tom knew he needed to see this church in Hyderabad that Lee Ruud kept talking about. Next to the church a well had been drilled and now people all over the slum area were coming for the fresh water. Tom told the others involved in the festival, "I'll do the first four nights and then I'm going to go to Hyderabad to see this church and well. You guys can finish up without me." Something inside of Tom was urging him to go to Hyderabad to see the church and well built in the slum area by the Christian Broadcasting Network (CBN).

Tom and Del went on to Hyderabad and met up with Lee. "Welcome to Hyderabad, Tom and Del. It's a pleasure to see you both again and show you what we're doing with churches and wells."

Del spoke up, "This is one big city! I'm used to living in a country suburb."

"Hyderabad *is* a big city, filled to the brim with 6.4 million people. It has a thriving middle class of professionals much like Bangalore. Hyderabad is also the largest center of Islam for southeastern India. Something like 40% Muslims live in this city. Did you know that Bangalore is known as the Silicon City of India, a sort of spin on our Silicon Valley in California, housing computer techs and software people? They take a lot of service calls from America and sometimes export their people to America to work."

"Wow, I never thought of India having a middle class with techies. What's the population of Bangalore?" Tom asked.

"About 5.4 million. The city of Bangalore is rich with Christian churches and agencies, yet as a region, the state of Karnataka is very unreached with the Gospel."

"What about the state that Hyderabad is in?" Del asked.

"That would be Andhra Pradesh. Actually, the Christian population has declined over the last twenty years, and yet there is a new harvest that is beginning to bump those numbers up again."

When Tom and Del came into the city of Hyderabad, it appeared at first to be a city of grandness, but as they wove their way through the congested streets, Tom began to notice the utter poverty around him. Soon a putrid odor filled his nostrils and there was no adjusting to it. The rancid smell seemed to worsen as they came into the heart of the slum area. Tom noticed a public latrine, but his guide cautioned him, "Don't go in there. It's an improvement for this area to have a public toilet, but it would not seem that way for you." Tom had observed that many people chose to simply squat alongside the road and then proceed on their way.

In the midst of the squalor, there arose a new building, a small seedling of hope growing in a place of despair. Lee explained, as they began to walk inside, “This 20x40-foot structure has an overlay of stucco over brick, and offers protection from the monsoons and the heat. It also gives the church a sense of credibility.”

Tom marveled at the simple elegant structure. There was peace in this place. “It makes a statement, doesn’t it, about the Christian God?”

“Yes, it does. It makes people ponder and ask, ‘Why would a God provide shelter and fresh water for me? I am only an outcast.’”

Tom stood at the door of the church; its shadow gave him refuge from the stinging heat of the day. Women and children were filling plastic and metal containers with the fresh clean water. The pump handle kept up its rhythm as sparkling water gushed out. His heart began to race with excitement: *This is like an oasis—a spiritual and physical oasis.*

Lee began to explain what a difference the well could make in a community. “Clean water is scarce in India. The World Health Organization will tell you that 80% of the world’s diseases stem from impure water. To give people clean water is a gift beyond what you can describe. In rural areas it is estimated that a village woman can spend up to four hours a day obtaining and purifying water for her family.”

“I can’t imagine Vicki spending four hours a day just working on providing clean water for us.”

Del laughed, “I think Wendy would rearrange that chore as everyone’s job!”

“So think of the implications for a woman to suddenly have this hand pump right in her own village. It will substantially reduce her time spent in hauling water to her home.”

Tom added softly, “And the water is fresh and clean. I like this idea.”

Tom would never forget this day in the slum. Its images and odors would be forever etched in his mind and heart. Could Tom have predicted that in five years Oasis would have thirty-seven churches built and over forty wells drilled? Probably not, but he was already getting the first glimpse of a ministry that would link people in India to partners in the West.

Over the course of the trip, Tom learned that not only was Rev. G. Peters the Superintendent for the state of Andhra Pradesh with the Assemblies of God, but he was also the president of a small, yet growing Bible college. His stature was taller and larger than other Indians, with an air of poise and humility. Because Tom sensed this man was both kind and wise, he did not hesitate to share his dreams with Rev. G. Peters. After presenting his idea of having festivals in outlying areas that had not been reached yet with the Gospel, Tom asked for input, "Could this work with what God is already doing in India with the national pastors and evangelists?"

Rev. G. Peters began to shake his head back and forth, which meant that he was in agreement. In his Indian-British accent, the superintendent shared his own vision of reaching hundreds of villages, putting pastors in each village. "I share your passion for the unreached areas. We could work together, Brother Tom. We could help you put together your ideas for the festivals, the churches, and the wells. My students at the Bible college could work with you in the festivals. It would be good training for them. And they could also go out amongst the villages. Once new believers form small congregations with a permanent pastor, they could look for land on which to build a church and drill a well. I would be able to watch and see which group of believers is stable and ready to take the step of looking for land."

Tom's interest was piqued, "How many believers would it take to make a decent size congregation?"

"I think thirty committed believers, strong in their faith, would be good."

Tom thought about what Rev. G. Peters had said. They continued to discuss ideas regarding the national pastors and some on-going training. A seminar during the day and a festival in the evening would be most helpful. The pastors could help with the follow-up of new believers as a result of the festivals. A friendship had been struck. An embryo…a rough sketch of plans had been drawn. But how would it all happen? Where would the funds for Tom's and Rev. G. Peter's dreams come from?

On the way home, flying over the Atlantic, Tom mulled over the last few weeks and wondered what the future held. Already in place were the evening festivals and the daytime seminars for pastors and leaders, including women. Now there was a new addition of church buildings and fresh water wells. Tom also sensed in a stronger way that what would set his particular ministry in India apart from his ministry in the past would be miracles of healing. It wasn't so much that he was after a healing ministry, but healing was a vehicle to help people understand the mercy of Christ. He prayed asking God to confirm to him his desire to see healings increased at the festivals and other venues of ministering to people. Were his motives right and pure before God? He wanted to be guided by scripture verses like the one in James: "It's his goodness and his mercy that leads us to repentance…." He prayed his reward would be to see God glorified, and not himself, nor Oasis World Ministries.

The miracles and healings Tom witnessed in India began to grow in numbers and types of healings. The openness the people had to a living God who wanted to heal them amazed Tom. He also began to see that along with worshiping millions of gods there was a spiritual bondage of appeasement, causing them to live their lives in fear. Where was the friendship with God in all of this? In contrast, believers in Jesus Christ had, as the scriptures taught, a peace that passed beyond any human attempt to create inner peace. It was truly from another world: God's kingdom.

After arriving in Minneapolis, Tom reported back to his churches, Northeast and Crystal, about his recent trip. "God did so much on this trip. Thank you for going with me in prayer and support. I keep learning about the Indian culture, one of which is, Indian people are very reserved with their emotions. You have to ask them, 'What did you feel?' Their culture teaches them to have strict control of their emotions."

He then reported on the large crowds of people at the festivals, faith commitments, and the healings. Then he introduced the new initiative: "Once I saw the church and well in Hyderabad, my mind began assessing all that could be done for such a modest cost. I thought to myself, 'We've just got to do this!'"

Tom's enthusiasm spilled out to the Sunday morning congregation. "This is how it works," he told them. "Once a group of believers reaches about thirty people and they have a pastor in place, the superintendent of Andhra Pradesh, Rev. G. Peters, decides where the churches should go because he knows best. He knows if the pastors are ready; he knows the spiritual climate and the demographics. That's the type of partnership we could have with Rev. G. Peters. So, with the current cost of construction and materials in India, it would cost just under $500 for the well and approximately $4,000 for the 20x40-foot church building."

People's faces and body language told Tom that they were with him. "To me it's kind of like the old adage, 'If we don't see that you care, then we don't care to listen.' The church is usually the nicest building in town and becomes a shelter. And imagine how much their lives will be improved with fresh, clean drinking water!"

Finally winter collapsed under the promise of spring with the scent of lilacs and fruit tree blossoms filling the Minnesota air. A future trip to India was being planned, including their first church and well project for sometime in November. However, along with all the excitement there were a few gnawing thoughts in Tom's mind. He shared these concerns with Vicki, Wendy, and Del, one night over a meal at the Elie home in New Hope. Although the trips to India infused Tom and the churches at Northeast and Crystal with spiritual vitality, he often struggled with being fair to the people at his own churches who looked to him as their spiritual leader. "I don't know. Maybe I should resign from Northeast and Crystal and go out on my own and allow both churches to have someone who is there full-time."

Tom took a sip of soda and continued, "Maybe they aren't willing to accept the fact that I'm gone so much. I think I am going to talk to the board about this. Everyone is so supportive of me and it's unusual for a church to be so willing to share their pastor so much. It's such a gift from the Lord, but I feel they deserve more."

"Are you getting a lot of complaints?" Del asked between bites of his cheeseburger.

"Or is it more nonverbal?" Wendy added.

Vicki jumped in with her thoughts, "I think Tom feels the tension of being responsible here at Crystal and also following God's call of evangelism in India. Isn't that it, honey?"

As usual, Vicki had put her finger on the problem for him. "Yes, you're right," Tom said. "I just feel this double burden of doing both, like I need to be in India when I'm here, and when I'm in India I need to be home."

Del looked at Tom, "Let's pray. God will show you the timing for everything. You bring back a lot to your people, Tom, and they know it. But you can't carry this double burden. Let's ask God to help you let *Him* carry it for a while."

Tom took the hand of his friends and wife. They had been through a lot together over the years.

Chapter Fourty Three

September 17, 1999

"Vicki," Wendy's voice came over the phone, "Del just slipped on the ice in the parking lot of the garden nursery that he makes deliveries for. I'm meeting him at the clinic. Please pray for wisdom and healing. Del's not one to go get checked out unless it's pretty bad."

"Sure, Wendy, is there anything I can do?"

"No, thanks though. I'll call later when we find out what's going on."

Vicki prayed as she continued about her day. Later that evening Wendy called back, "It's bad, his shoulder is completely ripped up. The doctor is recommending surgery, but there are a couple things we can do for home therapy first."

"Is he in a lot of pain?"

"Well, Del never says much when he is, but I can tell by the way he's favoring that arm, and he's kind of walking slow."

"I'll tell Tom, we'll be praying. Keep us updated."

Wendy called Vicki a few weeks later with the news, "Del needs surgery."

"Oh, Wendy, I'm so sorry to hear that. When is the surgery?"

"Well, they said July would be best, but Del wants to wait until after Josh's wedding, maybe in September."

Del and Wendy had lived in a mobile home for thirteen years. God worked out a series of financial miracles so the Grages family could move into a home in Big Lake. They had purchased the lot through a special lottery they had to bid on, similar to a silent auction. Then they ordered a pre-manufactured home that came in two halves, which were placed on a foundation on the city lot. The first weekend after the Grages house had been delivered, Tom and Vicki, together with the younger boys, drove out to Big Lake.

Tires crunched on the gravel into their driveway. "Look, there they are!" Vicki yelled out, "Oh, look at their house. It's beautiful."

Tom helped Del arrange the wicker lawn furniture Del had just picked up from the "lay-a-way" at K-Mart while the grill was heating up. "Say, Del, how's that shoulder of yours. Do you think it will hold up with moving everything into the house next week?"

"Oh, sure," Del shrugged it off. "I've made it this far and I'm having surgery after everything's done. The doc will fix me up and I'll be good for another 10,000 miles."

Before touring the house, Del made sure Tom saw the garage, pointing out where the workbench would go. "Well, let's go inside and you can see how it comes in two halves before they seal them up."

Soon the brats were sizzling brown with a delicious aroma and everyone gathered outside for the first official picnic at the Grages' new home. Tom prayed a blessing over the food and the new home.

Later, as Tom and Vicki were getting ready to leave, Wendy gave Vicki a farewell hug. "Thanks so much for coming out. You guys made it a special day for us."

Tom said, "We wouldn't miss it for the world. I can't wait to come and have another of Del's brats. Although with winter coming, we might have to move the lawn furniture into the house." As Tom was pulling out of the driveway he gave Del and Wendy one last wave. They looked so happy standing in front of their new home, arm in arm, both waving.

Two weeks later the phone rang. Vicki was in the kitchen making coffee and looked at her watch. It was 7:00 a.m. She took the call while Tom was getting dressed for the day. After coming into the kitchen, Tom glanced at Vicki. He knew that look. Something was wrong.

"Tom, that was Wendy. She was on her way to pick up Del this morning. They kept him overnight because he was in so much pain. The hospital just called and said there is an emergency medical situation and asked her to come down. She's already called Josh and Jessica and they insisted on going down there. Wendy asked if you could go to the hospital, because she is still a long way off. She wants someone there as soon as possible."

Tom's eyes met Vicki's. They had been in the ministry long enough to know what "medical emergency" meant.

"I wish I didn't have to get to work," Vicki fretted. "Make sure you call me right away and let me know how things are going. I'll be praying." Vicki's face creased with worry as she stood in the open doorway.

"I'll call you after I get there."

Tom headed down the driveway and immediately began praying in the heavenly language he had received years ago as a teenager, when the visiting evangelist had told about the power of the Holy Spirit assisting Christians in prayer. Something in his gut was tightening, but he kept praying. He reached Del's room in the intensive care unit before Wendy got there.

"Could you please tell me where Delroy Grages' room is? I'm his pastor. His wife called saying there was a medical emergency."

The nurse led him to the room where Tom saw a team of approximately eight nurses and doctors hovering over Del. Tom felt his eyes widen; his breathing accelerated. He hesitated for a moment before asking the nurse next to him, "What's going on?"

"A blood clot."

The team was pumping his chest, working smoothly at the CPR procedure for which they were all well-trained. Instinct took over for Tom and he walked over to Del and laid his hand on Del's forehead and began to pray. The lead doctor of the emergency team asked, "Does anyone oppose us stopping?" No one in the room said a word.

Tom stared in disbelief, "Wait a minute, you can't stop. You have to keep trying!"

Tom looked into their faces and quickly introduced himself. Everyone looked at the lead doctor, who said, "We've been trying for thirty to forty minutes and there is nothing happening. I'm sorry."

Tom watched as they disconnected all the machines and walked out of the room. Tom was alone with Del. He looked down at his friend.

Wendy was coming.

Tom began to pray over Del's body for a miracle. Then, in acceptance of God's will, he committed Del's spirit to the Lord, thanking God for this faithful humble servant who gave much and lived a life of active faith.

"Lord, give me strength to be there for his family. Help me when Wendy comes."

Tom was reluctant to leave Del's side, but he knew he had to be the first one to tell Wendy. He had to make sure she knew before she walked into the room. His thoughts were swirling: *How am I going to approach Wendy…and tell her she'll never have a chance to say good-bye to her husband?*

Tom waited in the hallway for Wendy.

He knew she knew something was wrong when she saw his face.

Their relationship had changed forever. In that moment she became as his sister and he became her brother. He reached for her arm, "Wendy, I've got to talk to you."

Tom was in a tunnel of emotions. He saw his hand reach for a chair. He heard his voice tell Wendy, "Here, sit down."

As the truth hit, Wendy collapsed. Tom gently caught her and guided her to sit down. He could tell her world was shattered; yet there was a measure of strength that remained. She wanted to see Del. The two walked side by side into the room.

As Wendy took Del's hand, she broke into sobs. Tom had quickly called Vicki before Wendy arrived at the hospital. He knew she was on her way and knew the situation, but Josh and Jessica were also on their way.

Somehow, Wendy found her voice and looked up at Tom, "How am I going to tell my kids? What am I going to tell my kids?"

Tom went out to meet Josh. Jessica was coming with Ryan. Soon Vicki was there, and together with Tom, the Elies, as Wendy would later recount, "took over" and assisted their friends however they could.

Vicki had kept a guarded watch over Wendy at the reviewal. Wendy had stood for nearly five hours receiving condolences from the line of friends and family stretched down the church lobby and out the front doors. Del had lived with a generosity toward people that endeared him to their hearts.

Tom officiated at the funeral. Vicki sat half listening, half thinking, of their cherished last visit with Del and Wendy. How pleased he had been with his new BBQ grill and his garage. Thoughts of how Wendy would be able to afford the mortgage payments along with the hospital bills swam in Vicki's mind. *Lord, you know they didn't have a lot of money, though they were rich in other ways. I'm worried about Wendy's future. I ask for your provision for her. I know you know all things. Help me to be her friend as we all mourn the loss of Del. I thank you that we will see him again, but it's hard for those of us left behind. Give us your peace, Lord.*

As people filed out of the church they made small talk. Some were reminiscing about Del. Memories through the years were being exchanged. Ryan shared his thoughts as well, "Del had such a simple love for people and a simple love for the Lord. He just wanted to do the Lord's will. He was generous, always happy; his laugh stands out to me. He just had this big belly laugh."

The others in the group agreed with nods and sad smiles.

"He was a good family man," someone else added.

Ryan laughed, "Jessica always gave him a run for his money. She always needed her car fixed or to be bailed out of something disastrous. Del was always right there." His smile faded as he thought of Jessica's future. Now the Heavenly Father would have to take over for Del.

A few weeks after the funeral, talk began about setting up a memorial for Del. His passion for church planting and providing fresh water through the wells, inspired a member of the Monticello-Big Lake Church, Mr. Kalonowski, to set up a replica of an old-fashioned well in the church lobby. Dubbed "Del's Well," it filled up fast with donations. Soon the amount needed to bore a fresh-water well was reached, but generosity in memory of Del kept coming.

Wendy began meeting with Tom and Vicki regularly after Del's passing. She needed the comfort and accountability of old friends. Sitting at a Mexican restaurant with Tom and Vicki, she talked about going to India again.

Tom was truly touched by her desire to go. "So, how are you feeling about going to India with out Del, Wendy? Are you sure you're up for this?"

Vicki's face showed her concern as well.

Wendy replied, "Well, Tom, it will be a few months down the road and it will be dedicated to Del's memory. I don't want to miss something like this. You, of all people, know how much the work of God's kingdom in India meant to Del."

"Yeah, I do. He felt it was India's time to come into her own revival. He saw himself as a partner with the Indian people, rather than having an imperialist mentality that sometimes outsiders can have. I heard the well has already been paid for. Isn't that great?"

Wendy smiled, but Tom and Vicki could tell she was still in deep mourning. "I miss him so much," she admitted. "The first week was a blur. It's like you're in this tunnel. But now the fog has lifted a bit and the reality of it all has settled in. This memorial for Del means a lot to me. It brings life to my soul. It's the only thing that excites me right now. Did you know that there is almost enough money to pay for a church, too?"

Vicki reached out her hand to Wendy's arm, "It will be a great tribute to Del, Wendy." There was a comfortable silence for a moment and Vicki's eyes began to fill with tears, "How are Josh and Jessica doing?"

"I don't know for sure," Wendy paused. "It's hard some days. Sometimes I think we all try to be brave for one another. There's a man at church, I don't know him very well, but I visited his wife, Marcia, in the hospital before she died from cancer in November. He has four small children, so I guess I should be grateful my children are older."

"Oh, my," Vicki remarked, "that's so sad."

Little did all three realize how significant the widower would become in the future. Their paths would cross in a way Wendy could never have imagined.

Chapter Fourty Four

The Pull of India

For three years, having Sunday morning services at both Northeast and Crystal worked out well, until Tom got his first invitation to India. He had begun to double his prayer time and that had continued to be his habit. After a couple of trips Tom had said to Vicki, "I'm bit, Vicki. I know I will keep going back there." How he was going to manage all three was becoming a larger concern to him, and Tom knew he had to keep asking God for divine guidance.

After Del's funeral Tom went to an Assemblies of God pastors' conference in Springfield, Missouri. Everything was in turmoil for him. He was in the process of doing the first official project of Oasis World Ministries. In November there would be two church and well dedications, along with evening festivals, daytime seminars with pastors and leaders, and visits to small outlying villages. Only, now Del would not be going with him. Tom thought back to the trips he had made with Del and wondered who his traveling partner would be. Vicki couldn't make it for the upcoming trip to Nalgonda and Vikarabad, so he would have to pray about a travel partner. Tom sensed that in the future he would be going more than once a year to India. Should he resign from the Northeast campus of Praise? He had spoken with the board, but he would have to talk with them again.

His heart ached with heaviness as he walked into the pastors' conference building late for the meeting. His flight had been delayed so he had missed the beginning of the opening session at the church. He needed some encouragement from the Lord. Was India really his calling after all? After Pastor Theresa D'Sousa-Greenhough was introduced, she began to preach and the room fell silent. It was clearly evident that this was a handmaiden of the Lord who knew her Savior intimately. The anointing of God's Spirit was strong and her words were not her own, but from the Spirit of the Lord. She didn't travel to the States much anymore. Her focus wasn't the speaker circuit. It was only a means to achieve her dream of serving the children of India. Raised in a loving Catholic family, she had had a deep spiritual awakening take place in their family kitchen. After that she had become a nun and began many years of serving God in the field of education. Gradually, she felt the desire to serve under Mother Teresa in caring for the lepers of Calcutta. Pastor Theresa stood straight, wearing an olive green Indian punjabi with her long raven-black hair falling to the middle of her back. Tom had never met her, but he enjoyed hearing her Indian-British accent. Her eyes sparkled with heavenly zeal as she told of the day Mother Teresa visited their convent and came to her small quaint room with a message from God for her. "Mother Teresa took my hand and said, 'My child, the time has not yet come for you to leave the convent. When the time comes, God himself will reveal his plans for you. For right now, stay where you are.' A few years later the vision came to leave the convent and my ministry had begun."

After she finished her message, there was a time of prayer for any pastor or leader who wanted a "touch" from the Lord, as they called it. Pastor Theresa prayed for Tom, went to the next person, and then came back to Tom and said, "The deaf will hear, the blind will see, the lame will walk, and many will find Christ."

The tall Norwegian child of God broke down and wept, knowing that she did not know anything about him.

Thank you, Lord! Thank you, Lord! I know you'll see us through. I know you know the desires of my heart and you are with us and will direct us! The harvest is before us and the healings will come from you.

What a confirmation this was to Tom—that he and Vicki were doing the right thing. Although they had never met and knew nothing of each other, in the future their lives would begin to cross more frequently as Pastor Theresa sought out Tom and Vicki to encourage them in their work in India, even spending personal one-on-one time with them. No matter how many years they had been in the ministry, Tom and Vicki still welcomed mentors into their lives.

A few months later, the heat was boring into the vehicle, even though the air-conditioning was on. The blue skies of India held no clouds as usual and let the sun have its way. Tom, his traveling partner, Fritz Kinney, and a team of Indian pastors, including Rev. G. Peters, drove about an hour to Nalgonda, a small village in the Andra Pradesh district. Along the way Tom pointed out to Fritz that two-thirds of India lived in rural settings, the other third living in mega-populous cities, such as Mumbai and Chennai, burgeoning with people. Tom had recently heard Fritz was into video production. Thinking that it would be good to capture on video what God was doing in India for the supporters back home, Tom had invited him to come along. He also knew Fritz had a pleasant disposition and could handle the rigors of India, which the video photographer did without complaint.

They pulled into the village and saw that the white building topped with two red crosses was completed, and so was the fresh water well. Oasis World Ministries had partnered with the small church of thirty people in this village and its pastor, as one of its first official projects as a non-profit organization. The church in Crystal, now called Praise

Christian Center, was the sponsor of the project in Nalgonda. Don and Kelly Newman and family, who had served in various ways over the years since the beginning of Praise, had sponsored the other project in Vikarabad. As the makeshift drape covering the dedication plaque was pulled back, the people applauded and Tom wept. Waves of emotion hit him as he realized what God had given him, Vicki, and all those who had donated the funds: this awesome privilege of blessing these dear brothers and sisters. And yet the Indian believers were blessing him. It was a two-way street—their faith inspired him to keep steady and faithful on his journey of destiny.

After a time of prayer, everyone proceeded into the church and Indian worship music began to fill the building. The scent of fresh paint lingered on the walls. At the front of the building, behind the altar, there was a bright wall mural of Indian artistry depicting designs with words of praise to the Lord Jesus. Christian scripture verses in Telegu painted with a flourish over vivid-colored rectangle shapes ran across the walls. Most of the people sat on mats and rugs on the floor.

Tom and the others sat on chairs in the front altar area. According to custom, laurel wreaths of yellow mum-like-flowers adorned the neck of each visitor, the superintendent, Rev. G. Peters and also the pastor, and his wife. It truly was a day of celebration, as thankful hearts gave gratitude to the Lord. After several people spoke and more worship music, Tom proceeded to preach about the Good News. Rather than talking negatively about the pitfalls of Hinduism and all of its millions of gods, Tom focused on Jesus. "Jesus is more powerful and loving. He was the only one who proved his love by dying for us. This payment is the only one that works to cleanse us of our sins. It stops reincarnation, because it is beyond reincarnation. It's not up to us to satisfy the anger of our wrong-doing by trying to perform certain rituals." Tom asked if anyone there had considered following Jesus and making him their One True God. Several people raised their hands and came forward to pray. These new believers would now be nurtured and loved by the believing community in that church.

Later, a simple meal of rice and curry sauce was served on organic plates of dark green banana leaves. Rev. G. Peters leaned over to Tom, "You know, Tom, this church will almost double in size now because of the building. It lends credibility to the pastor and Christianity is taken seriously."

Tom was awestruck by the whole day. Here was Christianity being lived out in the trenches of life and something stable had been anchored in the village. The people made up the living stones, but the building gave expression to that faith. It was such a simple structure of only 20x40-feet and yet it would bring so much life—abundant spiritual life—to the entire community.

Tom asked the pastor through a translator, "How much is the well being used?"

The pastor replied in Telegu, "They come every day. The well is God's gift to everyone who wants to come."

Tom thought of all the disease this well would help avoid. Dehydration was such a common ailment, along with other waterborne diseases caused by impure water used for eating, drinking, washing, and bathing.

It was a most satisfying day for Tom. He knew his Divine Call to India was being confirmed again. It wasn't for everyone. He had to laugh at some of the funny reactions he would get from people about him traveling to India, "What would you want to do that for?"

Others would comment, "I'm glad it's you and not me! I'll be praying for you, Pastor." Tom would often explain passionately, "I can put up with all of that because I know I'm able to reach thousands of people. And many are hearing of Jesus for the first time!"

Was it really that much to sacrifice? I guess it depended on what was focused on. The grace of God to fulfill a calling, to follow one's destiny, was amazing.

After Tom got back from India, he told Vicki everything that had happened in India and then voiced a decision, "I can't keep doing two churches and India. I don't think it's fair to the people. The Northeast church doesn't have a senior pastor who is really there. Looking back, we should have structured the two churches differently, by having two senior pastors instead of the two-campus structure. I could have been a preaching pastor who acted as a chairman of the board with the two churches in relationship with each other, like sister churches, doing a lot together, yet each a distinct church." Tom had prayed and discussed the situation with Vicki and now knew that God was guiding him to select one church to pastor.

The board members listened intently to Tom. "I'm resigning. I can't do two churches anymore and India. I feel like I am neglecting my duties as a pastor. The people at Northeast deserve their own senior pastor. You can either sell the building and come over to Crystal or get a senior pastor, but I am resigning here at Northeast and will only pastor the Crystal church."

The reaction of Tom's resignation from Northeast was mixed. Some saw it as the future Call of God on the direction for both churches to have their own identity, while others did not want the change. It took a while for everything to settle down in everyone's heart, including Vicki's. She and many other people had poured a lot of prayer, blood, sweat, and tears, into the people of Northeast. But she knew she had to let them go into the hands of the Lord.

At the last joint service of two churches, Vicki thought back to when they had first purchased the building on Monroe Street. She and Tom talked over the memories with those who had been there at the beginning and cried while saying good-bye to those who were staying. Although she knew they couldn't keep up the rigorous pace of two churches and Oasis World Ministries, she felt it was like having one of her own kids leaving the nest. God would have to help all of them during this new season of life. Their Heavenly Father certainly knew the beginning from the end, and his plans were always for good, not harm. So be it. Amen.

It took a while to build up the Crystal church, but the Northeast church, now called Northeast Assembly of God, sent over some people who helped serve Crystal. Pearl, Donny and Kelly Newman came, as well as Tom's sister, Beth, and her husband, Kevin. As expected, Tom's parents, Al and Ruth, joined the Crystal group. Ryan settled into his position as youth pastor for Spirit Fire and continued to lead worship with Vicki.

Wanting to make sure his congregation was with him, Tom began communicating as much as he could from the pulpit about the future. "I intend to go to India more than I have in the past: three to four times a year. I know this is not usual for the senior pastor of a church to do this, but I believe this is how God is leading me."

Tom looked over the entire room filled with people he loved. Would they continue to be understanding and supportive of Oasis World Ministries as his trips increased each year? "So this morning, I'm asking all of you if you will climb on board with Vicki and me in this vision of reaching out to the people of India with the Good News of the Gospel of Jesus Christ. Not only will I be preaching at evening festivals, but I will also be partnering with the Indian Christians in mentoring pastors, building new church buildings, and drilling fresh water wells. In the Four Gospels we read how Jesus met the needs of people spiritually and physically. It's not one or the other. We can do both! I believe this is a blessed nation and a blessed church. And I believe it is for a reason: to be a blessing to others, just like

Abraham was told in Genesis, chapter 12. Let's turn in our Bibles to Genesis 12:1-3:

> *The Lord said to Abram, Leave your country, your people and your father's household and go to the land I will show you. I will make you into a great nation and I will bless you; I will make your name great, and you will be a blessing. I will bless those who bless you, and whoever curses you I will curse; and all peoples on earth will be blessed through you. (NIV)*

We see here that God is making a covenant with Abraham, and God is also looking into the future. He is seeing Christ coming through Israel's descendents, and then from Christ, the first century church. We are a continuation of that covenant to be a blessing to all peoples on the earth. Now it's our turn to be that blessing, not only to people right here in the Twin Cities, but also to the people of India."

Chapter Fourty Five

Y2K and LUV

The New Year rolled in and the Y2K hysteria dissipated as people pushed unopened boxes of generators into a secluded spot in the garage and started eating their stockpiled rations with a little humble pie for dessert. A few months later, Tom and Vicki met with Wendy again, at a restaurant halfway between New Hope and Big Lake, to discuss the India trip. Enough money had been raised through Del's Well for both a well and a church building. Tom and Vicki embraced their friend and slipped into a booth near a window. They both noticed Wendy's countenance seemed noticeably improved. Tom felt a sigh of relief. He didn't know which hurt more, the loss of Del or watching Wendy and the kids suffer from their loss. The three discussed the kids and reminisced a bit about their anniversary trip together to Israel and India, laughing about the missing tickets episode. Life was hard. One never knows what lies around the corner, but there was some measure of comfort for all three of them knowing they had taken the big 25th and 30th anniversary trip together.

Wendy shifted a bit and cleared her throat, "Tom and Vicki, do you remember when I asked you both to be my accountability partners? Well, I need to run something by you."

"Okay, sure, Wendy," Tom replied.

"What is it Wendy?" Vicki asked.

"Well, remember that guy I told you about whose wife died and they had four young children?" Tom and Vicki nodded their heads, curiosity filling their eyes. Wendy plunged ahead, "Well, his name is Russ, and we went out for coffee just to talk, ya know, because we both have lost a spouse. We talked for a long time and decided to meet again. It was so nice to talk to someone who understands. And you know what else? We both miss talking to someone of the opposite sex. You don't realize how much the companionship means to you, the comparing of notes—just the interaction. I mean, I get a lot from my girlfriends and he does from his guy friends, but it's just not the same. I know it seems fast, but I feel like I am already having strong feelings for him."

Vicki's eyes widened, but Tom seemed to take it in stride. "We would be happy to meet him if that would help," offered Tom.

Vicki could see Wendy's face cloud up, "What is it, Wendy?"

"Do you think I'm being disloyal to Del's memory?"

Tom spoke first, "No, Wendy, I don't. You were married to Del for over thirty years and you were faithful to him. Everyone knows you were loyal to him, but he's gone now."

Vicki reached for Wendy's arm, "Wendy, the human heart is large enough to make room. You don't have to trade the love you've had for Del for someone new in your life. I don't think Del would want you to be by yourself for the rest of your life if you met someone special."

Wendy teared up, "I'll never stop missing Del. I realize that now. But I need to move on. I can't bring him back by not marrying someone else."

"That's right," Vicki wiped a tear away, feeling her friend's pain.

Wendy continued, "Russ and I have talked, and he will always miss Marcia too, so I feel like we will have an understanding of honoring our respective spouses' memories."

Tom said, "That's a good point, Wendy. We'll be standing with you in prayer. You're a godly woman; you'll make the right decision. The spirit of God is in you to guide and counsel you. And we can all meet together if that will be a help to you."

Vicki was a little more protective, "Let's set a date. I want to meet this guy."

Tom nodded. He had meant what he had just said about Wendy having a good head on her shoulders, but there was also a part of him that wanted to know just exactly who this guy was.

Later, in the car Tom and Vicki discussed the whole situation. Everything was happening so fast and yet this new friend of Wendy's had faithfully taken care of his wife and children while she had battled cancer for over seven years. He must be a solid guy to do that, right? A feeling of wanting somehow, for the sake of Del, to make sure nothing disastrous happened to Wendy took over, and by the time they got home neither one of them was too sure about this Russ guy anymore. Well, Del could count on them. They would do the best job they could praying for Wendy and thoroughly checking this guy out.

A few weeks passed and Vicki was over at Wendy's home in Big Lake helping her take care of some of Del's personal belongings. "Where did Tom go off to this time?" Wendy asked.

Tom had left for another road trip to preach and then share about Oasis World Ministries. "He's starting to go on the road more to raise funds for the churches and wells. People are so responsive when he shows the video footage. It helps them connect more with the Indian people." Vicki's face creased with doubt, "I don't feel like I'm doing too much to help you today."

"Vicki, it's a big help just having you here. I just couldn't bring myself to do it alone in this house. Besides, Russ will be over shortly. You can meet him and get to know him while we eat supper together."

Vicki's cell phone rang. "Oh look," she smiled, "it's Tom."

"Hi, honey, how's it going?" Vicki wandered back to one of the bedrooms while Wendy kept looking through the papers in Del's desk. Tom's voice sounded excited on the phone. "Everything's going good," he said. They chatted for a few minutes, "So, you're going to meet Wendy's mystery man tonight?"

"Yeah, I'll give you the full report later tonight. Just a minute, Tom, I heard the doorbell ring. Maybe it's him." Vicki glanced down the hallway and then continued with Tom, "Oh, it must be one of Josh's friends, he's pretty young-looking. Well, you take care, honey, and I'll call you later." Vicki strolled down the hallway.

"Oh, Vicki, I want you to meet Russ. Russ, this is my dear friend Vicki."

Vicki's mouth dropped open. She reached out her hand to shake Russ's hand, but she could feel her mind go numb. It was worse than she and Tom had feared. Wendy had been driven off the edge of sanity by her loneliness! Here was a young-looking man with golden highlights in his hair, trim and dark-featured, who looked like he had strolled out of a gentleman's fashion magazine. Did Josh set her up with one of his friends, or what?

Finally Vicki muttered, "Oh, uh, um, yes, hi."

Then she bore her eyes into Wendy, her emotions rising up like a volcano ready to explode. "Wendy, I need to talk with you for a minute—now!"

Vicki grabbed Wendy's hand and dragged her back to the bedroom where she had just spoken with Tom. Wendy's face now mirrored Vicki's look of shock and disbelief. Vicki wasted no time. They were old friends, as close as sisters, and she was ready to let it rip. "WENDY—you didn't tell you were dating a kid!"

Wendy threw back her own volley, "He's not a kid!"

The match continued, "Well, he looks like a kid!"

"He's got four kids, Vicki, remember?"

"Well, how old is he exactly?"

"He's ten years younger than me if you really want to know."

"Oh, well, okay then." Vicki gave up game point to Wendy and mildly followed her down the hallway back to a bewildered Russ.

Vicki noticed Wendy had a little twinkle in her eyes as she announced, "Well, now that we are finished with introductions, how about dinner?"

Several days later Tom pulled his car into the best parking spot he could find at the restaurant. Vicki prepped him, "Okay, Tom, brace yourself. He's very young-looking, but Wendy assured me he's only ten years younger than she is."

It would be Tom's first meeting with Wendy's prospective husband, Russ. After introductions Tom couldn't help but feel sorry for Russ. He was obviously nervous, as though he was meeting the Godfather, or something. Wendy must have told him that if they didn't approve of him, she would seriously question their future together. Tom tried to put him at ease. But he couldn't help feeling like he wanted to peel back Russ's outward appearance so he could see what was really inside the guy. Tom never realized how protective he felt over Wendy until that evening. After Tom asked Russ about his faith, his marriage, and then his kids, they moved on to softer subjects, such as hobbies.

"Ever play any golf, Russ?"

"Sure, I have a membership with a club in Elk River."

The next day Vicki called Wendy. "Nice choice, Wendy. He obviously has a strong love for the Lord and is devoted to his family. He's got to be a pretty committed guy to have taken care of his wife and kids during her time of sickness. He even seems interested in traveling overseas."

"So, did he pass the test with Tom?"

"Yes, with flying colors. Both Tom and I wish you and Russ the best. Had you talked about any dates yet?"

"Yes, actually we were thinking about getting married in December. Then I asked him to come with me to India the end of January, and he said he would!"

"You have got some planning ahead of you, girl! How are your kids and Russ's kids feeling about all of this?"

"It will be an adjustment. But I think we're all ready to make some kind of family out of what we both have left: kind of like the old TV show, the Brady Bunch."

"But Wendy, it's like you're going backwards. Instead of all the freedom you now have, you'll be back to a whole houseful of kids. Are you ready for this? Have you really thought it through?"

"Yes, I have, Vicki. I've sought the Lord on this and have asked him to give me a mother's heart for Russ's kids and I believe he has. It's hard to describe what I feel towards Russ's kids. It must be close to what adoptive parents go through. This child is not my birth child, but is mine anyway. It's funny, Del and I always talked about having more than two kids, but we never did. Now I'll have four more, talk about a double portion of blessings."

Chapter Fourty Six

It's Time

Once in a while Tom and his sister, Beth, would reminisce about the good old days of Jesus People Church, wondering how everyone was doing. Inside both of them there was a longing to somehow reconnect with everyone.

They didn't want to go back and relive JP, but they wanted to revisit the memories that were so significant in shaping their lives. It was the people. JP had been community, one that had served a larger cause, a focus greater than themselves.

God had done so much. It really was *His* church, after all. Time had mellowed thoughts and feelings and hindsight had given more understanding to what had happened and why the church had fallen apart. It wasn't so much who did what anymore. Years of church experience had taught them much about wrestling with the powers of darkness and that humans were just that—human.

God had brought healing in both Tom and his sister Beth's life, also with Vicki and Troy. But maybe there were others out there who still needed a touch from the Lord and a way to complete the healing process God had begun in their lives.

One winter day, after several years of thinking about the people from JP, Beth was struck with a deep desire to organize a JP Reunion. It persisted all day. Many years of longing to be reunited again culminated inside of her, until she couldn't stand it another minute. That afternoon, while gazing at the rest of winter quietness on the landscape of her yard, she grabbed a pen and pad of paper and began to write down everything she had been thinking about all day. More ideas came. She wrote and wrote, excitement filling her body. She would have to run it by Tom. That would be her confirmation if this was truly from the Lord or not. Beth prayed one more time, "Maybe this is your timing, Lord. Maybe the season is right for us to come together again." She knew one of her nephews was having a choir recital that night. She would tell Tom then and see what his reaction would be. In the meantime, she would pray.

Later that evening Tom walked into Armstrong High School and, after shaking off the chilly stroll from the parking lot, settled into a good spot to listen to Jon's choir performance. About five minutes before the performance began, Tom noticed his sister Beth working her way through the room searching for him. "Hi, Beth, you made it," Tom said, smiling at his sister.

She had barely sat down when out came, "Hey! You won't believe the idea I had today!"

Tom asked, "What?"

He was used to Beth's ideas. They had been collaborating on many things over the years and this was nothing new.

"A JP Reunion, that's what! I've got pages filled with ideas and plans!"

Tom's mouth opened slightly; he felt his breath catch. As Beth rattled off all the ideas she could think of, his eyes were boring holes into her. No, more like past her, to a deep place of thought. Observing his expression, she said, "Tom—what?"

She continued, "What? Say something! You're staring at me like

I'm crazy!"

Finally Tom responded, "Guess what I thought of today?"

"What?" Beth asked.

Tom asked another question, "Guess what I wrote down ideas for today?"

Now Beth was going crazy, but she suddenly was getting the picture and her reply came out in a hushed whisper, "What…?" There was an understanding in the silence.

Beth softly said, "*It's time.*"

Tom looked at his sister, "Let's move forward with this and see where God takes it. If it's the right timing, things will fall into place. If not, then we need to wait."

Beth was ready for action. "Okay, we can both call a few people, and a few of the old staff, to see what they think." She paused a moment, "I'll call Patti Worre. She has always expressed interest in a JP Reunion."

The next day Beth pressed the phone to her shoulder as she dialed Worre's number. "Hello," a familiar voice from the past answered the phone.

"Patti? This is Beth Hammer, Tom Elie's sister."

"Oh, I recognize the voice, Beth. How are you?"

After a few minutes of greetings, Beth told Patti about the day that both she and Tom had felt compelled to list out a rough sketch of ideas about having a JP Reunion. "So what I'm wondering, Patti, is if you think it's time and if you would consider helping us?"

Patti fired off her answer like a bullet, "Absolutely!"

Beth had to laugh, same old Patti, full of enthusiasm, "I'm so glad you can be part of this."

"You know, I've kept a lot of JP memorabilia. Maybe we could use it for some kind of walk-down-memory-lane-video."

"That's awesome, Patti, bring whatever you've got," Beth's pulse quickened with anticipation.

For the first planning meeting, about a dozen people gathered at Tom and Vicki's home in New Hope. They met several times over the next four months, and then a larger organizational meeting was planned for July 20th. The former JP staff members were contacted and those who wanted to come were to meet at the building with the large cream pillars, the one JP had previously owned on 24th and Nicollet in Minneapolis, which was now Twin Cities Fellowship Church. The meeting started with prayer that warm summer evening. Tom was at the piano leading the worship. Tom's parents, Al and Ruth, were there and marveled at how the worship was immediately in the heavens just like it was in the past at JP. Ruth looked around and saw the hunger of all the people there. They had a longing to worship together again in the Spirit as they used to. That deep hunger had lasted over fifteen years. And now in the presence of their spiritual enemies, those demons of darkness that had sought to destroy them, these Children of God sat down to a feast especially prepared by their Good Shepherd.

For Tom, it was more than just a chance to travel down memory lane. It was essential that the reunion would be a time of healing for people. He looked over the gathering in the room. Simply by word of mouth people had been contacted and in turn they had contacted others who might be interested in organizing the reunion. One hundred fifty people had come and offered to help. The former pastors were also there, helping wherever they could. A look of humility and servanthood, rather than an agenda of their own, was on their countenance and in their demeanor, as well as the others who had come to the meeting. They all just wanted to be together again. This wasn't another run-of-the-mill reunion. This was a *family* reunion.

Tom was at the piano, but he wasn't leading the meeting. One of the former senior pastors was sitting in the back, and after a time of worship someone called back to him asking if he would please come up to the front and pray. Dennis slowly walked to the front. When he reached the front, he looked out at everyone and was so overcome with emotion that he couldn't talk. Finally, he managed, "Let's just sing."

So they sang one of the old JP songs and after Dennis got himself under control enough to talk, he said, "I don't need any honor. And I don't deserve any honor. But I want to tell you what man deserves the honor. It's the guy behind the piano."

Dennis turned toward Tom and asked him to please come and stand by his side. The two men embraced and Dennis continued to hug Tom as if all the years were coming out of him. Tom was able to hug with true forgiveness. Never in his wildest dreams had he thought anything like this would ever happen. There were a few audible sobs of joyful crying around the room, but it was only the beginning of what God had planned for His Sheep.

After the time of worship, everyone settled into about a dozen committees to plan the practical logistics of the reunion. There would be music, a service of some type, a reception time, and what else? The date was set for September, with an outdoor picnic planned for the next day. The big question was, where would they hold the reunion? Should they charge people or take an offering? They needed a budget, didn't they? And how were they going to get the word out? Finally, the answer came for a location. Pastor Randy Morrison, who had been a part of the prayer ministry at Jesus People Church, heard about the JP Reunion and offered the use of the facilities at Speak the Word Church for the Friday night service on September 8, 2000.

One desire came to the forefront above all other planning details: a time of prayer, healing, and reconciliation would be made available. People contacted Beth with words of encouragement that

God wanted more than just the typical reunion. A letter came with the same scripture that had kept coming back to Beth over and over from Isaiah 61:1-3:

The Spirit of the Sovereign Lord is on me, because the Lord has anointed me to preach good news to the poor. He has sent me to bind up the brokenhearted, to proclaim freedom for the captives and release from darkness for the prisoners, to proclaim the year of the Lord's favor and the day of vengeance of our God, to comfort all who mourn, and provide for those who grieve in Zion—to bestow on them a crown of beauty instead of ashes, the oil of gladness instead of mourning, and a garment of praise instead of a spirit of despair. They will be called oaks of righteousness, a planting of the Lord for the display of his splendor. (NIV)

Another person called on the phone with the same scripture. Someone else called about a dream she had concerning the healing and reconciliation God wanted to do in people's lives, with each other and with God. People also kept telling Tom and Beth that it was the right timing. Even five years ago it would have been premature to have the reunion. God was in the midst of this reunion and it was according to his calendar. Ministry teams were arranged and people began to pray for God's Spirit to have his way at the JP Reunion.

As people began to leave that night, Beth and Tom caught sight of each other, "Oh, Tom, I can't believe we are back in the same JP Nicollet building together with all these familiar faces. The memories that came flooding back were incredible. And the worship—it was like we were there again!"

"I know. Isn't God good?" replied Tom. "And the response of everyone working together to help with the reunion—it was like the good old days when we worked together at JP."

Beth snickered, "Everyone looked a little older too."

Tom smiled, "You mean even me?"

Beth explained, "Well, I'm used to seeing you so…I mean, I know we are all older, but with you and Vicki it's been so gradual. Some of these people I haven't seen for almost fifteen years."

Vicki came over and asked, "What's going on over here?" her usual smile beaming. "Wasn't it great to see everybody?"

"Yeah, we were just discussing how young everyone still looks," Tom said with mock sincerity.

As Patti Worre left that night, she commented to the threesome, "What an evening! It was like a family who hadn't talked for a while and had to warm up to one another, even apologize and forgive a little. But once we all got going, it was like being transported back in time. It felt like we were part of this great cause again. God is in this reunion. I know he's going to do something absolutely amazing!"

Soon postcards were passed out or mailed, word of mouth traveled along a human web of connecting relationships across the Twin Cities, the nation, and the world. A web site was set up about the Jesus People Church Reunion. Was it really happening?

As word spread, people started making plans to travel from out of state, including George and Kathy Ridge who had been part of the JP Singers. They had been on the bus tour when Tom, standing in his bathrobe, had awoken everyone to morning taps on his trumpet.

Some, though, struggled about whether to come. One of the former pastors of JP looked at himself in the mirror hung in the dorm room at the recovery center. It felt strangely familiar to be here, as if he was repeating history. "Park House was a long time ago, wasn't it, buddy?" He asked out loud to no one.

He had been contacted about the reunion and it had sparked memories of JP. He could see Tom Elie flipping hamburgers in the kitchen at Park House and he smiled briefly. Part of him wanted desperately to see everyone and be with his old church family again, but the man who had shared the Gospel with people and seen thousands come to faith in Jesus Christ over the years, as one of JP's senior pastors, didn't exist anymore. No, he had better sit this one out. Then from somewhere inside of him came a prayer, "It's up to you, God. This one's in your hands."

Soon a call came. A friend would pick him up for the rehearsal and the reunion.

A rehearsal had been arranged the night before the reunion and Kathy and George Ridge had arrived from the Dallas area. It was decided that George and the JP Singers would begin the time for worship as they had done at JP for many years. Next, Tom, John Worre, and Jane Thompson, the vocal trio, Spirit and Truth, practiced each song a couple of times. It was as natural as if they had practiced together the previous week. It was all still there inside all three of them, just waiting to be sung together. They simply played a chord for the first song and began singing. Those around them in the room looked up mesmerized; some began tearing up while others smiled as if seeing a long-lost friend. People were commenting on how they should get that trio going again, maybe record again. At least tour a little.

The former senior pastors were milling around greeting people. Their faces were aglow with the beauty of the Lord, which comes from experiencing the mercy and forgiveness of the Lord. They were travel-weary souls of the world, but now they had come home. It was like a rest by the still waters that the Psalmist David wrote in Psalm 23 as a young shepherd. The past was in the past; they could go forward and so could Jesus People Church. What the devil had set out to destroy—God was restoring right before their eyes. There was much laughter and a sweet presence of the Lord filled the building that night as people rehearsed, got reacquainted, and prayed for the next day.

Beth would later recount, "The rehearsal was like a preview of the next day. It felt totally right, not rushed, not stressed or out of order, and without wrong motives. It all just fell into place."

On a beautiful late summer evening, Friday, September 8, 2000, the sanctuary at Speak the Word Church was comfortably filled with 1,000 people. Beth opened the service with the scripture from Isaiah 61 that had been confirmed to her by many others for this gathering, and then it was time to sing to the Lord. As George led the worship with the JP Singers, it was as if they were all transported through a time machine back to the days of JP. He even tried a few of his famous segues from song to song. But no one requested that he play his two standards from the earliest days: *Born Free* and *Greensleeves*. George had only known how to play these two songs on the organ and had rotated them for offering and service prelude at their first building off of Lake Street.

People's arms went up in praise to God. Ruth felt like a cloud opened up and the praise was ascending to the throne room. She noticed people crying all over the church auditorium. Many of the old tunes were sung again including some from the Jesus People music songbook published in 1980. Then the trio, Spirit and Truth, got in place on the platform. Tom couldn't believe he was standing there with Jane Thompson and John Worre. As they began to sing, the presence of the Lord seemed to hover and bring a hush to the room. Their voices still blended like a perfectly fitted garment. Many people began to cry, including John. The years melted away and they were three young kids again singing their hearts out for Jesus.

After the slide show of memories, one of the former senior pastors came up to the platform and looked over the crowd. He had aged, along with everyone else, but a youthful joy played in his eyes. Then it was as if he drew himself up from the ashes of the past and stated,

"I want you all to know: it is well with my soul."

Instantly, applause rang throughout the crowd. He then took a few minutes to relate how he had come back to the Lord and his new journey with the Lord of the Harvest. Then the other senior pastor walked up. As he stood before his former flock, he, too, took in the moment. Through the years he had left God, but God had not left him. "I just want you to know that the same is true for me. I'm back on the right track again."

Again the crowd responded. There had been so many questions over the years. To be certain, people had gone through feelings of anger and loss, but once they had worked through forgiveness toward their leaders, they began to see them as people who had become prisoners of darkness. Twenty years had taught everyone a lot about life. Each one could look back over the years and see things they wished they could have done differently too. Time had also taught them that leaders are people—not God. Their dependence must never rest on leaders or on the apparent success of a church, but on God alone. Through the humble words their former pastors spoke, came restoration and conclusion to their bittersweet journey of the past. The Holy Spirit had been preparing many hearts for this moment and people were ready.

At the close of the service, people were invited to the front altar area for prayer. Nearly fifty people broke into ministry teams with pamphlets of scriptures to be used for ministry and to be taken home for those who wanted them. Many people gathered around the altar to pray for one another. Some were in a place of spiritual discouragement, while others knew they needed to get back on their faith journey with God. The detour from God had to stop. Many who came to the front altar had slipped away from the Lord in the confusion surrounding the breakup of JP. Now they were hungry for the Lord and wanted a fresh start with him. As people prayed together, there were audible sobs as old wounds were healed and souls restored with the Great Shepherd.

For Tom, personally, his hurts of being let down by men he admired and trusted, and then himself being misunderstood by others and thought of as a traitor, finally dissipated into the winds of forgiveness. He had tried to walk in forgiveness as much as possible, but this day of reconciliation and restoration was like a day of independence! The captives were totally set free—wounds healed—his and others. He would no longer walk with a limp.

He still didn't totally understand why everything had happened, but he didn't have to understand it anymore. Joy was bursting out of his soul.

People lingered afterwards enjoying refreshments and their conversation continued. People simply could not bear to leave their spiritual relatives.

"How many years has it been since the break up of JP?"

"Close to fifteen years."

"I think one thing we realize now, since the demise of JP, is that, for the most part, people have held onto their faith. So many people I've talked to said that even though the hurts and disappointments were huge, over time they came to see that God was still with them."

One person reflected, "And I think people idolized the leaders a little bit. Our worship should be reserved for God alone, not spiritual leaders."

Another group, conversing at a table and sipping punch, concluded, as did so many other people that night: "So much energy was poured into those musicals and plays. Every member of JP was involved in some way. We all looked for the prize of the evening: watching spiritually hungry people find Christ and commit their lives to him."

One person joked, "Yeah, man, we were the hippie generation, no shoes for the ushers—"

"And no bras for the ladies!" someone else cut in amongst laughter.

"Then the sophisticated people came and we finally had class! The funny thing is, you would see fur coats next to sweatshirts and jeans, and it didn't matter to anyone."

"It was just so hard to be in community with all these people and then not see them anymore. Working shoulder to shoulder on so many events, and watching God work through our humble efforts, fused us into one piece. Then the bomb blew us into so many pieces."

"But it wasn't the end. God hadn't jumped ship. We just couldn't see through the fire and smoke that he was still there in our midst," someone else said.

One thoughtful, soft-spoken person interjected, "Even a destiny can be an idol. JP had a powerful history-making destiny. I think we could all sense that. Maybe we paid too much attention to how good that felt instead of setting our affections on the Lord."

Another added, "We'll never know what all played into the ending of JP, but we can learn from it."

"And praise God for all the good that came out of JP."

"You're right. There was a lot of good that came out of JP."

Meanwhile, Vicki continued her conversation with Patti Worre and a few others. "*Scrooge* was a good opportunity to bring friends or relatives to JP and see a first-rate production. It blew away their stereotype of a charismatic church: people swinging from the chandeliers and rolling in the aisles."

Patti began laughing, "Well, after all, with a name like Jesus People it did sound kind of weird back in those days. I remember comments like, 'Oh my goodness! She's going to church more than once a month and tithing?'"

"Mind control! A cult for sure!" Vicki pulled down her glasses to the end of her nose for extra emphasis.

"I can't believe how many times I had heard Jesus People described as some kind of cult," Patti responded.

It was hard to leave the reunion and the glow of the evening. People were still caught up in conversation, feeling the returned warmth of the glory days of Jesus People Church and all that it had stood for. When would they ever be together like this again? Even people who had totally walked away from Christianity came, "I felt compelled to be here. I heard about the reunion and something stirred up within me. I had been a part of a great cause. I just had to come. And I'm glad I did. I'm so glad I did!"

Finally, though, people began to disperse. Tom and John Worre had stopped to talk a moment between mingling with people and saying farewells, when Roger approached them. John put his hand on Roger's shoulder, "Roger, it's so good to have you here. I'm so glad you came."

Tom was looking on. He realized how much he loved these men—and all the former staff people. They had labored in God's harvest fields together. And it was fruit that had endured. Many people at the reunion were talking about all the people across the United States they had run into at various churches and other places that had been saved through the ministry of Jesus People Church.

Roger looked at Tom, "And you, you've been faithful all these years, Tom."

Tom didn't know what to say, he felt humbled by Roger's kind words. Here was a broken man before him, but one who knew the grace of the cross intimately. "It's how we finish, Roger." Tom and Roger shook hands and then they embraced for the last time.

George and Kathy Ridge were saying their good-byes to everyone and hugged Tom and Vicki before leaving the reunion. "Thanks, Tom and Vicki, for bringing us all together again," George said. "The same spirit that had been with us earlier was here today, as if time stood still, we all flowed together in the spirit and picked up where we left off."

Kathy added her thoughts, "It was such a blessing for us to see so many things that God had done over the years for our friends. What a joyous time of celebration that God had allowed us to be a part of such a great move of God. Thank you both so much."

George couldn't resist one last joke, "Maybe some JP Reunion T-shirts will soon be available. We could wear them and go on another hike together. Ha!" George was referring to the long hike with his wife, Kathy, and Vicki, when they were both very much with child.

Kathy gave him a playful shove on his arm, "Oh George! That was a horrible day!"

Tom and Vicki joined in the laughter, as they thought of the two militant hiker men encouraging their pregnant wives to keep up the pace.

Winter came with spring on its heels when Tom received a call while at home from the director of a Minneapolis Christian rehabilitation center for substance abuse. Tom sat in silence after learning that Roger had died from complications of pneumonia; his heart hadn't been able to take the backup of fluid in his lungs. The funeral would be later that week. Tom lamented the fact that he already had a trip to India in place and would have to miss the funeral. He ruminated on what the director had said about Roger: that Roger had been doing so well in the program and had sat in the front row eager to hear and learn. Tom reflected on God's grace to take Roger home at this point in his life.

The tragic news of Roger's death six months after the reunion brought a stunned appreciation of the timing of the reunion for Beth and many others. Beth's neighbors gathered regularly on Saturday mornings for a neighborhood Bible study and had been praying for the reunion during its planning. They were in shock at hearing about

Roger's death. Beth relayed the news to them slowly and methodically as she processed her thoughts, "For Tom and me, and the people involved in the JP Reunion—just to know you had the timing, and the right idea to have a reunion. God was so merciful before Roger died to have given him an opportunity to tell those at the reunion that he was back with the Lord." Beth continued with emotion in her face, "So many things that happened at the reunion were healing; it's amazing to see how God could use something like that."

Chapter Fourty Seven

First Corinthians 2:9

After getting home from another busy day at Praise, Tom opened the letter from James, dated January 1, 2001. The group photo caught his eye. Studying the picture, Tom smiled as he found James right in the middle holding a certificate. His brown face framed with short-cropped black hair and wire-rimmed glasses, held a thoughtful and happy countenance. The ethnically-mixed group of black and white men surrounding James wore celebratory expressions. A few were downright grinning from ear to ear, proud of their friend.

Old memories flooded Tom's mind as he sat down in a comfortable chair to read the letter. In his mind's eye, he could picture the neighborhood surrounding the Northeast building. It had been an interesting first meeting with James at his home with the dilapidated front porch. Agitated at first by the white preacher boy coming to his front door, James had eventually come to church a few times and had given his life to Christ. However, he had soon backslid into the drug culture again. But that hadn't deterred Tom from pursuing the relationship. Tom laughed as he remembered how the Holy Spirit would prompt him to go over and knock on doors and windows of that creepy house every Sunday morning, telling James to get up for church!

Dear Pastor Tom,

As the new year starts, I have been thinking about all that has happened in my life during the last few years. Pastor Tom, you have been so instrumental in helping to change my life from one of hopelessness to hope. I am writing to thank you for caring, for being persistent, and for helping me and many others.

Without your efforts, who knows where I would be today—perhaps in jail or dead. I remember all the times you persisted in coming to my home on Monroe Street. Sunday after Sunday you never gave up. You were a mentor for me, a man of God I could truly respect and appreciate. You kept urging me to get to know the Lord Jesus Christ. You arranged for me to come to Minnesota Teen Challenge, and when it did not work out the first time, you still did not give up. Within minutes after my telling you that I had a desire to return, you arranged for my re-entry. As you know, I went on to graduate, served a six-month internship, and have worked full-time with the men's program for over two years.

Today I can proudly say that the Lord leads my life. I have been totally free for almost four years. I have a fulfilling life working with others who face the same problems from which God delivered me. I am now helping to impart into their lives what God has imparted into mine. Leading others to Jesus is the greatest joy of my life.

This past year has been a true blessing in so many ways.... In December I received my ministerial license through the Pentecostal Church of God. I have now been offered an opportunity to speak at Stillwater Prison as well as start Sunday evening services at Bread of Life Church in Minneapolis. The Lord is opening new opportunities for sharing my story and the good news of His miraculous love and power.

Again, thank you, Pastor Tom, for following the Lord's command. I pray that I will be able to serve as an example of Christ's love as you have shown me. May God bless you, your family, and the ministry in 2001!

Your Brother in Christ,
James

Tom noticed a verse at the top of the letter highlighted in the decorative perimeter from First Corinthians 2:9 "No eye has seen, no ear has heard, no mind has conceived what God has prepared for those who love him." (NIV)

Chapter Fourty Eight

Del's Well

Ryan wanted to go to India. The youth group at Praise, known as Spirit Fire, had raised money for a church and a well. He began making plans and popped into his dad's office at the church, "Is Jessica going, Dad?"

"Yes, Wendy is going too, and they're going to dedicate a church and well in Del's memory. Russ is also coming along; this will be his first trip overseas."

"Sounds like a cool trip. I still remember my first missions trip to Mexico when Jessica and I sat together on the bus."

"India's different than Mexico, so you better get yourself ready to go in every way possible. Make sure you're prayed up, Ryan; it's a different spiritual climate than you've ever been in before."

Ryan honestly wondered if it could really be any worse than some of the other South American countries he had been to, but all he said was, "Okay, Dad." He knew his dad was a clean freak and got excited by blood and other things that didn't bother him, not to mention he was a lot younger than his dad. He would pray, he always did before every trip; only he just didn't think India would be the overwhelming challenge everyone made it out to be.

The doors of the car opened and there was the ramp to the stage. Just off the plane in India, Tom led the way for Ryan, Vicki, Wendy, Russ, and Jessica. They walked like zombies from the car to the platform for the first night of the festival. A crowd of several thousand Indian people had been singing for an hour while waiting for the white guests from America. The travelers had all slept in the car and now were fighting hard against the overwhelming effects of jet lag.

"Oh, my eyes," Ryan moaned. "My contacts are like dry eggs stuck on my eyes. I can…hardly...see anything." He knew he was in some city in the Andhra Pradesh state, but he couldn't recall the name at the moment.

The group weaved here and there making their way up the rocking gangplank to their row of seats at the back of the platform. Hand-woven rugs covered the somewhat rickety stage. People with dark faces, adorned in beautiful fabrics, watched with interest as they filed one by one into their seats. Vicki and Ryan watched Tom perk right up like a wind-up toy. He was here for this moment: to bring the Gospel to a dry and thirsty land, full of souls searching for spiritual truth.

Ryan leaned over to his mom, "He's a machine, Mom. How does he do it?"

"It's the Call of God inside him, Ryan. I don't know how he does it, either."

Despite the bright lights shining on the stage, one by one, members of the group bent their heads in apparent prayer while Tom preached. At the sound of Tom giving the altar call they all seemed a bit refreshed and watched as people took the courageous step of coming forward publicly to confess faith in Jesus Christ, "the One True God," as Tom had put it. Ryan sat back amazed. Over the years he had seen his dad do hundreds of altar calls, but never anything like this. The atmosphere was charged with a spiritual dimension he had never experienced. The anointing of God's presence was so strong.

Then Tom started praying for people to get healed. Since his first trip to India, Tom had seen many people healed in Jesus' name who had been deaf or blind. Ryan looked at their happy faces. This was true joy the whole world could not buy with all its wealth, stealth, and power.

The sun rose over India, as another day began for the group of Minnesotans far way from the hustle and bustle of the American suburbs. They climbed back in the car for another day of seminars, preaching in villages, women's meetings, and evening festivals.

"Ryan, how would you like to preach one night this week?"

Ryan hesitated, "I don't know, Dad, this is your gig, not mine. I'm just here for the youth group."

Tom told him to think about it and let him know. Ryan did think about it, and one night later that week he could feel the power of God inside as he preached to the sincere dark faces of the Indian people. They were obviously interested in what the son of the "American spiritual guru man" had to say. Working with the translator, Ryan preached the sermon he felt the Lord had given him for these people. Six hundred people responded to the call to follow Jesus, as the One True God. After praying with them to receive Jesus as their Lord and Savior, Ryan began asking people to come forward to be healed by the power of Jesus. A little boy, who hadn't walked since he was born, was carried by his father to the front of the stage. Ryan bent down and prayed for the little boy, his heart breaking with compassion. In a few minutes the boy's father was amazed as he watched his son walking, and then running back and forth across the stage.

Ryan asked the crowd, "Who healed this boy?"

The crowd understood. "Jesus!" they called back.

"That's right. It was Jesus. The same Jesus who died to make payment for your sins and mine. And after three days in a rock hollowed out for a grave, he came alive again to prove to the world that he was who he said he was, that he really did shed his blood on the cross for all of our sins. He is the One True God. This wonderful Jesus healed this little boy tonight. Let's say thank you to Jesus by clapping our hands."

Joyful exclamations erupted. Ryan clapped along with everyone. He would remember this night forever. People stood at the altar with tears streaming down their faces. They had just found the One True God: Jesus. Their searching was over. For years they had felt the heavy burden of appeasing angry gods; that burden was now lifted. And in its place was a love so deep and pure that words could not express what joy they now knew.

Tom turned toward his son, "Just think, Ryan, this is the first time many of these people have ever heard of Jesus."

"Wow, Dad, it just blows my mind. It's true; the fields of wheat are white, ready for harvest. People are waiting all over India to hear something that brings life to their souls."

On the way back to the hotel Tom explained the follow-up program to Ryan. "The directors do a good job working with all the pastors in the area who want to help, and the lay people help, too. It's a job for everyone to help these new believers grow in their faith."

Ryan was tired and ready for bed; yet there was a spark of excitement left in him wondering what tomorrow would bring.

Another day in India and Tom had just finished up with a night of preaching at the evening festival. He looked over the group of new believers who prayed to receive Jesus Christ as their Lord and Savior. Tom wanted to make sure they had really thought this whole thing through, instead of making an emotional decision based on the impulse of the moment. With the utmost respect he asked them, "Now, did you mean that with all your heart?"

They all nodded their heads; some had tears running down their warm brown faces. "Good. There are pastors here and other people who can help you to follow Jesus. Get to know them and start spending time with them. Another important thing to do is talk with Jesus every day about everything in your life and thank him for his love for you. You have been given a booklet to read—these are words from the Bible. Read from this booklet as much as you can or have someone else read it to you. Don't forget to meet with other people who believe in Jesus at a nearby church every Sunday."

Now he would have to entrust these new precious souls into God's care. His part was done. The rest was up to the indigenous believers. More and more people were being trained to mentor these new disciples of Christ. The pastors' and leaders' conferences during the day were packed full with men and women desiring to learn more and be part of what God was doing in their midst. For too long India had been a dark place with only a spattering of hope here and there. Maybe the revival everyone had been praying and hoping for had finally come.

The bright afternoon sun was beating down in a clear blue sky, baking the air. Ryan sat in the Jeep while it jostled through traffic and animals navigating through tangled streets filled with ruts of dust. He sat in stunned silence. Vicki looked over at him, "What's going on, honey?"

Ryan let out a sigh. He wasn't about to let his pride cover his ego at this point. "It's so completely different here. From the first moment you walk off the plane the air smells different," he said.

"You mean like the animals?"

"Not only that, but the cooking smells, the plants, the people, and even the dirt seems to smell different."

"Yes, you're right. You can go down a street and every block the smell will change from offensive to a fragrant floral scent, and then to curry cooking on a stove."

"Exactly! And not only that, I think, too, just the sense that this is a different spiritual place. I felt a little oppressed when I got off the airplane in Bombay, I mean Mumbai. In the last few days I keep thinking this is one "spiritually dark" place."

"That's true, but there is also hope and light. Every night when your dad calls people forward to receive Jesus, I see the light of the Gospel break through the darkness."

Wendy who had been listening added, "Yes, I can see it in their eyes. Before they pray they are dark and afraid, and after they pray to receive Jesus, the light of heaven is in their eyes. It's the most beautiful transformation. I'm so glad we have a seat on the platform. Just watching what the Holy Spirit does during the altar call is amazing."

Suddenly, a car pulled around another smaller car and headed straight for their vehicle. Everyone held their breath while the driver calmly pulled onto the side of the road at the last possible second. The roar of the engine blew past their ears.

"Man, that was close. I could have written my name in the dust on the side of that truck!" Ryan exclaimed. "That's another thing I don't get about India. Who taught these people to drive?"

Tom spoke up, "Ryan, sometimes I close my eyes. It's just their way. When you come to India you have to take it the way it is."

"Dad, how can you take it? I mean, you come here time after time."

"It's the people, Ryan. God loves them and wants them to find him. If I carry the gift of the Gospel with me, I think about how priceless that is and what a privilege it is to bring it to these people. Don't they deserve a chance to hear what I have heard, what you have heard, about the Lord being their salvation from sin and hell?"

Ryan thought for moment, "You really love these people, don't you, Dad? I mean, it's not about getting big evangelist notches on your Gospel gun belt, is it?"

"Ryan, I do love these people, and not because I have to. The more I learn about them, the more I find to respect about them. Of course, there are always deficiencies in every culture. America has its share of strengths and weaknesses, too."

Everyone fell silent for the remainder of the trip to the hotel as they passed by homes and shops mingled with people and animals.

•

The first week was almost over for the Minnesota travelers and now the day had finally come. Ryan smiled over at Jessica during the dedication service in memory of Del. Her chic black glasses matched her dark hair and features. She responded with a sad, but knowing look, that only long-time friends can exchange. They would each carve out their own lives as time went by, each one taking different paths, but there would always be that special bond forged over years as playmates, travel buddies, co-laborers in the youth ministry, and through the loss of her father.

Jessica smiled again, there was joy to be had this day. "My dad was such a great guy; I'm so proud of him. You know, he was always helping people, and to see a lasting legacy of his love for people means a lot to me."

"I think this is the way your dad would have wanted it, Jess. He would have taken his last few thousand bucks and built a church and a well for someone else." Ryan let out a sigh. Jessica went over to her mom and they hugged and cried as they read over the plaque one more time before leaving the village. In golden letters inscribed on a sleek black tile, it read, first in English and then in Telegu:

OASIS WORLD MINISTRIES
"Touching our World with God's Love"

In loving memory of
Pastor DELROY GRAGES
Big Lake, Minnesota, USA.

On 3rd February, 2001
Andhra Nagar, Nizamabad (Dist.) INDIA

Tom and Russ were looking over the mechanics of the well. "Russ, you're an amazing guy to come halfway around the world to watch your new wife dedicate a building and a well in honor of her first husband."

Russ squinted up at Tom in the bright sunshine. He lifted his hand to his dark eyebrows, "It's a privilege to be here, Tom; I'm really glad I came. Wendy lost Del and I lost Marcia. So, I guess we have an understanding of how you can still care about your first spouse and make room in your heart for someone else."

Vicki overheard what Russ had said as she walked over to the well. "It's a day of closure for both of them," she commented. "Another step in their journey of grief."

Wendy and Jessica slowly made their way back arm in arm to the group by the well. "What a day this has been," Wendy said.

Vicki gave her friend a warm hug and a sweet kiss, "You did such a good job today, Wendy. You were so gracious in sharing your heart with the people of this village. And the preaching you've done at the women's meetings has been excellent."

Ryan piped in his two cents worth, "I bet Del is looking down and just smiling away at you."

"Yeah, I think he is, Ryan," Jessica said. "I can feel him here with us today."

Before the group left, they learned of an interesting story about the well. The government had tried to drill a well seventeen times in that area. For Del's church, they came in and prayed over the well before they drilled and got fresh clean drinking water on the first try. Later, the people in the village were telling the Christians, "Your God knows where the water is! He can make it come!"

After dropping off the others at the airport, Tom, Ryan, and Jessica, along with their driver, wound through the maze of the city to meet up with the festival crew for another week of meetings and church dedications. It seemed oddly quiet in the car without Vicki and Wendy gasping about the traffic. Ryan began to feel queasy, "Oh, man, I think I'm getting carsick or something."

"After a whole week here?" Tom asked.

Jessica probed, "What did you eat last night?"

Ryan tried to think over yesterday's menu. The bumping of the uneven pavement didn't help matters. As they drove through the city to the place they would be staying, Ryan heard the call to prayer from the local mosque. Later on that night as he lay in bed, he heard it again. In the morning the loud Arabic chanting of call to prayer awakened him. It made him feel as though he was in the Middle East rather than in India. It didn't help his indigestion, either. Tom looked over at him from his chair. He had gotten up early to read his Bible and pray, "How's it going, son?"

"Not too good, Dad." Ryan shuffled off to the bathroom again. He caught a glance of himself in the mirror and thought his appearance matched how his stomach felt—disgusting. No matter, it was time to get on the road again and head for a village. He could hear his dad calling Jessica's room to make sure she was up for the day; then a voice through the bathroom door, "I'm going to head down to the lobby to meet with Pastor Thimothi. I'll see you down there, okay?"

"Yeah…I'm coming."

Despite his fragile stomach, Ryan's face lit up like a department store sign once he saw the plaque on the stucco wall of the church next to the double front doors.

Sponsored by Spirit Fire Youth Group
Minneapolis, Minnesota U.S.A.

To know that on the other side of the ocean, teens in his youth group had made this day possible, was more than he could contain. He let out a holler of praise and thanksgiving to God. This work of God would continue to touch the lives of the people in this village. Not only would the building be a blessing, but also clean drinking water would be available to everyone who needed it, free of charge, with no discrimination against race, class, or creed.

Ryan stood before all the faces of the Indian people gathered inside the church for the dedication. The young good-looking energetic twenty-two-year-old youth pastor had been asked to preach at the dedication service. Sitting on the floor, women and young girls were on one side of the room. The other half was filled with men and boys with clean-shaved faces and clean shirts tucked inside their trousers. They were all wondering the same thing: Why would a young white man come all the way to their village on behalf of his young people's church group?

Ryan was able to share his heart about the youth group, Spirit Fire. The young people in America had something in common with everyone in the room on this dedication day. In the mid-day Indian heat, Ryan explained the need of all people to come into a spiritual relationship with the One True God: Jesus Christ.

Even with all the wealth of America, and the ability to move up and down the class system, they still needed a spiritual healer: Someone to save them from thousands of years of reincarnation, or as many Americans believe—sudden death, game over. The death of

Jesus and his resurrection provided the way to find God and to know him. A living Heavenly Father whose character is full of mercy and forgiveness, as well as justice. As the Indian musicians played their South Asian melodies, Ryan prayed with those who wanted to follow the One True God of the universe.

After Ryan concluded, he sat down next to his dad while glancing at the simple roof and newly painted walls adorned with scripture in Telegu. "Dad, I feel so humbled. We need to do more to raise the funds for another church and well."

Jessica agreed, "I just couldn't imagine how much difference these projects can make in the lives of these people until now."

Ryan continued, "I'm never going to take our church building for granted ever again. Sometimes I wish it were bigger or in better shape or something, but I won't anymore. Well, except if the furnace goes out in the winter again."

Chapter Fourty Nine

Pressing On

After Tom had resigned from Northeast, he took a few more India trips and then approached the Crystal church board. "I've always thought that if I'm going to leave this church or any church, it has to be with the favor of all, like a send off in the Book of Acts, where it says, 'it seemed good to the brethren,' instead of leaving because I'm hurt or running away. I have had plenty of opportunities to be hurt, but I've always prayed and told the Lord, 'Where you lead me I will stay, until you lead me elsewhere.' In light of this, I think I should resign because I want to do evangelism across America and overseas. But I want you all to pray about it and think it through so it's a decision we make together."

A few weeks later, the church board and Tom met again. "We're honored to have you be our pastor. You're a world-class pastor. We want you to stay. Is there a way to do both, possibly up to half the time each month?"

Tom didn't know what to say. He hadn't expected a combination of doing both. "Are you sure about this? How do you see this working out practically speaking?"

Another gentleman spoke up, "We figured two weeks every month. We can increase the responsibilities of the associate pastors to fill in the gaps."

Tom spoke with gratitude in his heart, "I just want to say that I'm both honored and humbled by your response. Let's try it for six months. If this plan hurts the church, then we'll have to figure out something else."

Tom left the meeting full of thoughts. As he drove home, he realized how unique his church was. Usually pastors were so busy they didn't feel they had time to go away on a missions trip, or they didn't feel they could raise the funds.

At home Tom told Vicki what the board had said, "Do you think it will work? It's a bit of an odd arrangement."

Vicki sat down across from Tom and said to him, "I think the reason our congregation is so different is because when they first voted us in, all they had was thirty-two voting members. Remember?"

Tom smiled. They had proved to be good people just as their former pastor had predicted. Vicki continued, "With God's help, and others, we built the congregation over the years with unchurched people. This is all they've ever known. They haven't been "churched" like other people who come from other churches. They think it's normal that you do these things. I've heard them: 'Well, yes, Pastor goes out and shares the Gospel and Pastor does missions work.' It's a natural thing for them."

Tom countered, "But I still get some flak wondering when I'll be back, or comments like, 'Are you leaving us again?' I wonder if it's fair to them?"

"But, honey, you always let them know from the pulpit when you will be gone and where you're going. And I think it helps them feel connected to you when you're gone and they get updates read to them on Sunday mornings. They are willing to share you with the world, Tom. I know they are."

Tom's countenance brightened, "Maybe we could do a live phone call from India. I bet Tom Hendricks could rig something up."

So began pastoral care via the cell phone. During his next trip to India, Tom called the church right in the middle of the service. Anticipation filled the air as everyone began to sing worship songs, knowing their pastor would be calling that morning. A few minutes later, sure enough, the phone rang, and Tom greeted all the folks back home in Crystal. The sound was so good it was hard to believe he was calling from India.

"Thanks, everybody, for praying. Things are going well here. It's 10:30 at night, so we had Sunday morning service, and also our first night of the second festival. Yesterday we dedicated two churches and two wells. At last week's festival we saw over 3,000 people come forward and receive Christ. There were also several healings."

In response to Tom's update, spontaneous applause filled the sanctuary with praise to their God and Savior!

Six months had gone by since the church board had released Tom to do mission work up to half of his time. When Tom met with them, all were very optimistic. "Actually, the church has grown more in population in the last six months than it has in a while."

Tom joked, "Well, in that case, maybe if I leave, it will really grow."

Another board member added to the first comment, "Overall, has it hurt the church? We all agree that, no, it has had just the opposite effect. It's broadened the vision of our people. It's been a stretching time for them in a positive way. We have seen them grow in their generosity in giving to people they have never met before."

Another member spoke up, "I think overall the congregation is proud that Praise is an integral part of what's happening in India. They are living beyond themselves, instead of focusing only on their church. The Great Commission isn't only for the Twin Cities, it's for the world. You're the one who taught us this in the pulpit, Pastor, and we listened."

Tom was amazed at the generosity of the people at his church. Not only were they willing to share their pastor with the world, but they gave financially as well. For a small congregation, it wasn't uncommon to receive an offering of $3,000 before he would leave on one of his trips to India.

After Tom started going to India four times or more a year, he was going to churches to raise funds almost every weekend. On Sundays Tom would get up at 6:00 a.m. and get ready for Sunday morning services in Crystal. After a full morning of ministry at Praise, Tom would have lunch and then drive to churches in Duluth, or Wisconsin, and other locations. Most of the time he didn't get back home until 1:00 a.m. Sundays were becoming a long grueling day after traveling to churches all week.

"Look, Tom, I believe in what you're doing in India, but you're wearing yourself out! I don't like you driving home so late at night when you are already tired."

"I know, honey, it gets pretty late. I'm going to ask the Lord what to do. There's got to be a better way to raise some more funds."

Vicki nodded with interest. "Let's talk to Beth about it."

Another confirmation of this idea of raising funds in a different way came from a friend in ministry. "Tom, have you thought about doing a banquet? It's a great way to raise the funds needed in one night."

Tom called Beth and she agreed to brainstorm with Vicki and him about ways to do a banquet. They agreed to invite everybody they knew. The number of tables began to grow. Tom and Vicki met with Beth and went over more details. Tom was getting excited as May 17, 2001, was approaching. "Who else do we know?"

"Tom, I have already filled four tables with every friend, neighbor, and relative I could think of," Beth said, "and Mom and Dad have given me enough names to fill four more tables."

"Who else can we ask? What about people from Praise?"

"Many people have responded. You know how supportive people at Praise are, Tom."

"How many tables do we have then?"

"Almost twenty-five tables," Beth replied.

"Who else can we ask? What about the program? How is that coming along?"

"Besides getting radio D.J., Chuck Knapp, to emcee, I'm not quite sure. What were you going to do for your presentation?"

"I want to let people know through visual means what is happening with their investments in Oasis, using pictures and charts…and maybe even facts to show how a simple thing like a fresh water well can change the life of an entire village."

Beth's sandy-brown eyebrows pushed together in anxiety, "This is a huge undertaking, Tom. I hope it all works out."

Tom flashed his trademark smile at his sister, "It will! And we'll know more what to do for next year!"

Beth sighed, "Can we get through this one first?"

After the banquet Beth, Vicki, and Tom, gathered around the kitchen table discussing everything while steam rose from their coffee cups. Tom was overflowing with excitement, "I'm awestruck! People were so supportive and generous. It's amazing that we raised $35,000 in one night! Glory to God!"

Beth and Vicki had that post-event glow when things turn out positively. Beth gave her assessment: "I think most of it went well, but next year we need to change a few things."

"So that means you'll help us do another banquet, Beth?" Tom asked with a grin.

Beth continued her thoughts by deftly ignoring her older brother, "Was our focus clear to the people?"

Vicki jumped in the fray, "How can we widen the circle of people to invite? We've all exhausted our list of personal contacts at 200 people."

"We'll just have to pray and ask God for more people to come," Beth said, "Maybe everyone who came this year would be willing to invite a few friends for next year." Vicki leaned her head into her hand, "So what are we trying to accomplish by having an Oasis World Ministries Banquet?"

Tom pointed out, "I think we're trying to raise awareness, getting the word out about what God is doing in India. The time of the harvest is now. The fields are ripe. People are spiritually thirsty and Hinduism is being questioned in the minds of many people."

Vicki concluded, "This whole thing is bigger than one person. It's gaining momentum and we have to recognize that and shift our ways of thinking for raising funds. What else could we do besides a banquet?"

The three musketeers, ragamuffins for Jesus Christ and the Harvest, sat back, took a sip of coffee, and wrote down notes for next year.

Tom was dead tired after another grueling trip to India. It was a good exhaustion, though. He thought over the blessings of God: miracles, salvation for thousands, church and well dedications. The pastors' and leaders' seminar had gone well and his health had been good, too. He missed Vicki terribly and was looking forward to getting home. All he had to do was get through the long flight in coach seating, which was always too short for his long Norwegian frame unless he got a seat in the exit row. Talking with other passengers helped pass the time and Tom was always willing to share the Gospel if travelers seemed spiritually open. So Tom started a conversation with the man seated next to him, who happened to be from Apple Valley, Minnesota. The man explained that he had been on a spiritual trek through India. He was involved in all kinds of belief systems blended into an eclectic philosophy and had been traveling all over the world searching for spiritual significance. Tom didn't contest anything the man said about various spiritual paths and practices; instead he listened patiently, learning that the man had been a former Lutheran. Then Tom began witnessing to the man, getting bolder in his approach by the minute.

Suddenly the man locked his eyes on Tom and pointedly declared, "You will turn from this Jesus within five years."

Without even pausing to think, Tom shot back, "I rebuke that in Jesus' name."

Tom knew it had to be a lie from the enemy, but it had been said with such force that it shocked him. He felt as if he had just had a conversation with the devil himself. Yet, he comforted himself that he had immediately responded from the depth of his soul by rebuking those evil words in Jesus' name, the Name above all names. Silence fell like a wall between them for the rest of the nine-hour trip from Mumbai to Amsterdam.

After Vicki picked him up at the airport, Tom relayed the whole story to her. Vicki's eyes widened, "You better call in the intercessors, Tom."

After the group of prayer warriors had gathered, Tom relayed the whole story to them. Pearl spoke up, determination glinting through her wire-rimmed glasses, "This is going to be hard to forget, but you have to remember that this man is a liar."

"Yes," Tom agreed. "But I can think of a lot of good men who have gone down. I don't want anything in my life that would cause me to do the same."

Pearl reminded Tom about all the prayer covering over his life and his family. "Tom, we wrestle against an enemy, but we are protected by the Lord. Even if this man said this with authority, it was the authority of the devil, and God has authority over the enemy. Nothing can touch your life that easily without you knowing it. You know very well that that thing, whatever it was, a curse or false prophecy, was bound. We've always prayed that the devil would have no influence in your life and that the Holy Spirit would protect you wherever you go."

"That's right, Pearl, I'm confident in God's protection over me. I don't need to fear these kinds of things, knowing God's grace holds me tightly."

April came, and with it was the second banquet for Oasis World Ministries, held at North Heights Church in Arden Hills. Jeremy touched his mom's arm. Beth was busy with all the things going on around her at the Oasis banquet, but she took the time to turn around and look Jeremy in the eyes, "What is it, Jeremy?"

"Mom. I think God is telling me to give my life savings to Oasis World Ministries for the people of India."

Beth was a bit startled, "Oh, Jeremy, you're only eleven, and it has taken you eleven years to get this amount in your account." Beth saw the wind almost go out of the sails of Jeremy's faith. "Let me talk to Dad about it, okay?"

Beth found Kevin; his tall frame made him easy to spot in the crowd, and explained the situation. They were a matching couple, with warm sandy-colored features, both slender and poised. He thought a moment before giving her an answer, "Beth, you can't take this step of faith from Jeremy. He wants to give it on his own initiative. What's the worst thing that can happen if he gives it all away? Down the road, Jeremy is going to look back on this banquet for Oasis and he'll always remember, 'I felt God asking me to give this money and I did it because I wanted to.' We don't know what God is doing in his heart. We tell our kids to be generous, to be a blessing, and then when they act on it should we hinder them?"

Beth looked for Jeremy and knelt beside him, "All right, Jeremy, if that's what you want to give, go for it!"

Jeremy's eyes shone with delight as he heard the news. "Thanks, Mom." His faith was bolstered for the moment, and for something in the near future.

It was the beginning of 2003 when Tom went on his first trip of the year to India. He was happy to escape from the deep freeze of a Minnesota winter, that is, until he got violently sick. It was the first week of the trip and he was getting weaker and feeling dehydrated. "I know when it's time to go home and it's time to go home."

It broke his heart to leave, but he knew he had reached his limit. The hardest part was telling the festival director that he needed to turn back. All the hard work of the Indian Christians over the past few months would be weighing on his mind. He was always amazed every time he went, by their diligence and call to duty for the sake of the Gospel. They were remarkable people, truly a shining example of servants for the Lord.

Meanwhile, in Minnesota, people were concerned. They called one another to pray and get updates on Tom's condition. Pearl was in the middle of it all, checking up on Vicki, calling her on the phone, "Vicki, how are you taking it?"

"Pearl, this is serious. I'm calling people from coast to coast to pray for Tom. I'm cashing in on some favors."

Pearl couldn't help but smile at the tone of Vicki's voice. Her dander had been kicked up, and she was marching into a prayer battle on behalf of her husband, and nobody better get in her way.

Naturally, Vicki was worried about Tom. She had been to India and knew that eating different foods that Americans are not accustomed to can wreck havoc on the digestive system. Once dehydrated, the body would begin to deteriorate and become more susceptible to viruses and bacteria it normally would be able to fight off. She was relieved to know he was his way home, but what a long way to travel when you are so sick. She knew he would feel torn between being levelheaded about his health and believing God would see him through no matter how much discomfort he was in. Tom had never been a quitter and he didn't like letting people down. *Oh, Lord, bring my husband home safe, and help him to let go of what he has to leave behind. There's more combat duty for him now and he needs people on the front lines, in both India and America, praying for him and Oasis World Ministries.*

It took Tom a while to recover, but he kept making plans for the next trip in March 2003 with Russ and Wendy Cunningham. A prayer meeting was scheduled before the trip at Tom and Vicki's townhome in Champlin. After a time of worship, Tom told about his upcoming trip and passed out prayer cards the size of bookmarkers, with the dates and locations of the festivals and dedications of church buildings and wells. "Please pray that God will do what he needs to do in my body to get it ready before I go to India again."

Pearl was among the group of prayer partners, "We need to also pray for Vicki. Many wives could not do what she does, letting him go to India four or five times a year, and praying for her husband's safety." Then Pearl remembered something, "Vicki, how is your back pain?"

"Well, it's been bad since Jon and Joy's wedding, which was August 2001. That's when I first started having pain in my hip. The doctor said it was from disintegrating discs in my back and suggested surgery. So in April of last year, I had surgery and they put in hardware, it almost looked like a couple of door bolts, and after that I got a staph infection. Then they had to reopen the area and clean out the infection. I was on two bags of intravenous medications a day for thirty days. I got very weak, but all I kept thinking to myself was, 'I'm a wife, a mother, and a grandmother—I can't die!' Unfortunately, the pain in my back isn't any better. I'm thankful I don't have to lift anything at my new job with the airlines."

Tom spoke up now, "It's challenging to us personally when we see incredible miracles in India, watching God open eyes and ears and healing people of tumors while our own health is poor. I don't pretend to understand it all. I only know to follow the Lord and keep praying and trusting him."

Vicki took Tom's hand in hers, "Sometimes I get frustrated hearing about the healings and the fact that I can't travel with Tom more, especially now that the kids are raised. The back pain really limits me." Her voiced cracked with emotion, "But we press on. God will see us through. He always has and he always will."

Chapter Fifty

Treasures of Heaven

For Lakshamakka, it was a day that started like all other days. And yet it was not like other days in any other respect. Today they were coming. Today was the day to celebrate the goodness of God in answering her prayers. Quickly she kneeled and lowered the contrasting purple-trimmed pallev over her head from the trail of her cream colored saree and began to pray joyfully in Telegu, "Oh, Lord of the Universe, how can I thank you adequately for what will take place today? You have been faithful through the years and now today." Tears began flowing as she thought over the years since her childhood wonderings, and then her husband's interest in the old preacher Samuel. Oh, how she longed to see her husband again! Matthaiah would have been so pleased today about the celebration. Samuel's words about their son had come true and what a fine pastor he had become.

Lakshamakka could hear people stirring in the village getting things ready. Last minute touches were added to the paint inside the newly-built church. Food was being prepared using almost every pot in the village, filling them with cooking rice and vegetables. The yellow-flowered leis were ready to honor the foreigners and the other pastors for their presence at the celebration. Quickly, she gathered her saree about her and stepped out into the bright sunshine filling the crystal blue sky. Somehow, it seemed brighter today as if joining in her happiness. A slight breeze moved across the fields as the oxen plodded back and forth at the command of their masters. She greeted the women gathered by the new well. Now they all could get water right in the middle of the village. How absolutely overcome with joy she had been the day her son told her the news that Sirivaram had been selected to get a church and well if the land could be secured by their small home church. The cold clear water was being pumped all day long and its beauty often mesmerized her when she filled her container each day. What a simple thing water is, and yet how powerful it is to give life. Her days of long walks to use the low-caste well were over.

Would the high-caste families come for the celebration today?

What would the foreigners look like?

A few hours later the preparations were complete and the wondering was over. Two large white vehicles covered in dust, rolled into the village right up to the edge of the church, under the shade of a sparsely-leafed tree. All the children came running. Crowds of people gathered to watch the strange white people from America get out of the vehicles.

Some were as tall as trees and some were shorter, some looked as if they had enough food to eat many times a day. There was even a tall lady like the tall man.

The introductions began and soon strange sounding gibberish was coming from their mouths. Several people couldn't help laughing at these foreigners with their different hair, clothing, and talking without moving their heads from side to side. Were they agreeing with nothing the others said? Yes, they must be agreeing, because they are all happy with one another and laughing.

Lakshamakka felt she would burst if she did not tell her story to them. This was such a day like none other! After her son was done with the introductions, she approached him, "Will you help me talk to the American woman? I want to tell her what God has done."

Yesaiah smiled down at his aging mother. Her gray hair shone in the sunshine like a crown of glory, "Yes, of course, I will take you to her."

Lakshamakka bowed slightly when they were introduced, and was happy to shake the hand of Mrs. Wendy. Lakshamakka looked past the woman's glasses into the windows of her soul and saw life. She could feel her voice quiver slightly as she began to tell this kind woman all that the Lord had done in her life, finishing with, "I have prayed seventeen years for a building to meet in, and today I see the answer before my eyes. The Lord is good."

The foreign woman, Mrs. Wendy, spoke in reply, her eyes filling with tears of joy. Her words were translated into Telegu, "I can tell by the look on your face that you love Jesus and have learned to trust him. How proud you must be of your son."

Lakshamakka moved her head from side to side in agreement as she listened to the translation. She was basking in the fulfillment of God's promises to her and it radiated for all to see.

There the two women stood. Worlds apart, yet both experiencing the joys and sorrows of life. Both knowing the King of Kings and Lord of Lords, whose name took away their sin and shame by the shedding of his blood, lying in a grave for three days, and rising to life and eternal victory for all mankind.

A call was given to gather around the plaque outside the front door of the church. How proud and strong the building looked with all the important guests in front of it. A cloth had been laid over the dedication plaque for the ceremony. Everyone in the village had read it by now, but the white people had not seen it yet, so it would be a surprise for them.

The tall slim man with the light eyes seemed friendly and spoke before he took off the cloth. She was surprised and pleased that he knew a few greetings in Telegu.

"I greet you in the name of our Lord Jesus Christ!"

Lakshamakka listened, her heart beating with joy. Mrs. Wendy and her husband, Mr. Russ, stood to the left as Rev. Tom Elie drew back the cloth. Mrs. Wendy clapped her hands with joy as if it were her church and had prayed and waited for seventeen years. The sun glinted off the black plaque edged in red. In gold lettering was the name of their church, Bethel A.G., Sirivaram, and the dedication day, March 20, 2003. Above it was the name of the sponsoring business, which she learned belonged to Mr. Russ Cunningham and his business partner. Yes, the name of the business on the plaque, Victory Tool, Inc., was appropriate for the day. It was a day of victory in physical and spiritual ways. Lakshamakka relished this moment, etching it into her memory forever.

Rev. Tom Elie said his good-byes and excused himself, along with a few other men, to go to another village that was waiting for them. Mrs. Wendy and Mr. Russ then cut the red ribbon over the mustard-colored double doors and the couple proceeded up to the front of the church to sit on the platform. Everyone crowded into the 20x40-foot building, with the men sitting on the right and the women on the left. Only the elderly in the back and the people on the platform had chairs to sit on. The beat of the treble congo drum mingled with the timbrel as they sang songs of worship. Then Mrs. Wendy and Mr. Russ began to speak words and someone translated in Telegu for all to hear. Lakshamakka glanced around at the room packed with almost two hundred people. Even some high-caste people had come and they were listening intently. Inside this church they were all equal in the sight of the Lord.

At the end of the service, several people came forward to profess faith in Jesus Christ, including members from high-caste families. The daughter of one of the leaders in the village became a believer, and eventually attended Bible school, and entered the ministry. Many in the village would comment with awe, "It is God's miracle because of the high-caste regulations of untouchability. Who would have thought that high-caste people would attend church regularly, sitting with low-caste people in church, and now even in the village busses!"

The service ended and the meal was about to begin when Lakshamakka learned Mrs. Wendy and Mr. Russ would not be staying. They needed to meet Rev. Tom Elie in another village. She stood watching the second vehicle leave. She had never ridden in such a fine vehicle. Her feet were used to walking everywhere she went. Neither had she flown in an airplane. Yet there was a kindred spirit, a fellowship in the Lord, and one day they would dwell in the house of the Lord together in eternity. Perhaps they would meet on the shores of the shining sea or near the trees with healing in their leaves. Then they could have a long visit about everything. About how this day came to be and how faithful their God had been.

Chapter Fifty One

Living the Dream!

At the Chanhassen Dinner Theater, Tom and Beth were walking around looking at the different theater rooms for the upcoming Oasis World Ministries banquet in November 2003. The theme was, "Blessed to be a Blessing," and was scheduled on the heels of Tom's trip to Guntakal and another city in India. Would enough people come to offset the cost of the dinner and theater rental?

Beth looked at the seating chart and the stage at the Chanhassen Dinner Theater. Tom was looking around, lost in his thoughts. Beth watched him for a second and then asked him, "Does this bring back memories?"

"Oh, yeah," Tom responded softly, "a lot of good memories."

It was like yesterday when they were here doing Christmas musicals with Jesus People Church. He could hear the music in his head, see the costumed characters singing and dancing. "So many lives were transformed by the power of God."

"Yeah, God did do a lot here."

"And now what happens next month at the banquet will help transform lives in India."

"Just think in 2001, when we held the Oasis banquet at North

Heights, we had 210 people come and now this year we're looking at 400 people!"

The buzz of excitement was in the air as Tom and Beth discussed all the details of the banquet. Tom still enjoyed planning and watching an event come together, and with Beth and Vicki handling most of the details, it was pure enjoyment. "Thanks again, Beth. People will have a chance to invest in the lives of others in India and hopefully it will be an inspirational night for them as well."

"Well, we still have a lot to do before the 10th of November. Tom, you thrive under deadlines more than I do!"

"I guess I do. How many people do you think we'll have attending next year?"

Beth shot him a look that only a sister can give a brother.

Over the years Tom began bringing people with him to India from all walks of life and Christian backgrounds. His current travel team consisted of a pastor and a young firefighter, both from Iowa; and a couple from Minnesota, a business owner and his wife. Despite feeling the jet lag in his body after the transatlantic flights, Tom felt the anticipation of the upcoming week. He noticed all the advertising for the evening festival in Guntakal. "The posters are plastered everywhere! How many did you print?"

The festival director, Pastor Thimothi Rao smiled, his warm brown eyes flashed with amusement, "Why, I think 3,000, Pastor. Do you think this is enough?"

Tom knew he was being teased, "Yes, Brother Thimothi, I think it will suffice. How is the set-up going?"

"The generator is up and running and all the floodlights are set up. The stage is done and the sound and speakers are almost ready to go."

"What about the city officials?"

"They are coming and will be on the stage the first night."

"Good," Tom said with relief. Whenever the city officials were included in the festival everything went better. Not only did it give the festival credibility, but also it was respectful in their culture. Tom enjoyed meeting the city officials, whether on or off the festival platform, and often offered to pray with them for help in governing their city.

The horn continued to sound as the vehicle wove through the Guntakal traffic. Finally, into view came an open expanse surrounded by cyclone fencing of various metals and woods normally used for soccer games.

"Pastor Tom, here is the festival site. What do you think?" asked Pastor Thimothi Rao.

Tom looked it over. The sparsely-grassed soccer field would soon be covered with large natural woven rugs in the middle for thousands of people to sit on and plastic chairs for some people on the sides. Many important people in the city would sit in a special section reserved for them. Space would be left between the stage and the seating area for the altar call at the end of the service. They drove around behind the stage. A prayer tent had been set up where prayer teams would be interceding for the people coming, the worship team, the skits, Tom's message, the translators, and finally the altar call, and the healing of physical needs.

"What's the atmosphere right now in the town?" Tom asked.

"Oh, everyone is talking about the festival. Everyone has been asking who is doing this event. They are asking, 'Is it really the Christians doing this? But they are such a small group. How can they do this large thing?'" Pastor Thimothi Rao replied.

"It's because they have a big God," Tom answered.

"Yes, we do," agreed Pastor Thimothi Rao. Although his stature was shorter than Tom's, their compassion for souls was equal.

Tom thought back to a previous festival, where the former state senator brought his four bodyguards armed with machine guns right up on the stage and sat for the duration of the meeting. After the sermon and altar call, the former state senator requested a decision card, filled it out, and left. Tom hadn't been sure if the city official felt threatened for his safety, or perhaps just wanted to flex his political prowess a bit. For whatever reason, it helped the festival to be permitted in a predominately Hindu city, and Tom had felt grateful. Opposition could get intense at times and nothing was taken for granted when it came to getting permits to conduct festivals. Oftentimes at night, militant opposing groups would set off fireworks during the festivals, trying to distract the crowds from listening. Some people would incite others to not purchase from shop owners who attended the festivals. Tom knew there were many festivals in India that had been shut down by radical Hindus and Muslims who whipped up people into frenzied riots. Working with the leaders of the city in advance helped to prevent disturbances and build a more peaceful climate in which to conduct the festival.

Tom flew back into the Twin Cities, spent one night in his own bed, got dressed in a dark suit and headed for the Chanhassen Dinner Theater. Wearing a formal black dress with sheer full-length sleeves, Vicki was talking with people at the banquet, "To hear the concept of a God loving them is unique. The gods they know are demanding, harsh, and cruel."

Vicki finished up her conversation and met with another group in the theater lobby. After greeting them and thanking them for their support, she continued with her stories about India. "One time Tom noticed a pastor who was not showing any affection to his son, so Tom took this pastor aside and told him, 'You need to hug him, encourage him. It's okay to hug him and encourage him.'"

Vicki added, "You can see how the pastors look to Tom as a spiritual father. They are so thankful, because they don't have the resources or the role models that we do in America. You should see how dedicated the pastors are at the seminars. They take notes and listen so intently. You can see it on their faces. The Indian pastors pay for half of their ride to the seminar. Oasis World Ministries pays for the other half of transportation to the seminar, their food, the lodging and the seminar. Last month at the seminar in Guntakal, three study books were given to pastors and leaders in the Telegu language."

Soon people were seated in the spacious theater room with table candles glowing next to white coffee cups. After radio D.J., Chuck Knapp, gave a few greetings, he warmly asked the audience, "Would you please welcome with me, Tom Elie, just back from India!"

Tom stood before the banquet audience. Their faces were mostly Caucasian. What a contrast from last week when he was in India. "Good evening, everyone, and thanks for coming out for the night! Thank you for praying for us while we were in India. God did miraculous things. Many heard about Jesus for the first time in their lives. I have asked you this question in many different ways before: 'Do people deserve to hear about Jesus?' And you have answered, 'yes' by partnering with Vicki, and me, to bring the Gospel to India. Let's rejoice today in our great and loving God!"

After the chicken dinner and entertainment, Tom came out to greet the crowd again and gave an overview of Oasis World Ministries in India. A slide came up on the screen. "This is the main thrust of what we do together as partners with Indian Christians.

One week in India typically consists of a five-night festival, dedications of churches and wells, a three-day seminar for pastors and leaders, and last, but not least, indigenous evangelists. Oasis sponsors seven Indian pastors to go out once or twice a month to small villages. They also do mini-festivals."

Tom clicked to a few slides showing pictures from India,

"Oasis World Ministries funds the nationals because they already know the culture and language. However, doing the larger-type festivals is where the Americans can help. But we don't come in as the experts. First we learn, and then we partner with our Indian brothers and sisters."

Tom showed his most recent pictures. "This is the city of Guntakal, a population of 200,000, which in India is considered a small city compared to places like Mumbai. We just did this festival during the latter part of October. There had never been a massive open-air festival for the whole city. The festival in Guntakal included thirty pastors from outlying villages and from the city."

More pictures came up on the screen, and Tom continued, "Trucks come in from outlying villages. By the fifth night, there will be 60-80 vehicles, some pulling wagons. They pack them out like it's the State Fair. It's a very celebratory atmosphere. Vendor tables are set up outside the main entrance, selling all kinds of merchandise and food."

Tom wrapped up his presentation with one last statistic. "The festival directors tell me, 'Half of the people here are hearing the Gospel of Jesus Christ for the first time ever.' On the fifth night, the attendance will be from 3,000 to 15,000, depending on the site location. We are seeing an average of 3,000 people make confessions of faith in Jesus Christ per week. Two months later the festival team will go back to every city where Oasis has done a festival, to survey the local pastors about increased church attendance. The average right now is 1,000 people added to the local churches that are within walking distance of the city. Of course, this doesn't figure in the people who come in from outlying villages on the trucks and wagons."

After the banquet Ryan remarked to his dad, "Dad, I didn't even know there were this many people who like us! Ha!"

"Well, Ryan, there's a lot of good in the ministry and the good always outweighs the bad. It's amazing to me how many people are here and how much they care. Oasis couldn't continue without them."

Christmas and the New Year came and went, and Tom had just come back from India. At his church he gave testimony of all the decisions to follow Jesus Christ and also about the healings. Then he went on to show footage of several church and well dedications. Jeremy was sitting next to his mom, Beth, in the church pew. It had been two years since eleven-year-old Jeremy had given his life savings to Oasis. For two years, he had done paper routes, babysitting, and stopped buying candy at the store. When his parents would hand out the weekly allowance of three dollars, Jeremy would say, "Put it in the bank for India, Mom. I'm going someday with Uncle Tom. I just know it."

Beth would put it in the bank and keep checking his savings account. After two years Jeremy's account showed that he had doubled the same amount he had given at the Oasis banquet two years ago—an amount that had previously taken him eleven years to save!

His eyes were fixed on Tom and the video. He hung onto every word Tom said. Overcome with passion, he grabbed his mom's arm in a tight squeeze and whispered not too softly, "Mom! I've got to go! I gotta go to India!"

Beth looked down at her son, "I know. You'll go. I don't know when, but you'll go." And she meant it. Ryan had taken her older son on a mission's trip. It was Jeremy's turn next.

In April, Tom and Vicki began realizing that it was time to resign from Praise. Vicki kept thinking about past memories of Praise and all the people and how much she loved them. She began to worry about what would happen to them with all the changes that would occur. She kept going to the Lord about her concerns until one day during prayer at home the Lord spoke to her heart, and said,

Vicki, who loves this church more?

"Okay, God, I know you do." Vicki was in grief. Letting go was difficult, she felt so protective of their flock.

Later she relayed to Tom, "I finally had a breakthrough in resigning from Praise. God encouraged me. He said that He loved them more, and that he would take care of them; that this would be a time of growing in him and trusting him for the people of Praise. I needed to let go and let God do *His* work in the people; that it would be hard for them and us, but God would work it in our lives for his purpose!"

Tom mused with thoughtful eyes, "It will be an adjustment for all of us. Change can be hard, even forward change. Embracing a Call is never easy, even when it's the right thing to do."

When Tom and Vicki broke the news to family members at a gathering at Beth's home, the hostess started crying, "I know I have to let you go as my pastor. I know God is calling you into Oasis full-time. It's just that…well…because of what happened with JP, it's so hard for me to trust spiritual leaders."

Tom hugged his younger sister, "I know, Beth. We all are more cautious now. But I always tell myself that I can get better or bitter from the disappointments in life. We are human, after all. I've made my share of mistakes, and over the years I've disappointed people, too. We have to move forward in forgiveness and let God sort out the details."

Beth nodded and hugged Tom one more time for good measure. Then he laughed, "Come on, Beth, it's not like we aren't going to see each other again. How's the Oasis banquet coming along?"

"Oh, Tom, stop it will you? Let me deal with one thing at time." A smile was beginning to form at the corners of Beth's mouth.

Chapter Fifty Two

One Million for the One

The music was playing as the guests were seated for Ryan and Tara's wedding. Family and friends on both sides of the wedding party filled the church with 500 guests. In walked Tom and nine groomsmen. Jon and Darren took their places alongside Troy, the best man. They waited for nine attendants to make their walk down the aisle. One of the other groomsmen looked at Ryan and thought back to the days when Ryan bounded downstairs to the recliner in Tom and Vicki's basement to help feed and dress him after his car accident. Steve Wadja, who had on one occasion preached to bats and on another had witnessed the infamous cannonball baptism of T.L., felt the lump in his throat, wondering where all the years had gone. He used to babysit these guys: Troy, Ryan, Jon, and Darren, and now, in the blink of an eye, it seemed, here he was standing with men. *Here he was with family again.*

Nine attendants now flanked each side of the groom. The dresses were a coral iridescent salmon color, contrasting elegantly with the black tuxes. The music rose to a stirring crescendo and down the aisle softly glided the bride, beautifully adorned in a spotless white gown. She had waited. He had waited, sometimes very impatiently for this day. There was a presence that lingered during the ceremony taking one's thoughts to heavenly matters. Oh, the Glorious Romance of Christ and his future bride, those who call Jesus Christ their Lord. One day *He* would come for *His* bride.

Later on that night, Tom and Vicki sat exhausted in their townhome in Champlin, basking in the glow of the wedding. Vicki let out a sigh of contentment, "What a beautiful day. I enjoyed every moment of it."

Tom looked over at his wife, "The years have just flown by haven't they, honey? Today I was thinking about us walking around Lake Calhoun, our wedding...our first house."

"Yes, and bringing home Troy. Remember how much Beth enjoyed helping with him?"

"Now look at her with four kids of her own."

"I'm so glad Jeremy gets to go to India with you, Tom. It will mean so much to him. I know he's young, but maybe God is wanting to plant some seeds for future ministry in his heart."

"When I think of how much money that young man saved up to invest into eternal riches, instead of using it to buy something he would have probably had a ton of fun with—I'm just in awe of that kid's heart."

Vicki looked over at Tom, who wore that expression she had seen a thousand times, his piercing hazel eyes squinting in serious thought and then enlarging in excitement with gray hair at the temples. He was still as charming to her as ever. "Well, honey, he's seen the video tapes of your trips, and Beth and Kevin have done a good job of instilling the value that as Americans we're blessed to be a blessing."

"Yeah, so many people 'blab it and grab it,' thinking the blessings of God are only for their personal needs. They seem to think God is only there to serve them, and not the other way around. God does want to take care of us, all of us, even those in India. The more I go there the more I realize there are millions of people there who need to hear his life-giving message of eternal salvation. Not only that, but if we can't meet a simple basic need like fresh water from the drilled wells…what right do we have to say we know about the love of God?"

Vicki's heart began to show on her face, her soft brown hair with golden highlights surrounded eyes of compassion, "That's why I'm able to send you off on every trip with your suitcase filled with tuna packs and teaching materials. It's not easy, but I know it's God's plan for our lives right now."

There wasn't a dry eye in the house of God in Crystal that Sunday morning, September 12, 2004, as Tom and Vicki, along with Ryan and Tara, said their good-byes to everyone at Praise. Tom had thought Ryan would eventually pastor at Praise, maybe even take his place one day. But it wasn't to be. "Dad, I'm called to youth. I don't want to pastor Praise. I really think the Lord is calling me to Indianapolis; I'm sorry."

"Ryan, we want you to stay, but if you feel the Lord is calling you to Indianapolis, we'll support you 110%."

"Thanks, Dad, I knew I could count on you and Mom."

In the midst of all of this, Tom and Vicki set up their first official Oasis World Ministries (OWM) office in a Twin Cities suburb. One of the OWM board members had graciously offered free office space for the maturing non-profit organization that was leaving the nest of Praise Christian Center in Crystal. It was a small office room, but it was a grand beginning for Tom and Vicki. When they had their next OWM board meeting, true to form, Vicki cried as she thanked the man for his generosity. "I'm sorry I'm crying so much the first time I meet you, but I'm so appreciative of what you are doing for us and Oasis. It's such an answer to prayer. I'm overcome with thankfulness to the Lord. He has always met us each step of the way with so many things over the years, and now with Oasis."

After setting up shop for OWM, they prepared for their next trip to India in October. Tom and Vicki were about to step into the final season of their journey in ministry. Now by faith they would trust God for provision not only for their personal needs, but also for the work in India, and their Indian co-workers in the Harvest.

Tom and Vicki leaned their heads back on the airplane seat as the plane took off from Indian soil. Despite her back problems, Vicki had been determined to push through the pain and not miss this trip. Holding hands, they glanced across the aisle at Tom's sister, Beth and her son, Jeremy. Russ and Wendy had come along again and a women's seminar had been hastily put together, giving a two-day notice for the women to come. To everyone's amazement, 500 women showed up hungry to hear the Word of God. Tom was wondering how they could fit lunch for all the women into the trip budget, when Russ stepped forward to pay the $250 for the food and preparation. "I only wish I could get by this cheap for my son's graduation open house."

Then Wendy had to come up with several hours of teachings at the women's seminar after being told it would last three hours with a lunch break. Vicki and Beth said they only had prepared for thirty minutes each because of the time translators took. After finishing that day, Wendy commented, "What I love about India is that all I rely on is stripped away, and I have to rely on God for all I do!"

Fourteen-year-old Jeremy and his mother, Beth, "took to India like ducks to water," as Wendy observed during the trip. During the festivals, both mother and son had helped Tom and Vicki with praise and worship and praying with people after the festival. Jeremy adapted so well to the culture that he even wore the traditional garb with a men's sash cummerbund. He also helped with taking the offering one night at the festival. People were curious about this young man from America. After putting in their offering, they would shake his hand. He was the only white person out in the sea of Indian people. Pastor Thimothi Rao's son, Jimmy Moses, smiled over at his new friend, Jeremy, who was two years older. He had heard that Rev. Tom Elie's nephew was coming and, after spending a week with Jeremy, declared in his Indian-British accent, "Jeremy, you should come back here for a summer and stay in India and we'll have you speaking Telegu by the end of the summer."

Back at the hotel the group ate their late-night dinner of chicken and rice. "So, Beth, what do you think about your first time in India?" Tom asked.

Beth's smile said it all. "Meeting the team you work with was wonderful. They are such servants with great happiness and contentment. And Jeremy and Jimmy Moses have really hit it off. Who knows what God has in store with that friendship down the road? I also liked the seminars with pastors and leaders; they seemed to soak in everything, and they really enjoy the light, funny moments, the worship, and they love the Word of God."

Vicki, Russ, and Wendy, listened to the first-time visitor, thinking back to their first trip to India, while Tom kept the conversation rolling. "Jeremy, you had the opportunity to speak with an interpreter to schoolchildren. How did that go for you?"

Jeremy spoke up with eagerness, "I had an 'evangelism cube' and told the story of Jesus' life, death, and resurrection, using the different colored sides to coincide with each part of it. My knees were knocking because I was so nervous, but I was thankful for an interpreter so I had time to plan what I was going to say next!"

Beth offered more of her thoughts. "The difference in culture is incredible. I think this week we realized we didn't have much to complain about at home, didn't we Jeremy? It was especially interesting traveling into the rural areas, like stepping back in time with all the animals and how they work in the fields."

Vicki said, "I still remember my first trip, seeing women walking down the roads carrying large loads on their heads, and some working at construction sites all day long."

Wendy nodded, "Ya know, we can leave the hotel in the morning and there will be a woman in a saree working on a pile of sand that is used to make concrete at a construction project nearby, and in the late afternoon, after the pastors' and leaders' seminar is done, she is still working. It's amazing how hard they work."

Russ spoke up, "So how does it feel to be doing Oasis full-time?"

Vicki was the first to respond, "If someone would have told me nine months ago we would be resigning from Praise and going full-time with Oasis, I would have said, 'You're crazy!' We have been pastoring for thirty years, so this is going to be a big change. I'm so relational and the loss of the church community, you know, sharing daily joys and burdens together, is going to be an adjustment for me. The Lord is just going to have to help me remember it's *His* church, and not ours to look after."

"He'll do a good job," someone offered, and everyone laughed as Tom responded with, "Yes, I suppose he can figure all that out now, can't he."

The drone of the plane's engines brought Tom's thoughts back to his seat in the airplane. He stretched his long legs out and smiled. Tom was living his dream. He smiled and thought of all the so-called detours he had taken in obedience to God, instead of fulfilling his own dreams as to what he thought his Call of an evangelist should look like. Silently Tom prayed, giving thanks for what God had done since 1996 and that first trip with Del. Now there was a full program in place with pastors and evangelists sharing the Gospel. As many as ten churches and fifteen wells were built every year, depending on the financial support. Del would be happy knowing how far Oasis had come since then, and also about Wendy. Here his widow had found an authentic companion who would help her carry on the torch for India. With this last trip, Wendy had gone more times than Del had.

Tom had wanted to have Oasis bigger than one denomination. A plan began to take shape in his mind. What if he began networking with other churches across denominational lines and came alongside them, as a resident evangelist, sort of like a coach? Instead of blowing in and out for one Sunday, he could partner with them for three years by using the gift of an evangelist to assist the local church in their quest to be a witness for Christ. Tom looked over at Vicki; she had her eyes closed. He would discuss it with her later. He could already picture her face as he told her about another one of his new ideas!

As Tom flew across nations toward Amsterdam and the approaching year of 2005, he would soon see what God had prepared for those who love Him, as stated in First Corinthians 2:9. Healings would increase in measure in America, and Vicki's back pain would also be resolved after surgery to remove the excessively large hardware from her lower back. She would eventually quit her job at the airlines, only working flexible hours, so she could begin traveling with Tom more and more. Together, as husband and wife, they would keep pressing on toward the goal of one million souls for the One.

Down through the years, by the grace of God, and with support from family and friends, Tom and Vicki had been faithful to the Call of their lives. They had done the best job they knew how to do as people with limited strengths and weaknesses. Now they would look to the future: Traveling around their home country, America, preaching, praying for healings, encouraging pastors, assisting churches with evangelism, sharing the vision of a million souls, and raising funds for their other homeland: India. Together with family, friends, and ministry partners all around the world, they would help spiritually thirsty people meet Jesus Christ and leave a legacy that would echo in eternity.

Questions about Christianity and how to follow Jesus Christ?

Making Christ your own is as simple as admitting you have gone your own way (sinned) and admitting you need him as your Savior because he paid the price for your sins by dying for you. But first, think it through, the cost of serving Christ is dying to your self (ask him to help you with this). If you do this you will have a new life in him, the One True God.

If this is something you are ready to do, pray and ask Jesus Christ to be your Lord and Savior. Admit that at times you have missed the mark (even if you are a basically good person). Then find an easy to understand version of the Bible and begin reading about Jesus Christ in the New Testament. And find others who follow the teachings of Jesus with love, grace, and kindness. Ask God your Father to help you understand what you read in the Bible, and to help you make friends with others who love Jesus Christ and have made Him their own. A destiny is waiting for you.

Consider visiting the Oasis World Ministries website or writing to them at the address below. Someone is waiting to hear from you.

Thinking about how you might partner with Oasis World Ministries? Someone is available to answer any questions you may have.

Email: info.owm@juno.com
www.oasisworldministries.org

Oasis World Ministries
P.O. Box 27893
Minneapolis, MN 55427

ACKNOWLEDGEMENTS

The author wishes to extend warm gratitude to all those who helped to make this book a reality. First to my husband, Sheldon Halberg, who has come home numerous times to find a mad typist in the middle of a paper tornado instead of dinner. And to all my content readers who read my rough drafts and gave the feedback I needed to refine this project into a reader friendly book. You know who you are and a special reward awaits you in heaven I am sure, but for now may you know that you have contributed to the Kingdom of God in a way that will touch lives for eternity. A special thanks to my Writer's Group, Joleen Kubiszewski and Pat Wheaton, who lifted my spirits when they were at their low times and to Stacy Bellward, who really knows how to use the red pen (thanks for letting me argue my thoughts back and forth!). Also, thank you to Julie Bosacker for detailed proofreading. And to all of those who prayed or had words of encouragement: I thank you for being an important part of my writing journey on my first book. Lastly, I would like to thank Tom, Vicki, their sons and spouses, family, friends, and all the other people I interviewed or called/e-mailed for questions and clarifications. Tom, Vicki, Troy, Ryan, Jon, and Darren, how can I properly show appreciation for letting me invade your privacy and learn about your lives? In the words of Patti Worre: "It was no small thing."

KIM HALBERG has written in some shape or form her whole life before taking a risk of her own and writing her first book: *Meet Me at the Oasis: Leaving a Legacy to Echo in Eternity*. She makes her home in Minnesota with her husband, their last son in the nest, and their orange tabby cat: Freddy. When she is not writing you may find her walking along park trails, gardening, trying new ethnic recipes, or going out for dinner with friends. She also enjoys hanging out with her three sons, daughter-in-law, grandson, and her husband, Sheldon (who sometimes whisks her off sailing).

Over the years Kim has traveled to many countries including India. She is currently on the leadership team at The Creek Community Church in Maple Grove, Minnesota. You may contact her through mail or her website: kimhalberg.com

Kim Halberg

PO Box 48340

Minneapolis MN 55448-0340